M·T
Mary

Where is my son?

Where is my son?

Owen Sheridan

CHALWAR

Chalwar Publishing Ltd.,
42 Villiers Road,
Kingston Upon Thames.
KT1 3AR

Sales enquiries: enquiries@chalwar.com

ISBN NO 0-9537728-0-2

All rights reserved
Copyright © Owen Sheridan 2001
Cover design © Owen Sheridan

The author welcomes comments
and suggestions by e-mail:
owensheridan@chalwar.com

Contents

1. A holiday romance — 9
2. Gordon Road — 18
3. Two weddings — 24
4. Turning sour — 29
5. Pregnancy — 41
6. Matthew — 52
7. Storm clouds — 59
8. Salvage — 74
9. The year of conflict — 84
10. In court and out — 95
11. Silver lining — 108
12. Grasping at straws — 118
13. A gun to my head — 128
14. The dark days — 140
15. Access — 151
16. 'I want my daddy' — 160
17. Aftermath — 177
18. The dispossessed — 186
19. Making a life — 196
20. The professionals — 205
21. Baptism of fire — 218
22. Countdown — 226
23. The halls of justice — 237
24. Appeal — 249
25. Standing alone — 259
26. Where is my son? — 270

The following is a true story.
Names of places and
people have been changed.

CHAPTER 1

A holiday romance

Daydreaming broke the tedium of my journey; it's the comfort of travellers. This year the public speaking finals were in Oxford. It was March; the weather had been bad and traces of snow were still on the ground - just the right time for a break from work, from London. I had visited the university before but never stayed, and as the train slowed down, it was an effort to drag myself back to reality, away from John Wycliffe and Evelyn Waugh...

We were staying an old college built of creamy stone. My room was tiny, one of two that shared an enormous study. Frank Collins had the other; we had kept in touch since our schooldays in Limerick. The reunion had already started in 'The Plough and Harrow' and Frank was in a hurry. He left me to admire the surroundings and the old photos on the walls.

The *buzz* from the pub could be heard outside the door. Inside, competitors and their supporters were calling across the bar and old friends were introducing new friends to one another. That was how I met Brenda.

'Owen! Over here! We kept a seat for you.'

'Hang on Frank! - Just want to try a pint of that Oxford Ale. I suppose you have enough for the moment?'

A few minutes later, Frank pulled out a chair for me as he saw me approaching - a pint of Oxford Ale in one hand and a pint of Guinness in the other. Brenda was sitting opposite me. Taller than the other women, she looked energetic and strong. Her hair was long, fair and wavy; it had caught my eye, a second before Frank's shout on my way in. She was dressed in cream and brown.

One of the nice things about moving is your friends no longer take you for granted. That evening I was not short of attention. I gave myself up to the merrymaking, joining in the craic wholeheartedly and contributing to the singsong, which lasted until the early hours of the morning. But a touch of disappointment dampened my mood as Brenda left the table to go to bed, even though my party piece had just gone down well and we hadn't been talking during the evening.

*

In my late twenties, I had taken off around the world. America seemed the natural place to start, and my first two years were spent travelling and working around the United States and Canada. After that I moved to Australia and stayed there for most of nineteen eighty-seven.

My knowledge of carpentry got me work in most places, and where it didn't there was labouring, house painting or truck driving. Being brought up on a farm on the side of a hill has several advantages. Money was scarce and we had to do most jobs ourselves

Singing came naturally to me thanks to my mother, and learning songs was easy thanks to the endless memorising that was part of an Irish education. It helped me to meet many more people. To work, earn my living, have workmates, to have fun, make friends and share their way of life: these were my reasons for travelling - and my skills could not have been better suited. Those years left me some very happy memories; it was the time of my life.

I came to live in London by accident. My flight from Melbourne landed in Gatwick Airport shortly after the big storm of 1987. Sevenoaks, Kent, we were told, was now 'One Oak.' Before taking the train to Victoria, I arranged to meet Joe Healy, a neighbour from Limerick. Joe is a builder, and

A holiday romance

since work was scarce in Ireland at the time, he had taken on a contract in Battersea. The job was finishing and he was looking forward to going back home to his wife and their two small children. We met in 'The Duke of Cornwall.'

'London is booming' he said. 'There's a pile of work around.' He arranged for me to stay with a friend of his called Jimmy Nagle. Jimmy's marriage had broken up, and he had a large four-bedroom apartment almost empty. He was interested in renting rooms.

We got on immediately. He is from County Cavan, small and very clean and tidy. A steelfixer by trade, he was turning fifty at the time. With his droll speech and sharp wit he became well known and remembered in the building trade, where many people move on and are forgotten.

'I can get you a job in the morning, Owen' he said. 'But your best bet is to go down to Docklands. That's where the money is. They're rebuilding the whole place. You'll get top rate, time and a half on Saturday and double time on Sunday, plus all the overtime you'll ever want.'

'Why aren't you down there yourself, Jimmy?' I said smiling.

'Ah well I'm past it. You know I'm not as good as I once was.' He winked – *But I'm as good once as I ever was.*

The following day, carrying my tools with me, I made my way to Docklands. Jimmy was right. When they saw the carpentry tools they didn't want me to go home. The pay was excellent - more money than I ever made in my life. It was no hard decision to stay on.

My friends were mostly Irish at first, but later on, having discovered what a truly international city London is, I became friendly with people from all parts of the world.

Stephen Clarke, a carpenter from County Clare was working with me on the job. Intelligent and well read, he could talk about all kinds of subjects from socialism to North American Indians even though he had left school at fifteen. Before long, we were working together on contract. So, having meant to spend only a few days in London, two years later I was still there, working in Docklands and living in Battersea.

*

As single men, we had often discussed the mysteries of 'scoring' with a woman. How many times had we gone out determined to meet someone at all costs - and come back empty handed? Then at other times it just seemed to 'click' for no reason at all. At thirty-three years of age it was still a mystery to me.

What Brenda and I did not know was that other factors were driving us together. She was living in Limerick, my home county, and interested in moving to London; we were both in good physical shape and 'on the rebound' after relationships that had gone wrong. The following day we found ourselves sitting side by side at the competition, and we couldn't be torn apart for the remaining twenty-four hours. Early on Monday, I was on the phone to Limerick and a few weeks later during Easter, a short visit to my father at my old home on the Cork border stretched out until it was nearly a fortnight long.

Brenda brought me to meet her parents and her brother Cecil at their holiday cottage in West Clare. Seamus Newman was a tall thin solicitor with an interest in history. We got into a conversation about Eamon De Valera who also came from the borders of Limerick and Cork and we got on well together. Margaret Newman was gracious and agreeable.

*

Back in London, over the summer we were in contact almost daily. We made last minute arrangements to meet frequently (but not too frequently), usually at weekends. When Brenda went on a fortnight's holiday to Greece with her mother, I flew out there and joined them for a week. It was mad, it was passionate, it was thrilling! It was a really good holiday romance. We could only have each other in small doses and they were never enough. We found things in common, a liking for old houses, and a love of books and reading. Neither of us could wait for my next trip to Ireland at the end of July. We spoke on the phone every night, and then Brenda told me she was applying for jobs in London. God was in his heaven!

My visits to Limerick tended to stretch anyway. Living and working in a big city has helped me appreciate the countryside where I grew up, especially since every lane, every house is alive with history and tradition. Older societies had people who were natural recorders. They kept track of genealogies, of events and characters and wove them into stories. Men and women with good memories and an interest in people, they filled a very important social role. By putting their lives into perspective, they gave a kind of structure, a meaning to the people who lived and died around them. My father is such a person and I believe he has passed it on to me.

He was an older dad, forty-three when I was born, and we were very close when I was a small child. James, my younger brother was born a twin. Small and delicate at first, his twin brother died after a few days and my mother had to devote most of her time to taking care of him. So my father was given the job of looking after me. Following him around the yard and up the hill, milking cows, feeding calves, driving the tractor, I learned to do all these things at the age of three. We used to feed the cattle and sheep with me driving the tractor while he stood in the trailer and pitched out the turnips or hay. I was four years of age. Dangerous? Perhaps - but there were no accidents. He did not play football with us or take us swimming; but he gave me a knowledge of another time and another set of people long dead. I never missed the football.

So my holidays back to my father tend to get prolonged. But this visit was special. Things moved very swiftly. Desperate for each other's company Brenda and I spent nearly every night together. Then we decided to go away one weekend, and on the way home almost without realising it I found myself asking her to marry me. She accepted straight away. We knew one another four months.

The following day passed in a kind of daze. Me! Married? It just didn't seem real. To be fair to Brenda, she did say that if I wasn't sure, she wouldn't hold me to it and there would be no hard feelings. But that was the furthest thing from my mind. I felt dizzy, unreal and embarrassed - but no regrets.

Earlier in the summer, I bought a cream-coloured Volvo station wagon and now we took advantage of the long evenings to drive around Tipperary and Clare. One day, on our way to Miltown Malbay, we stopped in Ennis for a quick cup of coffee at a pub. The girl behind the bar was about seventeen. She was about to put the two cups down in front of us when I heard Brenda saying *'Would you mind wiping the counter first?'* It was the way she said it, her tone of voice that jarred me. The girl reddened, stammered an apology and wiped the counter down.

Brenda decided to accept a job in London and we arranged to travel back together. It was time to announce our news to her family, so the following Monday, she phoned with an invitation to dinner at her parents' house on the Ennis Road.

Before the meal Margaret took me to one side; she had guessed what was coming.

'Owen! We need to know how you are fixed to provide for Brenda.' she asked me bluntly.

Having been brought up in a culture where marriages, until recently, had been arranged, the question did not seem strange. Anyway my circumstances at the time were nothing to be ashamed of.

'Well, right now I have fifty thousand pounds in the bank and I can earn very good money in London' was my answer. She nodded, smiled and went back into the dining room.

It was a lovely day when the boat sailed from Rosslare; the crossing was perfect.

*

Telling my friends made me blush. It took all my courage but it became easier after the first few days. We had driven down from the ferry and stayed the night with Brenda's brother Timmy in Ealing. Feeling very responsible, I made up my mind to find accommodation and work as soon as possible.

The recession in the building trade had started to bite at the beginning of the year when Stephen Clarke was with me 'first-fixing' flats in Docklands. There seemed to no end to the work. We put down the floors in each flat, fitted the stairs (they were two storey), the doorframes and hundreds of timber noggins to take the plasterboard slabs.

One day in May the general foreman called me into his office. 'Owen' he said. 'When will you have the flat finished?'

'Well Nigel... I planned for Tuesday, but if there's a push on, maybe we could have it done for Saturday by staying on a few evenings.'

'It's not that. But when it's done, I'm afraid there just aren't any more. They're not selling and we're not getting funds to finish the others.'

It was as sudden as that. Of course I knew about the recession but until then there was no recession for me. Now its claws could be felt all at once. People in the building trade are philosophical about these things and Stephen and I looked on it as just another job finished. We signed on as two carpenters with an agency and stayed working together for about a month. After that we went our separate ways.

The cutbacks made me a little apprehensive about getting work. But there was no need to worry. The second agency on my list offered me a job the same day. Brenda had a job waiting for her - and a good one. A solicitor like her father, she eventually came to specialise in family law. Her firm was based in Guildford, Surrey. From the beginning, there were problems with her boss. She wasn't used to the legal procedures in the UK and he had very little patience about explaining them, so they had a number of disputes.

It was a measure of my feelings that I shrugged the work situation off without worrying and also took another problem in my stride. We were homeless - or almost. Up to the end of June I had been renting a little studio flat. Then the Mortgage Company decided to repossess it from my landlord. Luckily Jimmy Nagle came to the rescue and offered me a room for the few weeks before my trip to Ireland.

We were about to approach him again when Timmy offered to keep us while we looked for a place of our own. His painting and decorating business was also suffering from the recession, and he was glad of the rent we paid him.

Brenda and I started work on the same day. My firm was refurbishing a large old house near Kensington and we finished at 4.30 p.m. each afternoon. The lack of overtime was a sure sign that the recession was beginning to make itself felt. But now it suited me, as it left plenty of time for flat hunting with Brenda. Being early August, there was a long stretch of daylight in the evenings. We usually met at about 5.30pm and spent an hour or so looking at places before having something to eat and going back to Ealing.

It took us longer than we thought because we were really doing two jobs. Our immediate objective was to find a place to rent but we were also on the lookout for a house to buy. With prices falling, there seemed to be no problem affording it. And with my experience, we were quite happy to buy a place that needed fixing up.

Meanwhile Brenda and Timmy were getting on each other's nerves, so when Stephen Clarke told me about an apartment for rent near his job in Balham, we went to see it the same evening. It turned out to be a very nice conversion on the first floor of a Victorian house. We saw it on Thursday, paid a deposit on Friday, and on Saturday we moved in. At last we had a place to ourselves!

This was the happiest time of our relationship. We looked forward to seeing one another in the evenings after work; we used to go for long walks after dinner and for trips away at weekends. I had a companion to share my activities and ideas. Our friends said we were the perfect couple.

CHAPTER 2

Gordon Road

Now that I was going to be a responsible married man, it was time to put my knowledge of building to good use.

In the summer of 1990 house prices had taken a drastic drop all across London. They had fallen by between a quarter and a third of their former value; it was the time to buy. Wandsworth seemed the ideal place. We had friends living there and it is very convenient for travelling to other parts of London, an important consideration if you work in the building trade.

At first, Brenda balked at the financial risk. It was her training, especially as house prices in London were so much higher than in Limerick. But she soon warmed to the idea and began to make plans for the kind of home she would like. We decided to buy a property in a run-down condition and fix it up ourselves. Of course Brenda had very little idea of the time or the work this would take, so if anything she was more enthusiastic about the project than I was - at first.

We looked at about thirty properties before seeing the house in Gordon Road. It was a little Victorian mid-terrace, on a crescent not far from the railway station, in terrible condition. The roof was leaking, plaster was falling off the walls, the wiring was dangerous, there was no proper bathroom and the kitchen was unusable. The good side was that there were very few signs of the butchery that had been done to so many of these little houses when they weren't valued as they are now. No PVC windows, no concrete tiles on the roof, no 'through lounge' and best of all no pebbledash covering the old brick walls.

Gordon Road

It would have to be wired, plumbed, heated, plastered - and then my work would begin. The job was going to be tremendous. Every wall and floor needed attention; the roof, on closer inspection, would have to be re-slated, the garden was a mass of briars and half the ceilings were falling in. But we could both see a lovely Victorian cottage at the end of all our labours, hanging baskets on the walls, a picket fence and garden outside. That vision was to keep me going through years of hard work.

We began negotiating and haggling. Two years before, the going rate for similar houses in good condition was £120,000. Even houses in poor repair were selling for £90,000 - £100,000 as builders were buying them up, decorating them and selling them on for a profit. They were a good investment then, but not any more.

Eventually after a full survey and much bargaining we settled on a price of £69,000 for the house and contents. These included some old chests and sideboards that were interesting, if not particularly valuable and a large cupboard full of old tools which pleased me thoroughly. We made the bargain in October, just a few weeks after moving into the flat in Balham.

Brenda had £3,500 saved up and I matched that with the same amount out of my savings. Moving in cost us £1,000, which meant we had to borrow £63,000.

Getting a mortgage was no problem. Interest rates at the time were high, and mortgage companies were bending over backwards to try to get people to take out loans at fourteen or fifteen percent. Normally, being self-employed in the building trade was a serious obstacle to getting a home loan, but when they saw Brenda's job-title, all the lenders were anxious to do business. We negotiated a cut of one per cent in the interest rate and because of a mistake in setting up our mortgage we were paying back interest only. This brought our repayments to £630 per month - only a few pounds more than the cost of renting the flat in Balham. Not bad at all!

With my contacts in the building trade it was easy to have an electrician, a plumber and a plasterer ready as soon as we could close the sale. With Christmas in the middle of the process, this did not take place until the eleventh of January, so we made plans to start work on the twelfth.

At Christmas we went to Limerick again. Brenda and her mother had preparations to make for the wedding and since it was only two years since my mother died, my father needed some company. The holidays passed quickly; friends came to congratulate us and to wish us well.

Then, a few days before going back there was a bombshell. Brenda's boss called her on the telephone - she had just lost her job. Afterwards, she seemed subdued but not very surprised; their relationship had never run smoothly.

With over £40,000 in the bank and confident of getting work, it didn't upset me. Brenda was quite concerned however, and vowed to go waitressing if necessary. She began to have second thoughts about buying the house, but soon realised that there was nothing we could do. Her mood seemed happy enough two days later as we drove to the ferry.

Things began to happen quickly after that. On the Friday we signed the final papers and closed the sale. Early on Saturday morning we left our flat in Balham in time to find a big skip being delivered to Number 20 Gordon Road. That day was one of the happiest and most fulfilling of my life. We stripped wallpaper, tore up layers of lino and carpet and pulled out the old kitchen and bathroom. I demolished a wall and hacked the plaster off another. The plumber and electrician also came and started work. Brenda stayed with me until seven in the evening and by then we were both exhausted.

It was a marvellous feeling, fatigue mixed with euphoria. Having spent years working on other people's houses, at last I was putting my ideas into practice on my own project - building our home!

The next morning we met some kitchen suppliers. Thanks to the recession in the building trade (now in it's second year and beginning to make it self felt) we were able to negotiate an excellent price, 60% off list. Then back to Gordon Road and more demolishing and clearing. Those days lasted until

Gordon Road

my next job on site, about a week later. It would have suited me better to leave it a bit longer and spend at least another week on my pride and joy. But Brenda was still anxious about neither of us earning money; so I went back to work.

It was hard to wait until five o'clock every day, to rush home, grab something to eat, then off to Gordon Road until after twelve, hacking down walls or fixing floorboards. My energy was boundless.

Brenda had set her heart on moving in on Valentine's Day; so by the first week in February things were really humming. In order to get more time for Gordon Road, I worked at two jobs for a few days, and then took a week off. My first 'shift' in Piccadilly lasted from midnight until eight and the other job in Holborn until five in the afternoon. After that I would go home to Balham and sleep until eleven. The days passed quickly. The next week was spent entirely in Gordon Road, clearing up, organising materials and doing anything that needed to be done.

It was pure joy, but one thing took the edge off my happiness. Brenda and I had our first row.

In the two weeks up to the move she had been growing increasingly impatient and bad tempered but I was so happy and wrapped up in the project that her words ran off me like water. However coming from Balham, a day or two before we moved in, one particularly nasty remark of hers struck home. Stopping the car, I suddenly became conscious of all the other things she had been saying. Switching off the engine, I looked over at Brenda and just said, 'You ought to do some serious thinking about the way you are talking to me.'

She didn't reply, so after a few seconds, I started the engine and continued on the journey.

On the way back she snapped at me again, this time about my driving, so pulling the car in from the traffic I said.

'Brenda! Up to now we have always taken it for granted that getting married was a good idea. But if we are making a mistake, now is the time to decide - before it is too late.'

Once more she said nothing, and that was the end of the nasty remarks for the time being. I was happy – and not really serious about pulling out of the marriage. But mentioning it gave voice to a fear that we *were* making a mistake. It was unthinkable; we never mentioned it again.

By the thirteenth, the house had been rewired, there was a new water main and the heating had been installed on the ground floor. A temporary kitchen had also been set up, and the whole place had been made generally habitable. The new kitchen would be arriving soon and the phone was about to be connected.

On the morning of the fourteenth, it was clear that we were going to make it apart from the bathroom. Dave Buckley, the plumber told me that it was going to be midday on the fifteenth before he could have the new system up and running. Brenda was adamant. We were moving in on Valentine's night - bathroom or no bathroom! So we bought a mattress and put it on the floor of the main bedroom.

The night was cold. It was a long trek to the downstairs toilet in the middle of the night and I'd have paid serious money for a chamber pot. But we did it! We were in our own home in Gordon Road for Valentine's night, having carried out a huge amount of work. It was no bad achievement.

*

The following morning, the house felt different. Until then it had been a project, a job. Now it was our home. It was time for a huge clean up. By about three o' clock Dave had finished and there was a bathroom across the landing. Luxury!

We worked until nine. There seemed to be no limit to the amount of work to be done, or to my supply of energy. Eventually Brenda suggested that we call it a day. 'How about a walk?' she said 'and a quiet drink somewhere afterwards.' It was a good idea, but it took an effort to drag myself away.

Our evening walks became a pattern, something to look forward to when working on the house. We tried to take a different route each time, to get to know the area around our new home. The brighter evenings enabled us to walk further and we were pleasantly surprised at the number of footpaths and walkways.

One of the first places we discovered was a little wine bar called 'Gustav's' round the corner from Gordon Road. It was in a small side street and its old fashioned awning gave it a distinctly Parisian flavour. The name, we soon discovered was no marketing ploy. Behind the counter was a huge man with a great bushy beard and not a rib of hair on top of his head. He spoke with a German accent and introduced himself as 'Gustav, all the way from Bavaria.'

'And we're Brenda and Owen - all the way from Limerick' I countered, smiling.

It was a relief to discover that he sold beer as well as wine and on the way out I joked 'You know you might even find us back here - if you're not careful.'

He wasn't; so he had to take the consequences. Gustav was quite a character. Like me he had worked all over the world and he took his holidays in West Cork. Born on a farm near the Czech border he had the countryman's contempt for rules and regulations. When working late, he often gave me a pint after hours. There was a cheerful atmosphere about his place and the odd singsong, unusual for London pub. Brenda was with me one Friday evening in March when a customer whom we recognised as a neighbour came over and introduced himself.

'You must find it difficult, settling into a new area' he said politely. 'Having to get used to all the different places and people.'

'Difficult? Good God no!' I answered, genuinely surprised. 'It feels like I've come home.'

CHAPTER 3

Two weddings

*I*t was unusual for my father to phone. A large official envelope had arrived with my name on it, and he wanted our new address, so he could post it on.

'Open it!' I suggested. It was from the United States Embassy, allocating me a green card. Four years after my application, it came as quite a surprise.

I was busy. Stephen Clarke had sent word that extra carpenters were needed in Central London, and for a few weeks we were working together again. In the evenings, it was hard to decide which was the most urgent job to do on Gordon Road. Gradually I fixed the leaks in the roof, the worst of the floorboards and the doors and windows. We even painted our bedroom and the little living room.

But the kitchen was a disaster. There had been problems with the delivery and when it did arrive in mid-March, we still weren't ready to fit it. The single-storey annex where it was to go was in terrible condition. I estimated that it would take at least a month before the new kitchen was in and working. In the meantime we were living and cooking in the small living room at the back of the house. Dave Buckley had fitted the old stone sink from the annex to one of the walls and Brenda had brought her little Baby-Belling cooker from Limerick. We still ate well and we had an impressive new bathroom to wash in. I didn't mind.

Brenda however was not happy at all. She became tense and irritable and she was very self-conscious about people calling. On one of our walks I tried to make her see that there was nothing to be ashamed of.

'Brenda!' I said. 'It's no disgrace having a house that's unfinished. Anyway we're making great progress. Look at what we've done in a matter of weeks! It's going to be lovely!'

But she was unconvinced. In fact she became worse in the days that followed.

The living room ceiling had to come down - before it fell down by itself. One day I took out the furniture and sealed the door to the hallway. In half an hour the remains of the lath and plaster were on the floor waiting to be bagged. It was quick and relatively painless. When the dust settled I opened the door.

Brenda came in and looked round distastefully. 'You're very good at *pulling down*' was all she said.

For the next few weeks she entered a protective phase trying to stop me replacing anything in the house whatsoever. Most of the things she was trying to preserve were cheap replacements put in since the Second World War and I began to lose patience. On the one hand she was very anxious to get the house finished, on the other she was making the job impossible. One Saturday she found me scraping paint off the stairs, using an old ceramic pot to hold the paint stripper. When she saw the pot she became furious calling me every name she could think of. Tired and irritable, I had had enough.

Crash! My hammer smashed the pot into a dozen pieces on the floor. As my eyes searched the room for another container, a sound behind me made me turn.

'What...!'

Brenda was swinging a metal dustpan in the direction of my head. Instinctively my left hand came up to deflect the blow. The dustpan hit the top of my middle finger. The skin was hard and callused from all the work; it came off in one piece, an 'umbrella'.

'Christ! Were you trying to kill me?' I shouted. She turned her back and walked away. She refused to talk about it afterwards, but at least she let me get on with the job.

My father's news meant that we had to get married if Brenda's name was to go on the green card. Margaret had phoned a few weeks earlier and asked me if I had any objection to having the wedding at the end of June.

'None whatsoever, Margaret!' I replied.

Now we had to be married by mid-April, at the latest. We telephoned the local registry office and arranged a date in late March. Four of our friends came along and afterwards we all went out for dinner.

For me that was the wedding. Anything afterwards was just a party for family and friends. But Brenda was determined that the civil ceremony be kept top secret and that we remove the wedding rings put on earlier in the day. I reluctantly agreed. In April we both went to Dublin and collected our papers at the U.S. Embassy after a great deal of red tape. We were registered aliens at last.

Back in Gordon Road the time flew. I liked the job in Central London and the people working with me. One of them was a big brickie from Dagenham called Sam Bowman.

'What are you eating?' he demanded one day as Stephen Clarke came into the canteen. 'I could nearly blow you over!'

'Think so?' said Stephen smiling. 'Let me tell you I'm stronger than you think. I'm able to do between two and three hundred press-ups, and a fiver says so!' Pulling out a five-pound note from his pocket, he laid it ceremoniously on the table.

Big Sam had very little choice but to match it with one of his own and Stephen got down on the ground on his hands and toes. He raised himself up.

'One!' we shouted. It was agonisingly slow. Down and up again. 'Two!' Then down and up. 'Three!' - the slowest of all. When he had completed his third press-up, he calmly got up and put the two fivers into his pocket.

'Hey! What are you doing?' Sam demanded belligerently.

'Taking my money of course' Stephen replied. 'I said between two and three hundred press-ups, Well *three* is between two and three hundred. Good job I didn't say between three and four hundred! I'd never have managed the fourth one.'

Ten days before the wedding, Stephen quit the job along with me to help with the house. Between us, we got several projects done, including a complete refurbishment of the stairs. Then Brenda had a stroke of luck. Having been out of work for nearly six months she was finally offered a job with a firm in Bromley, starting in August. She was delighted. Our financial worries seemed to be over.

Before we knew it, it was time to go back to Limerick. Our wedding was to be on the longest day of the year, a Saturday, so we flew over the weekend before. Seamus Newman was determined to 'do the right thing' by his daughter and the wedding was expensive and elaborate. We were dressed in morning suits and Brenda and her bridesmaids in lovely frocks and flowers. Margaret had booked one of the new plush hotels on the road to Shannon. The expense made me uneasy, but Brenda, like most women, wanted her special day and since the Newman family was hosting the wedding, it was not my business to interfere.

We had a blessing in the little church near where Brenda grew up. The city was now reaching out its tentacles, ready to swallow it together with the fields and hedges alongside. 'A shame!' I thought, my country background overcoming my years in the building trade. The priest was Father Michael Newman, Seamus's brother all the way from Chicago. We took to one another at once. One of the few clergymen to welcome real discussion on the subject of religion, he got some great talks going in the days coming up to the wedding.

It was a happy day - even though we could hardly eat our food and my speech was a bit 'wooden'. But afterwards we could all relax and join the fun. When the meal is over, the custom is that the friends of the bride and groom are invited to 'the afters' i.e. the dancing and celebrating which often last until the early hours of the morning.

My friends came from far and wide. They spilled out of the ballroom and the bar, overflowing even the huge landing and gathering down along the stairs and in the hotel foyer. There were over six hundred people in all. The manager eventually opened a smaller ballroom with another bar and it was filled to capacity.

My father was in his element. At seventy-eight he was livelier than most people. He is not able to sing but he has an endless repertoire of recitations and stories. Brenda and I went to bed exhausted, shortly after two. But my father, my brother, my sister and many of the guests stayed up another four hours singing, reciting and playing music. It was a wedding to remember.

The following day we went back to London and from there to America for the honeymoon. We spent the first week in New Orleans, the second in Boston (my old home) and the third travelling across Massachusetts in a motor-caravan - or as it is called in the U.S. a 'recreational vehicle'. This was Brenda's idea and the most memorable part of the holiday.

Strangely enough, of the two of us, I was the more irritable during the trip. Why? Was it just tiredness? It had been the most strenuous six months of my life. Or was it my subconscious mind telling me that something was wrong? It's hard to know; but consciously I felt very satisfied. One morning, driving westwards from Boston, my mood was so foul that we barely spoke a word to one another. A tense silence filled the vehicle. But after lunch, feeling sorry and ashamed, I apologised to Brenda and made it up to her for the rest of the journey. After that, we relaxed and enjoyed the last few days of our honeymoon.

Finally it was time to fly back to London, to Brenda's new job and her new kitchen (which I had promised to finish at all costs); to Gordon Road and to our future life together. We were both looking forward to it.

CHAPTER 4

Turning sour

Rows had been cropping up between us ever since the move to Gordon Road; but as yet they were no more than that - rows. When they were over we would have a laugh and enjoy one another's company again.

Brenda started work a few days after the honeymoon, and my priority was to get the kitchen ready. The first morning, having dropped her to the office, I arrived home and began to examine the little extension where the kitchen was to go. After five minutes it became clear that two walls would have to be substantially demolished and a new roof put on.

'Why? Oh why didn't we start it before the wedding?' I wondered aloud. The answer was that there just wasn't time. We had deliberately shied away from anything that might have remotely suggested a new project in order to squeeze in all the jobs at hand.

Now here it was, and it couldn't be ignored; so I set to work clearing everything out and telephoned Stephen Clarke to know when he could give me a hand.

'I can give you two days Owen, starting tomorrow,' he said. 'Then I'm off to a job in Streatham.'

'Great! I'll pick you up in the morning at nine.'

Nine o'clock was late for a builder; but Stephen never liked to start too early and the quality of his work was more than enough to offset the late starting time. It was a stroke of luck that he was free. Now materials had to be bought and delivered to Gordon Road by the next day, so I let Brenda know that I couldn't be able to collect her from work and set off in the car.

Back at Gordon Road, things needed to be made ready for Stephen. First I ripped out the rotten door and windows and hauled them to the bottom of the garden ready for burning later that evening. 'Thank God for bonfires!' I thought. 'Otherwise skips would cost me an arm and a leg.'

The time seemed to fly. Looking at my watch it said half-past-two - time for some lunch. Thanks to Brenda's sandwich toaster, I was back working again before three. Now the ceiling had to be hacked down with a spade (filthy job!). Then it all had to be sorted - the wooden laths to the bonfire and the rest of the rubble into bags. Next, the old cast-iron gutters and the fascia boards had to be prised off before removing the slates from the roof. The roof at the rear of the building was low and could be reached from a stepladder. The bottom row of slates was barely done when Brenda appeared behind me. She saved me countless trips up and down the ladder by taking each slate from me and laying it on the ground. We had the whole roof off in less than an hour.

She enjoyed it; we both did. Even though a little disappointed at the amount of work to get the kitchen ready, she still accepted it in good spirits.

Three weeks later Brenda was standing in her 'state of the art' kitchen, having just transferred all the food into the new fridge. It was looking very well. The ugly white appliances were all concealed behind doors of polished oak and we had a high-level oven - important because Brenda suffered from a bad back. She seemed pleased and in good humour.

My customary few days with my father were now due and I was looking forward to the rest. Brenda couldn't leave her new job, so I travelled on my own. We telephoned one another every day.

There was no rest in Limerick. The fences in my father's place were in a bad state and some cattle had broken into the neighbours' fields. He was quite embarrassed about it, so the posts and wire were bought and ready before my arrival. It was great exercise, satisfying, but tiring.

Turning sour

Back in London, my hands were cut from the barbed wire and I was burnt out, spending days lying in bed reading books. Brenda did not take a sympathetic view.

'How do you think it makes me feel?' she complained. 'Going off to work every day knowing that you're lounging around the house. It's not healthy anyway, all this reading.'

'Thanks for the support,' I replied.

'Oh for God's sake stop whinging!'

I said no more.

Soon afterwards, in the car, Brenda brought up the subject of the war in the Balkans and I began to explain the history of what happened. After about a minute she cut across me impatiently.

'Oh let's drop it. I can't follow what you're saying. You never make it sound interesting, like Cecil does.'

It was the way she said it. There was no regard for my feelings at all. Once more I said nothing. What could I say?

'All my friends got married and moved into *beautiful* houses'

We were on our way out to meet friends and she had seen me working all day on Gordon Road.

'What's going on?' I thought. 'Was it *meant* to hurt?'

*

These three incidents were the turning point; they started a pattern that I tried desperately to understand in the months ahead. But there was one other quarrel that was significant in its own way. It began simply enough.

The microwave needed a shelf and there was a handy piece of board left over; so one evening I cut it to fit into the kitchen corner. It was not a straightforward job as the corner was not a right angle but it was finished by ten o' clock.

'Brenda!' I called.

She came into the kitchen where I proudly presented the microwave sitting on its new shelf above the uncluttered work surface. To my surprise she frowned and pointed to the dust and shavings lying around.

'Can't you see the mess?' she snapped.

'Can't *you* see *that*?' I was pointing to the shelf.

'I suppose now you expect me to clean up after you.'

'I'm not expecting anyone to do anything!' I took a deep breath. 'Look! You get the dustpan! I'll get the Hoover. In five minutes we'll be done.'

'Clean it up yourself! I'm sick of cleaning up messes for you.'

'For me? Don't you think it benefits you at all?'

'That's not what I mean! It's your mess; you put it there.'

'I put the shelf there too. You can't change the shape of a piece of wood without a bit of dust!'

'A bit of dust! This whole house has been full of dust ever since we moved in. I'm sick of it! It never seems to end, and now I come down to find the kitchen a mess. Well, I have no intention of cleaning up any more after you!' She turned on her heel and marched up the stairs leaving me furious beside my evening's work.

It was the intensity that was different. This time she was not just annoyed; she was really angry.

'About what?' I asked myself, calming down. 'Surely not about some dust?' The next time I would have to talk to her. It was no good saying nothing and just hoping those scenes would just go away. They seemed to be getting worse.

There was no problem getting an opportunity to talk to her. Over the next few weeks she got angry several times, but I shied away from bringing it up. Was it that I sensed what the result would be? Or was it just my upbringing? In rural Ireland, giving offence was always a last resort. You offended someone if and when you were ready to come to blows, not before.

But my patience gave out in the end. We were looking at the little hallway inside the front door and I said it was 'too narra' to do anything with it.' Brenda turned on me.

'Would it cost you much effort to say "narrow" like everybody else' she said.

'Probably not. "Narra" is just the way I first heard it pronounced. It's dialect, a more direct descendant of Middle English 'narwe', so strictly speaking it's not even grammatically wrong.'

Brenda's expression changed from mild disdain to savage anger. She *hated* to be corrected on any point of knowledge. She actually lifted her hand to strike me but now I was angry too. The offence had been deliberate; but in my direct way I had concentrated first on the question as it was put.

'Don't even *think* about it,' I growled. She let her hand fall; then turning round, she banged the kitchen door and went out to the garden.

What was going on? Who could I talk to? Before long Jimmy Nagle came to mind. Jimmy's marriage had ended five years before. Picking up the phone I had a brief chat with him exchanging news, and then asked him out for a drink. He said we were due one for a while.

Men don't usually talk about these things, and when we met I hesitated to bring the matter up. But he gave me the cue; he didn't miss much.

'Well how's Brenda?' he said.

'She's a bit cranky at the moment Jimmy, It's hard to know what to make of it.' I gave him the gist of the last incident and the one before that.

'I'm not sure Owen,' he said thoughtfully, 'but one thing I'd say to you.'

'What's that?'

'You're very quick with your tongue. Maybe if you didn't always have the answer ready, you might be better off. Women like to have the last word and they get very worked up when they don't.'

'So what's the best thing to do, the next time she acts up?'

'Nothing! Let her act up and then let it die down again. She'll be sorry when it's all over. You'll find life very pleasant then for another while.'

Chapter 4

'You mean a man shouldn't defend himself when a woman abuses him?'

'Not when he has to live with her, he shouldn't.'

'But will she have any respect for him if he just puts up with it?'

'Owen if you're bothered about respect from women, your best bet is to stay away from them. The only man a woman respects, is the man she can't get.'

'But what about *mutual* respect, equality and all that?'

'Ah what about Santa Claus! Look Owen! You've got to realise it's the women who call the shots. A man doesn't pick his woman; she picks him. And when a man and a woman go to bed, it's not the man who starts it - we start the obvious part at the very end. And a woman will be boss in her own house; it's no good arguing with them. The best thing a man can do is to give in gracefully and stay well out of their way. Go out and have a few pints for yourself and let her calm down.'

'And did you always give in to your wife, let her boss you around?'

'I did, until I had a few drinks taken - and you can see where that got me!'

I had probably asked one question too many, but there seemed to be no ill will. Jimmy obviously sympathised with me and the conversation moved on to other matters.

But on the way home I brooded over all he had said. *Her house*! Damn it! Wasn't it my house as well? *Don't answer her back?* Surely, if I just sit there and take all the abuse she will despise me for it. Or will she? *Let her be the boss?* Do the same as Jimmy did except when he'd had a drink? Was he better off out of marriage? Perhaps I would be too. I had always respected Jimmy's intelligence. But was he talking about the same level of anger? Somewhat doubtfully I decided to give his advice a try and see would it change things. There didn't seem to be a great deal to lose.

It wasn't easy. Over the next few weeks there were unpleasant scenes about all kinds of things. The state of the house dominated the list of complaints, followed by the dust that appeared every time I set about changing it; it was hard to win! Brenda accused me of being a male chauvinist because I 'did nothing round the house.' Here Jimmy's advice got thrown to the winds as she was reminded of several things in as many seconds. The result was an angry silence. Taking Jimmy's advice literally, I tended to go round to Gustav's whenever things were becoming ugly, - but then she criticised me for spending too much time in the pub.

It wasn't working. Brenda's anger was not settling down; it was becoming more frequent. Even worse she began to make sneering and hurtful remarks when she didn't seem to be angry at all. It began one day when she made a throwaway remark about how little I was earning. It had been a particularly bad week. I winced, hurt by her tone, and she noticed. Over the next few weeks the little 'barbs' came frequently in my direction.

Of course there were good times still. We enjoyed going to the odd film and we still went for walks. But I never knew when things would turn nasty, and there was never an apology, no expression of remorse or anything to make good the hurt that had been done. One wound was festering, as the next was inflicted. The shadow of our quarrels was always there.

And there seemed to be no reason for them. Jimmy's advice was no good to me; his experiences were different to mine. He was probably dealing with a different sort of anger. It made me feel helpless and bullied - and then angry at what I was going through. Having brooded over each and every incident for a whole day, I made up my mind to have a battle royal the next time it happened. I was looking forward to it. But something intervened just in time.

Brenda had been accepted into the British Law Society, which meant that she could now practice as a solicitor in England and Wales. There was a ceremony which Seamus and Margaret came over to attend. We all had a good day and Brenda seemed to be happy. She even had me try on her gown and took my photo in it. We had a laugh. After her parents left, her behaviour changed abruptly. They obviously had had a word with her in private when they noticed what was going on; so things were easier again.

At last our life settled into a kind of rhythm. The recession in the building trade was getting worse but by signing on with a few agencies, work was still available. Brenda kept a curb on her anger and I could look forward to the next week instead of dreading the next row.

But by the middle of December things were getting worse again. She was controlling her anger, not eliminating it and it began to erupt without warning over issues that seemed very trivial to me. One of these was a silly disagreement over prose and poetry. We were discussing 'Les Miserables' and I made the statement that 'verse set to music must be the most powerful way of conveying emotion.'

'I don't agree,' she interjected quickly. 'You can describe it better in ordinary text.'

'You mean the best way to convey emotion is in *prose?*' My tone was incredulous but it was an honest question, without malice. She didn't answer and wouldn't talk to me for the rest of the day.

Worst of all were the bad 'vibes'. These came mostly midweek, in the evenings after work. I would come home to an atmosphere so tense that I could almost physically *feel it*. It was horrible! And it remained until we went to bed. But invariably, when we woke up the following morning, it had mysteriously disappeared.

Things were becoming unbearable. Three evenings like that in two weeks made up my mind to confront her, the next time it happened. There wasn't long to wait. A few days later I could sense it even before opening the door. 'Right! I've had enough of this!' I said to myself, and marched up to her boldly.

'Hello! Picture no sound?' I said, sounding stronger than I felt. There was no reply.

'Brenda do you have something to talk about?' There was still no reply, so I continued.

Turning sour

"Look! I'm coming home here to this kind of thing every second evening and I've had enough! It's time we had a talk.' Brenda's face became disdainful; still she said nothing.

'Brenda! Do you hear me talking to you? If you think you can intimidate me like that you can think again. I want to know what's going on. I'm just about sick of it!' My voice was genuinely angry now. Brenda, still ignoring me, adopted an even more contemptuous expression and walked around me towards the door. That did it!

Stepping to the left I blocked her way.

'You've been treating me like dirt for months. Now please tell me what's going on because I'm **damned** if I'm putting up with any more of it! - And don't ignore me when I'm speaking to you!' The words came through my teeth.

'Look! Can we talk about it some other time?' She was actually talking to me. Was that what it took?

'Fine!' I said, glad to calm down. 'But can we settle the time now? When is it going to happen?'

KNOCK! KNOCK! My head turned instinctively; it came from the front door. Brenda took advantage of my indecision to slip round me and admit a neighbour who wanted me to replace a broken pane of glass. Perhaps it was unfortunate, but it was doubtful if our talk would have taken place anyway. My mind was anxious to let go of the subject too. I remember reflecting how, when angry, I adopted the archaic speech of my father.

There's a saying I picked up in America. "You can do what you want to an orange but what comes out is always orange juice; that's what's inside!" With my marriage, the story was the same. The 'bad vibes' stopped all right to my relief; but a few days later I became conscious of something else. Brenda had taken to snapping angrily at me over small mistakes. Spilling some coffee or dropping my keys provoked a very irritable 'be careful'; a verbal mistake and I was 'an idiot'. She spat the words out making me feel 'on edge' like a schoolboy waiting for the teacher to correct him. She had to be confronted again but I hated the thought of it.

Chapter 4

Brenda made up my mind for me a few days later. A customer was speaking to me on the phone and I described something as 'part of the course'. When the call was over Brenda told me that it's 'par for the course.' She added 'it's an expression *we* use in golf.' It was her tone of voice; it couldn't have been nastier. It was time to take the bull by the horns.

'Brenda, we're going to have to talk about this. You're snapping and snarling at me for weeks! This can't go on!'

The waves of opposition and anger rose to meet me. *It felt like I was doing something wrong!* It made me falter for a moment, but plucking up courage I continued. 'You can't talk to a human being like that, I've had enough of it!'

'Oh for God's sake Owen! You make me sick! Always whinging and whining like an old woman!'

'Look are you prepared to talk about this or not?' I said, already knowing the answer.

'I'm certainly not going to be bullied by you into anything!' she responded and walked out of the room her head in the air.

She left me more puzzled than angry. On my way into the kitchen to make myself a cup of tea, my mind was alive with questions. What was going on? Why wouldn't she talk to me? Where was all this anger coming from? Why was she treating me with contempt? Was it my fault? Should I be stronger? Must I get really angry to get a response? Aren't couples supposed to talk things out? So why was she making it feel so wrong? What was the best way to handle it? What was going on?

What?

No answers came but one thing was clear. This anger was not coming from me; there was no doubt about that now. Also Brenda's anger was unusual; other women did not have it. But as regards explaining it or knowing what to do, I was as wise as ever.

Christmas came almost before we knew it. We were lucky to get a place on the ferry from Pembroke to Rosslare. Then there was the drive to Dungarvan in the Volvo, a right turn at Fermoy, and before long we were up among the hills. It felt good to be back. Our first Christmas as a married couple!

There were several friends to meet including Joe Healy and his wife Maura. They had built a new house on the next hill. We could see it from my father's even though it was four or five miles away by road. Joe and Maura took us on a tour of their new home and it was certainly very impressive.

'Just as well you're in the trade, Joe,' I said looking at the drawing room. They both smiled, well pleased.

Brenda and Maura seemed to be having a great chat, so Joe winked at me. 'Will we go up the road?'

'Twist my arm' I replied.

Kennedys' pub hadn't changed at all, and we had three very pleasant pints of Guinness before leaving at around eleven o' clock. I was glowing with contentment and good humour. When we got back to the house Brenda said it was time to go, even though eleven is quite early to leave in that part of Ireland, especially coming up to Christmas.

We were in the car before I sensed it. Was it that the two women didn't get on? Or maybe the house had made Brenda jealous. Whatever it was, the atmosphere was foul.

'How much drink did you have?' she demanded. 'Should you be driving?'

I slowed down. 'You drive if you want.' My good humour was leaving me all too soon.

'No! Just be careful!' she snapped. It was not the right time; it was anything but the right time. She was robbing me of my evening, poisoning things *again*. We drove home in angry silence.

In the old family room of my father's house, she started once more.

'*How dare you* walk out on me like that and leave me alone with some strange woman!'

I glowered, my anger boiling. Mistaking my silence for weakness she carried on, her voice becoming louder.

'If this is the way I'm going to be treated I'm going to spend Christmas with my own family.'

'**Out**! Get outside the door you selfish little bitch! You'll wake my father!'

She took no notice; she even tried to push me out of her way. I retaliated in kind, catching her by the arm and propelling her out the door, across and into the laneway beyond. When she found her balance, she gave a little growl of rage and tried to barge past me again.

Clack!

It was my palm across her right cheek; it makes a sound like no other. For a moment she stood in shock; then with a growling sound she made two fists out of her hands and flung herself at me in fury. But now I was as angry as she was. Grabbing her two wrists I pushed her roughly back; she staggered, then found her balance again.

'Listen you spoilt filthy little brat! You want to go to your parents' place? Then let's go right now! The best thing you can do is to stay there! And I'm going to wake both your parents up and tell them what you've been up to. You think you can treat people anyway you like. You're not prepared to talk to me about it; well maybe you'll talk to them. Come on! Get your bags! I've had enough of you!'

For a few moments she did nothing. Then she began to cry. For ten minutes she stood there in the lane sobbing. My anger soon died down, and of course I didn't go through with the threat to take her into Limerick. I never really wanted to. We made a cup of tea when we went back into the house.

For the rest of the holiday Brenda was graciousness itself. She made a good impression on all my friends and she was particularly nice to my father. There was a lot of visiting and she always seemed in the best of humour. We had a good Christmas.

CHAPTER 5

Pregnancy

*B*renda had to be back at work on the thirtieth; so we asked my father if he would like to come to London with us for the New Year. It was forty years since he had been out of Ireland, and he accepted the invitation cheerfully, travelling back with us in the car. We arrived early on the morning of the twenty-ninth.

He is a great walker and soon got to know the neighbourhood. Gustav's, he found very pleasant but he was not impressed with the Guinness. Brenda had to work on New Years Eve, so it was nearly ten o' clock when we went round to Gustav's to celebrate. We the best New Year's Eve I can remember. My singing voice was never better, Brenda joined in all the choruses and my father even recited 'The Cremation of Sam Magee' to a big round of applause.

The following day, he announced that he had found a pub where they served Irish Guinness brought over from Dublin. The pub was about a mile away, he told me, giving me the name and address.

'Good God! That's over in Fulham, across Wandsworth Bridge!' I said. 'We'll pass about twenty pubs to get there!'

'And what about it? A mile is a mile! Less than I have to go to Kennedys'. Leveller walk too!'

There was nothing for it but to go with him. He was seventy-eight years old and I was thirty-four; it would hardly do to let him go on his own.

The reason it is so clear in my mind is that it was the day things changed again. One of Gustav's regulars had asked me to fit some kitchen units and when I reached home the atmosphere in the house was terrible. There seemed to be no reason for it and it couldn't be brought up without creating a scene in front of my father.

Since the awful row before Christmas the whole thing had been put to the back of my mind. We had had a few 'teething problems' in our marriage that was all! Now here it was back once more bringing me close to despair. All of a sudden, the year ahead looked very different. It was all I could do to hide my state of mind from my father as we set off.

The drink did me good, so did the walk.

*

'I'm pregnant!'

It was less than a week after my father had gone back, his first time on a plane. 'Like a big bus,' he told me afterwards. He had enjoyed his visit, and it gave him the confidence to do some more travelling. He had a pensioner's pass, which meant he could travel all over Ireland for free by bus and train, and now he decided to make use of it.

The thing noticeably missing from Brenda's voice was enthusiasm. She sounded like a cyclist who has just noticed his front tyre getting flatter and flatter.

'Do you know for certain?' My tone was even, but there was a little thrill rising inside me that was hard to conceal. I was pleased, very pleased in fact. Surprised at the strength of my feelings I looked to see if Brenda noticed.

She did! And judging by the scowl coming over her face it gave her no pleasure at all.

'Yes' she said, 'I've been to the doctor.'

'Oh right! Well at least there's time to make plans, get ourselves organised.'

'Valerie will be furious!'

Brenda's boss, a very capable solicitor, took a dim view of unplanned pregnancy. There had been one in the office the previous year and the unfortunate employee, a black girl from Ghana, had felt the rough edge of Valerie's tongue for months afterwards.

'What are we going to do?'

'Do? There's very little we can do now. After you check again, we can look at hospitals and things.'

She turned away. The mood was bad and it was not the time for talking. I read a book until bedtime.

The following evening things were not much better. There was very little talk and by half past ten it seemed a good idea to slip round to Gustav's for a pint. Going out the door I heard her pick up the phone. An hour later she was still on her seat with the telephone in her hand, talking to Margaret, her mother. The conversation ended shortly after that and she went to bed without a word. Slightly earlier the following evening I got the distinct feeling that it was time to leave once again. This time the lights were out when I came home.

'We'd better discuss having a baby.' She said it in a matter of fact kind of way, the following morning. But it meant the tension was over, time to breathe a sigh of relief. Also, she was now plainly reconciled to the idea of being pregnant, not angry about it any longer. Margaret could take the credit here; there was very little doubt about that.

It was what I wanted to hear. Since the walk to the pub with my father, my mind had been in turmoil. That night, and for the next week, I had resigned myself to the idea that our marriage was doomed, but Brenda's news made me determined that it must work at all costs. At least, if she was no longer angry about being pregnant, then we were in with a chance.

*

As far as work was concerned, things were very satisfactory. Two days after my father had gone home, Jimmy Nagle phoned to tell me about a carpentry job in Fenchurch Street Station. The station was being completely refurbished and there was at least six months work ahead. In fact the job lasted until mid-August. With both Brenda and myself earning, we were comfortable for the rest of the year.

Chapter 5

In late February I suggested a break, a long weekend in Bruges, Belgium from Thursday until Sunday. Being the off-season, there was no problem booking the holiday at a week's notice.

Bruges is very pretty and interesting and all Friday and Saturday we had a very enjoyable time. However on Saturday evening, on the way back to our hotel, I could sense Brenda's mood changing. Casting my mind through the events of the day I tried anxiously to work out the cause of the change, but without success. Wisely, I kept the conversation to a minimum until we went to bed.

It was at breakfast the following morning that the storm clouds broke. I made the chance remark that we came from 'fairly similar backgrounds', thinking that this was pretty safe ground. She laughed derisively and said I 'hadn't a clue what I was talking about' and in a loud voice told me how our backgrounds were totally different and how absurd it was to think anything else.

I was determined not to get angry. The marriage had to survive now - no matter what! The holiday and the rest also helped me to feel relaxed and strong. So it was not too difficult to stay calm, responding unemotionally to every point she made. It lasted the whole day. My mind desperately tried to come to grips with what was going on. One thing was sure; this was not about family backgrounds or what our fathers did for a living.

It ended when we were on the boat back to Dover. Brenda went up to the toilet on the next floor and when she came back the bad atmosphere was gone. Her face wore a different expression and her voice had a different tone; it was all over. It left me more puzzled than ever. Part of me cried out for answers, wanted to take the bull by the horns and demand to know what the hell it was all about. But I guessed that it would only lead to a return of the foul mood and she wouldn't tell me anyway. I took the easy way out.

It was like that for most of the year. Good days and bad days followed each other unpredictably and for no apparent reason. It was like being married to two people. Before long I did demand answers, but all I got were jeers about 'whinging and complaining' and it seemed to make Brenda even angrier. But there were the good days too; days when we had fun together, when we were the best of friends, when it seemed as if we'd never had a row. Our day at the Ideal Homes exhibition in Earl's Court was like that. We were relaxed and happy, wandering among the stands, eating hot dogs and frozen yoghurt. At one stall, a big cheerful man with a strong Cockney accent tried to sell me a diamond-covered sharpening stone for sixty pounds.

'Bargain it is guv!' he said. 'Hun'red pound in the shops! And your tool bag will be so much lighter going to work. See how light it is!' he recited, picking the stone up.

'At that price, the bag would be even lighter coming home,' was my reply.

There were many days like that, short trips, evenings with friends, happy times in Gordon Road. And there was no day that I did not phone her at work. At half past twelve I would go round to the phonebox before having my lunch. My job was going well and Brenda's even better; there were no money worries. She still hadn't told Valerie about being pregnant, but felt she could handle it now.

Still the rows continued. Often they would erupt at unexpected times and about subjects that seemed to be harmless. We had always disagreed about the subject of modern art but our disagreements were pretty amicable. So when I arrived home, one evening and told her about a piece of graffiti at the job, I expected her to be amused. The graffiti artist was evidently familiar with the tastes and peculiarities of the art world for he had drawn something like this:

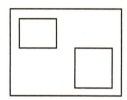

Underneath was the caption: *"BALLS - by Picasso."*

Chapter 5

It kept me chuckling all day but Brenda was not amused. 'I'm afraid I don't see the joke' she said coldly. It was a long evening.

We quarrelled a lot about the house and its unfinished state. Brenda said she was ashamed to bring her friends in the front door. She had a point; the door opened into a narrow hall, really no more than a corridor. The partition between this hallway and the drawing room rested on a very uneven wooden floor. The boards had been sawn and refitted many times over the years, to fit pipes and cables. The partition really needed to come down, so new floorboards could be laid.

The problem was Brenda was totally opposed to it. 'We're not starting any new projects - making a mess!' she insisted. 'We can lay a carpet over the boards.'

It was no good trying to explain to her that we couldn't do anything with that floor as it was, and that it would be cheaper to do the job properly. She was having none of it! So for a while the floor stayed uneven. At last I grew tired of waiting and arranged for Stephen Clarke and his brother Terry to come and help me the following Monday when Brenda went to work. When she arrived home the partition was in rubble bags out in the little front garden.

To my amazement she looked round and smiled. 'I really like it this way,' she said. 'So nice and airy. I don't think we'll put a partition back there at all.' She even took a day off work, a few weeks later, to help sand and varnish the new floorboards.

The baby was due in September and the hospital had a 'parentcraft' class starting in mid-June, one evening a week for eight weeks. Brenda used to meet me there after work. She liked to sit behind me, so that when she noticed me to nodding off, she could surreptitiously prod me awake with a pen. Not that the classes were boring, it was just that I had been on my feet since seven in the morning. In fact we both found them very helpful. Afterwards we often had a meal in one of the small restaurants on the way home. Before the classes I had never visualised a real baby. Now we jokingly referred to Brenda's bump as 'Pyracantha' and I actually began to grow fond of 'her.'

If only we didn't have the rows! They threw a shadow over everything. It was impossible to predict when they were going to flare up, so the tension was always there. Worse than that, Brenda refused point blank to discuss them after they were over. Now, committed to making the marriage work, I tried to insist that we talk about them. Couldn't we talk things over, find out what was wrong, clear the air and become friends again? But her response was a stone wall: no communication of any kind, nothing! We never made good a single row, never made up or said we were sorry. Our quarrels never ended. Strain and anger were there, waiting to explode the next time.

It began to wear me down, to make me feel helpless and vulnerable. One Saturday morning in July, the ugly atmosphere met me on my way down the stairs; by now it was all too familiar. Brenda was in the kitchen and greeted me with a scowl. Determined not to give in to her mood, I broke the silence.

'Lovely day!'

No answer! Brenda's scowl intensified. I found myself feeling guilty and defensive. Maybe going out for a pint the previous night wasn't fair to her. Or had I said or done something wrong? Forgotten something perhaps? With a feeling of annoyance I realised that I was allowing myself to be intimidated. This mental bullying had gone on for long enough! It had to be confronted sooner or later - and now was as good a time as any!

'Brenda! Is there something wrong?' It was difficult to keep my voice even. There was no answer, no acknowledgement except that her face took on a scornful look. The anger boiled inside me.

'Brenda! Answer me when I'm talking to you!' My voice was not even now.

Still no response.

'Brenda! I'm talking to you. If something is wrong, please tell me! I will not be treated like this without some kind of explanation.'

'Do you ever get tired of whinging?' Can't you act like a man?' My anger subsided a little. It was clear enough what she was doing - trying to upset me, turn me away from the subject, anything to avoid the discussion.

Sensing my uncertainty, she walked to one side of me towards the door and if her face had not held on to the disdainful look she would have made it. As it was all my anger was kindled again; my foot in the door stopped her in her tracks. She dropped the scornful expression and her face took on the look of a cornered animal. With her right hand she made a fist and swung it at me. She is a big strong woman and if the fist had connected it would have made its mark for days to come. But I parried the blow easily with my left arm and the hard bone of my wrist bit into her forearm. It hurt! The shock drained her of energy and she stood there helplessly.

My anger was evaporating too - but this might be my only chance to press ahead.

'Listen!' I said, trying to sound angry still. 'We have to talk about this! What are you are so afraid of?'

'Okay!' she responded in a choking tone. 'Can we walk? I need to get out of here!'

I nodded, so we walked all along Gordon Road, up to the main street and round the block until before I knew it, we were back home again. All the way she kept up a conversation about nothing in particular. My anger had evaporated by now, leaving me ashamed of having lost my temper and unable to insist on discussing our rows. She was being particularly pleasant as well, creating the kind of atmosphere I hated to spoil.

Coming in the door I knew I was going to let it go. Brenda went into the kitchen; she made us a cup of tea.

*

Pregnancy

It was like living in a different house. Of course there was the odd 'hurry up!' and 'be sure to hoover up the dust!' but in a very different tone from before. And there were no scornful looks, no bad 'vibes', no deadly silences. Still uneasy that Brenda had not talked things over, I had nothing like the thoughtless optimism of the New Year. But she seemed to be working hard at the relationship - and the baby would bring an even greater sense of responsibility to both of us. Cautiously, I began to believe that we could work things out, that our marriage would survive!

At work the job was nearly over. When they needed a steelfixer for a week I got the job for Jimmy Nagle; one good turn deserved another. Jimmy's droll manner and witty remarks made him very popular with the lads on site.

One day a gaunt young man came into the canteen as we were having breakfast. He had the pale look of a heavy cannabis smoker. He was selling tools, he told us. His eye lit upon Jimmy and, mistaking him for a brickie, he pulled a trowel out of his bag. Handing it to Jimmy he said, 'Good bargain here mate! Top quality steel!'

Jimmy brought the trowel down sharply on the corner of the table. He looked down at the trowel and his eye caught a small dent.

'Might have been *stolen*,' he said. 'That's about the only relationship it ever had to *steal*.'

The whole canteen shook with laughter. No sale was made.

*

'Owen'
'Yes...Oh hello Tim!'

It was Brenda's brother on the Saturday of the August bank holiday weekend. He had interrupted my thoughts about 'Pyracantha' and the fragile peace between us.

'Are you very busy? I need a hand with a ladder.'
'To hold it? Where are you?'

Chapter 5

'I'm here in Hammersmith, but there's no need to hold it. The job is finished. All I need to do is to take the ladder away. Any chance you could give me a hand with the Volvo. It'll only take half an hour.'

'Ok! So where are you?'

He gave me directions and I got there in just over twenty minutes. The ladder was up on a low flat-roofed extension, leaning against the main building. I pulled the Volvo half way up on the kerb and Timmy, quick as a goat had clambered onto the flat roof using a stepladder. Deftly he pulled in the extension piece and took the ladder away from the wall. Then he handed it down to me. In less than a minute it was tied on my roof rack ready to go.

The extension was in fact a shop front. It had been built over what was evidently a small front garden like the one in Gordon Road. An old lady now came out of the shop and started a conversation. I like talking to old people and began to chat easily with her. Timmy began shuffling impatiently beside the car; it made me feel mildly irritated. After all hadn't I come to oblige him? What was his hurry? We'd get to his place soon enough.

He caught my eye and beckoned me urgently. He seemed to be in some kind of hurry. Reluctantly, I said goodbye to the old lady and climbed into the car.

'You're somewhere down this direction aren't you?'

'Well I was thinking it would be better off in your place.'

'My place? But don't you want it handy for your next job?'

'I have no place to store it.'

'But where do you keep...?' Suddenly I realised what was going on. 'Oh shit Tim! If anyone took my number! What the hell do you think you're doing?'

'He caught me in my wages, promised me fifty a day - then only paid me forty. He even tried thirty-five!'

It was a common trick among unscrupulous builders at the time. Written contracts were few. I could sympathise with him. All the same...

'Damn it Tim! You could have got us both locked up. The Old Bill would hardly be likely to believe me. "You see Constable, I never knew the ladder didn't belong to him. Honestly I didn't! Do I know him? Well actually... he's my brother-in-law." That would sound really great!'

But Tim was unrepentant. 'Haven't you a fine ladder for nothing? And you'll hardly stop me from using it every now and then. It'll come in very handy.'

Tim is one of those people with whom it is impossible to be angry. Anyway there were bigger things on my mind.

'You should know Timmy by now,' Brenda said later. 'You walked into it like a child.'

But she was laughing. At least she didn't get angry!

Maybe there was hope for us after all.

CHAPTER 6

Matthew

Matthew arrived with very little warning.
One Saturday in early September, as I was installing a kitchen a few streets away from Gordon Road, Brenda called round. It was lunchtime and she wanted to know when I would be ready. She even helped me to grout some tiles before we walked home. A few weeks earlier she had taken maternity leave from her job, and her mother was due to fly in from Limerick that afternoon. As we were getting ready to meet her at the airport Brenda noticed her trousers were wet; her waters had broken. There was still no pain and very little feeling. We telephoned the hospital, threw a few things in a bag and set off in the car.

Driving along beside the Thames, the traffic slowed down and eventually came to a standstill. I got out of the car and looked around. Another driver a couple of cars further on looked out of his window and, noticing my bewilderment, told me that there was a huge demonstration further ahead. Apparently some pro-fascist group was holding a musical concert that attracted a demonstration, which brought a counter demonstration in turn. Gripping the wheel I cursed all fascists and anyone else I could think of. After a while the cars moved on again at a snail's pace.

'Christ! This is only supposed to happen in films,' I thought to myself, 'not in real life.'

It was hard to hide my anxiety. What if the pains started while we were still stuck in the car? However I kept up a steady patter of conversation with Brenda and she responded in a similar tone. No pains yet!

Another twenty minutes brought us to the pedestrian entrance to the hospital. I turned to Brenda.

'You'd better go in this way. We may be another half hour getting round to the car-park.'

My tone of voice betrayed my concern, and for the first time she looked worried. A few yards further on the cars stopped again; so grabbing her bag, she made her way carefully from the car up to the hospital door.

Margaret was waiting for me at the airport.

'Is everything all right?' she said, seeing me alone.

'Everything's fine! Brenda's just gone into hospital but there are no pains yet.'

I was not feeling as confident as I sounded. 'Perhaps the baby is already there by now,' would have been nearer to what was going through my mind. We were both too worked up to think of using the phone, so it was after another stressful hour of driving through London traffic that we found out how things were.

Brenda was installed in a comfortable room overlooking the Thames. Sitting up in bed, she smiled as we came into the room. From across the river we could hear Big Ben; it was seven o'clock in the evening. There was no danger yet, the nurse told us, so Margaret came back with me to Gordon Road. Hungry and very tired, I made myself a quick snack and fell asleep on a chair.

At ten o' clock the phone rang; Brenda's pains had started. There were no traffic problems now, and by half past I was walking along the corridor that led to Brenda's room. Margaret was not allowed into the delivery room, so she stayed behind at Gordon Road, having given me instructions to phone her every two hours.

Brenda was propped up on the bed, holding a small black box with several strings attached. The instructor had shown us one of these in parenting class. It was called a 'tense machine' because it is supposed to relieve pain and tension in some strange way. She was also connected to a huge monitor with various screens and dials.

'There was no pain 'til they switched that damn thing on,' she grumbled.

As the night wore on the pains became worse, so I asked her if she still felt the same way about the epidural injection.

'I told you no one is going to stick needles in my back!' she said.

The nurse kindly mentioned that pethadine, the painkiller that Brenda had agreed to take, was very effective and that, at least, was reassuring. Brenda had made very clear decisions about coping with the pain. On one hand she had no intention of trying to be a hero by giving birth without pain relief of any kind; but on the other she had decided to draw the line at 'needles in the back', and she stuck to her decision - pain or no pain.

It was a long night and not for the faint hearted. There are advantages to being born the son of a hill-farmer. It's not uncommon for the more sheltered 'yuppie' dads to get physically sick at the sight of all the blood and slime. But I had seen too many cows calving, sheep lambing and mares foaling to get upset *that* easily.

By five o' clock however, I was worried. The baby's head appeared to be bigger than normal. ('A family trait,' I thought guiltily) and Brenda was getting very tired. Shortly afterwards she wasn't able to push any longer and soon the monitor showed the baby's heartbeat decreasing rapidly. The midwife immediately sent for the doctor who produced a device like a tongs with large cupped ends and set to work. I watched in horror as the baby's head appeared and had to look away as his neck stretched and stretched. It seemed that that his little head would be torn off.

Suddenly it was all over. The nurse in front of me was holding a baby. For a while it was hard to take it in. This was different! Suddenly there was *a presence*, another human being in the room - and he didn't come in by the door! There is something special about the human spirit. It was nothing like seeing a calf being born, nothing at all!

'It's a boy!' the nurse called, bringing me back to reality. That itself was a surprise. Having grown fond of 'Pyracantha' during the pregnancy I expected a little girl. Still a little dazed I noticed the doctor with a pair of scissors in his hand about to cut the cord.

'Let me!' I said a little shakily and then again as though he hadn't heard me 'Let me!'

Without a word he handed me the scissors and I carefully cut Matthew's umbilical cord up close to his belly and then handed them back.

Matthew! Matthew's cord! He was already a person; he had his name. Calling him 'the baby' always seemed wrong. Dazed or not, it was quite clear in my mind that he was going to be called after my father. Brenda had agreed to that, months earlier, and now his little identity was fixed firmly in my mind.

Taking him from the nurse, I held him in my arms briefly, and then carried him over to Brenda. For a while she held on to him before handing him back to me. In a cubicle just outside the delivery room, he was weighed, measured and all his details entered in the computer. Both his parents had bonded with Matthew as soon as he was born. It was just as well.

My first job was to phone Margaret and after that one of the nurses gave me a cup of tea. When she arrived I went down to call my father and to tell him about his first baby grandson. He was delighted and even began to ask me questions about flights to London! That made me smile, tired or not. It was daytime now; the morning sun was shining on the Thames, nearly seven o' clock.

It was nine before I got to bed, still too excited to sleep properly. At two in the afternoon Margaret set off with me for the hospital again. It would be nice to be able to say that the first time I held my little son in my arms a great rush of love and tenderness came over me. But the fact is, earlier that morning my mind was too numb to be aware of a great deal of affection.

It was now, the second time that I began to notice feelings that lay buried inside me for years. He was so small and helpless that all my protective instincts were aroused at once. Picking him up and holding him brought back my experiences that morning, but now I was able to process my feelings and express them.

First there was the joy, the sheer joy of parenthood, of having my own tiny little child in my arms. For parents the phrase 'pride and joy' is no cliché. Both feelings seemed to come together. My pride in my little son was uncontainable; it just bubbled out of me, stronger than any pride I have known, a sense of triumph, of victory! When Brenda took Matthew back, I couldn't stand still.

Leaving the three generations for a while, I went downstairs to a public phone and telephoned everybody who came into my head, in London, in Ireland, even my sister and some friends in the U.S. until all the coins in my pocket were gone.

The following morning, Margaret came with me to the hospital and we made a second visit late in the afternoon. About ten in the evening I decided to go round to Gustav's for a quiet beer to celebrate. At the bar Gustav was quick to spot the mood and asked me the news.

'I'm celebrating tonight Gustav,' I said. 'We have a baby boy since yesterday morning. He's called Matthew.'

His face broke into a huge grin of pleasure. 'Congratulations!' he boomed, his voice filling the bar. It had been quiet until then, being Monday evening and there were no more than ten customers inside. Now they all looked up, glad of a bit of excitement.

'Owen has some good news, he is a daddy since yesterday' he went on as my face turned scarlet. There was a cheer from the tables and all the heads were now turned towards me.

'Tell you what! I'll buy you all a drink if you stop making noise and give a man a bit of peace. What'll it be Gustav?'

'No deal, Owen! No way!' the lads were saying. 'You can't just become a daddy and then spoil our fun. You must put up with your hard time like the rest of us.'

Gustav grinned. He and the others were out for some fun. One thing for sure, it was going to be no quiet drink.

'Well so what! Why spoil the fun? And I feel like celebrating anyway,' I said to myself.

So we drank 'to Matthew!' 'To Matthew!' again and at least twice more. To be fair to Gustav he didn't just make the announcement to sell more drink. Sometime around midnight he put a line of glasses along the counter. Then he broke open a brand new bottle of Irish whiskey and poured it across the glasses until the bottle was empty. The glasses were touching, so he didn't spill a drop and they seemed remarkably equal in contents; he had evidently done this before.

'May he have a long and happy life,' he said. I could have hugged him. As a matter of fact I think I did!

We all sang songs, told jokes and philosophised grandly until nearly half past two; then it was time to head for home. On my way to bed I noticed Margaret's light on.

'G'night Margaret! We were celebrating' I explained helpfully.

'I'd never have guessed! Goodnight now Owen!' she laughed, 'I'll see you in the morning.'

*

'Dim drums throbbing, in the hills half-heard.'

Chesterton's 'Lepanto' came into my head very soon after waking up, and stayed with me all day, probably because it described what I was feeling. A dull throbbing pain in my temples eclipsed all other thoughts in my mind. Even Matthew was temporarily forgotten.

Margaret was up before me. She had made tea and poured me a cup. 'You had a good night' she said good-humouredly. The tea did the trick. It soaked into my dehydrated body like a balm.

'Oh, Tom O'Hara called, he's meeting you in Fulham at ten'

I groaned. Of course! We had made the arrangement for yesterday. Then I had put it off until today and he was now on his way from Norwich. There was no way out of it.

'You'll have no trouble finding the hospital?'

'None, Owen but I'll leave it for an hour or so; you'd better get a move on!'

'Oh to be twenty five!' Back then, I could go for a night's drinking and still feel human the following morning. Now ten years later two or three pints were quite enough! I picked up my toolbag (it seemed twice as heavy as usual) and set off for the bus stop.

It was a long day. Tom had acquired a new studio apartment (the attic of a three-story building in Ellis Road) and he wanted it rented out as quickly as possible. We worked until eight o' clock that evening. Then I changed my clothes and went straight to the hospital leaving my tools on the job and promising myself never to touch alcohol again!

The following day, Wednesday, we finished early. Margaret drove with me to the hospital where Brenda was dressed and ready. Feeling great, I picked Matthew up in my arms and carried him out to the car with Margaret and Brenda on either side of me. He was an exceptionally well formed little baby, with a wisp of red hair and no wrinkles whatsoever on his skin. Carrying him made me feel as proud as Punch.

As we walked slowly along the corridor the head of midwifery appeared accompanied by a visitor.

'What a lovely baby!' she said seeing him in my arms. 'What's he called?'

'Matthew,' I replied smugly, 'Matthew Sheridan.'

CHAPTER 7

Storm clouds

I was no self-conscious dad, afraid to be seen changing a nappy or pushing a pram. Parenting came easily to me, like something I had been doing all my life. Matthew slept in a Moses basket beside the bed, and seeing him and Brenda together each morning, it was an effort to drag myself away to work.

But money had to be made; there is no paternity leave when you are self-employed and no unemployment benefit either. By Saturday afternoon Tom's flat was finished and rented out at a hundred and ten pounds a week. He seemed unusually pleased and happy enough to postpone the next job until Wednesday allowing me to take Monday and Tuesday off.

Margaret and Brenda were glad to have me around, especially as Brenda had decided to breastfeed.

'They just dried us up in my time and showed us how to mix the bottle,' Margaret said. 'So I'm afraid I'm no good to you.'

My knowledge of things like mastitis and colostrum came as a surprise to everybody, not least to myself and they both depended on me. My first job was to buy a changing mat, more nappies, a breast pump, and two bottles. They made life easier, especially on Brenda.

The thing that took me by surprise, was the strength of my own feelings. I had always been cool, and analytical.

'You have lukewarm emotions Owen,' a prospective girlfriend had told me once, as she rejected my advances. It was true and I knew it.

It was hardly surprising. Children were not exactly mollycoddled in my time, except among the very wealthy. Parents didn't believe in it. And of course it didn't help to be the first child, a heavy baby with a big wide head. My birth was also by forceps - and it wasn't over anything like as soon as Matthew's. No wonder my mother had a problem bonding with me; there wasn't much support around then, or sympathy. Doctors tended to say things like 'Pull yourself together woman! Isn't he a fine healthy child? If you were like the poor woman down the ward, you'd have something to worry about! Her child has a clubfoot!' Breastfeeding tended to iron out these bonding problems, but that was out of fashion when I was a baby.

The result was a thinker, an analyst, good at school and anxious to measure up and be accepted, but afraid of emotion, keeping it buried as much as possible in his subconscious mind. Now, bonding with my own little son, all my feelings came out in a gush. For the first time in my life I knew what love was. I was crazy about him, totally captivated and fiercely protective. When he was asleep in his cradle I would look in anxiously to see that he was still breathing.

Once when the three of us took a walk along Wandsworth High Street, we saw an Asian driver having trouble getting his car into gear. Another car pulled up close behind him and began to 'toot' angrily at being held up. Then, leaning out the window he yelled something about getting out of the way. Matthew sensed the anger and began to cry fearfully in his buggy.

'Can't you see he's not able to get it going?' I growled through the open window.

'That's not my problem,' he snapped back. That did it!

'You make my baby cry again - it's going to be your problem!'

I'd like to think it was the force of my personality, but it was more likely the sight of this big Irish construction worker that did the trick. Anyway the tooting stopped, so did the yells.

Sadly, it *was* the first time I knew what love was. Being in touch with my feelings brought a new awareness about a lot of things. One of them was the poignant knowledge that I had little or no feelings for Brenda. There was a strong physical attraction in the beginning, then a sense of companionship, but nothing more.

It made me feel guilty at first, but all the sneers and hurts of the past year were enough to make me realise that there were two sides to the story. After all they were hardly the behaviour of a loving spouse either. A spouse hurt and bitter at being unloved - perhaps, but a loving spouse - no! Anyway, so what if we didn't love each other! Neither did most couples! And there was nothing we could do about it; the idea of breaking up Matthew's home was unthinkable! So I just put the whole thing to the back of my mind, turning my thoughts to more immediate, practical matters. It had always been my way.

The recession was now with us in earnest and work was getting scarce. Tom O'Hara had some more repairs to do on his flats, but after that it looked as if I would have to sign on the dole. However as luck would have it, a call came from Stephen Clarke, telling me to have my tools outside Bond Street Tube Station at a quarter to eight the following morning. A French bank was having its offices refurbished and there would be plenty of work available.

There was: eight until six on Sunday; eight until eight on Saturday; and eight until ten during the week, for two weeks. The pay worked out at over five hundred a week after - not an offer to refuse, so I had my tools in Bond Street.

Margaret went home soon afterwards. She was barely gone when my father telephoned us and announced that he would be arriving in two days time.

'Well! That beats all!' I said, putting down the phone. 'Booked his own flight and everything all by himself! Not bad for seventy nine!'

'When is he coming?' Brenda sounded less than enthusiastic.

'The day after tomorrow. Now please don't do anything to hurt his feelings! He's an old man and he wants to see his grandson. If you must be snotty with anyone, be snotty with me! I don't object when your relatives call. And you're glad to accept my father's hospitality when we go to Limerick.'

That was that! On the Monday evening, the foreman allowed me to finish 'early' at 7:00pm in order to meet him at Heathrow Airport. He was thrilled to see Little Matthew, his namesake, and really enjoyed his stay. He made friends with Gustav and he had a habit of calling there about two in the afternoon 'for a quick ball of malt' When I mentioned the idea of taking a few days off while he was in London he wouldn't hear of it. 'You don't throw a job like that away! That's not the way you were brought up,' he said.

The following night, Tuesday, I got home from work shortly after ten. Brenda had telephoned Stephen Clarke and he had called with Jimmy Nagle. They were down in Gustav's with my father celebrating and we could both join them, as she had a babysitter. Brenda had made some dinner and it was eaten in ten minutes. We strolled round the corner to Gustav's. As we went in the door we got a shout from the corner.

'The prodigal, home at last!'

'How are you Jimmy? Are you working?'

'I am not! What they're offering you lately is a joke! A bloke rang me a few days ago looking for a steelfixer and when he said what the pay was, you know what I told him?'

'No, Jimmy.'

'I told him I wouldn't *turn* in the bed for it, not to mind getting up!'

The laughing set the mood for the rest of the evening. It was less than an hour before we had to leave, but we all enjoyed ourselves thoroughly. It was Brenda's first night out since the hospital and she had a great time. We walked home arm-in-arm. Looking back, it was one of the happiest nights of our marriage.

By the end of the week my father's visit was over and so was the Bond Street job. Brenda seemed to be getting more angry and sorry for herself again, but working the long hours I saw little of her and tried to keep out of her way. The first morning after the job finished I didn't wake up until almost ten. Coming down the stairs I felt really pleased with myself. After all, wasn't there a cheque for over a thousand pounds in the drawer? Suddenly the bathroom door opened and Brenda came storming out. Turning round, I was met with a hard slap across my face.

'You swine! You're just like all men! What you're doing isn't good enough at all!'

She took one look at my face and ran back into the bathroom as abruptly as she had come out. My foot in the door prevented it from closing. Furiously, I caught her by the shoulders and shook her as I shouted:

'What do you mean not good enough? You spoilt angry bitch! I've been working night and day to look after you. You're just a spoilt child! You don't know what gratitude is! Nothing is ever good enough for you, is it?'

The sheer energy calmed me down. Feeling ashamed at having lost my temper, I turned away and walked downstairs without saying a word. Brenda followed me shortly afterwards.

'Look Brenda, I'm sorry for losing my temper. Let's try and talk about it! It's about time all these rows were sorted out once and for all.'

Silence. Her lips tightened into a thin stubborn line. It was her way of baiting me, always the same.

'Come on Brenda! We have to sort this out. We have a small child to consider now; it's not just the two of us any more. Stop trying to hurt me for once and think of the marriage! Think of Matthew!'

The line of her mouth seemed to widen slightly into half-smile. She was winning; getting to me.

'Damn it! Can you not stop trying to hurt me this once? Don't you realise how important it is? And your own behaviour wasn't exactly ladylike; maybe you could have the decency to apologise the same as I did!'

Not a word! I was getting nowhere, just working myself up and making myself frustrated and angry for nothing. The best thing to do was to let it alone for now and deal with it later when Brenda's bitterness had died down. After all she had to realise that we had to sort this out - or Matthew mightn't have a home.

I waited until nine that evening, when Matthew was asleep in his basket.

'Brenda!' I began and then hesitated, already sensing the 'vibes' of opposition rising to meet me. But it was important to push on.

'Look! We're going to have to discuss these rows sooner or later. Let's deal with them now. We need to have a proper home for our son.'

'Don't you think you've done enough already today?' It was her way of trying to intimidate me but I wasn't going to let it work, not tonight anyway!

'So did you; we both did enough! More than enough in fact! And if we want to stop doing more than enough, we'd better try and talk about it.'

'I have nothing to say to you.' Then she turned her back to me and walked out of the room.

That was that. I couldn't make her talk and she knew it. My fists tightened in helpless frustration. Grabbing my coat I walked out the door and round the corner to Gustav's for an hour. Gustav had a good chat with me, speaking in general rather than about the exact problem, as men do. He advised me to 'let her be'. She would talk about it in her own time and then we could sort it out.

The following day things were back to 'normal'; in fact Brenda broke the ice. In a tone of voice that was not unfriendly, she complained that we had never brought the central heating upstairs. Winter was coming on, and now there was a small child in the house. Since 'we had a few bob' wasn't it a good time to call Dave Buckley, the plumber and get him to put in radiators upstairs?

Storm clouds

It was disconcerting to hear her speak like this, as though we had never said an angry word to one another. But at least it brought the atmosphere back to normal and I phoned Dave almost immediately. The heating was in and working that weekend. But once again the quarrel was not made good. It was just brushed over, waiting to come to the surface again - next time in a different disguise. And the right time for her to talk about it didn't arrive; I never really believed it would.

Matthew was changing. He was becoming more aware and he had just begun to smile. We both found him more and more delightful. I loved to take him for walks in the pram or to pick him up to show him off to friends when they called. He was used to my smell, my touch, and the sound of my strong rural tones. When he was six weeks old, Brenda said that we must buy him a cot. One day she bought a copy of 'LOOT' the London free ad's paper and when I arrived home she announced that she had answered an ad, from a couple selling a wooden cot in West London. All three of us drove off in the Volvo.

A week earlier Brenda had given up breast feeding because of mastitis, so now Matthew was being fed by bottle. As we were looking at the cot, he woke up and began to whimper. I picked him up and gave him the bottle without thinking, pleasantly surprised at the murmurs of approval from the couple and the two grandparents. Picking up my little son and feeding him seemed the most natural thing in the world. Most dads feel the same.

Changing nappies was no great problem either. Brenda had become interested in a women's group which did not agree with disposable nappies and she made a convincing case against non-biodegradable waste. The result was that most of our nappy changing involved the old fashioned nappies with the pins. That didn't put me off one little bit. When she came home with a big pile of towelling, one Saturday afternoon, we enjoyed learning how to change them; it was fun.

One evening I remember taking off the dirty nappy and going 'POOH!' Do you know what? They would never have gone to the trouble of inventing poison gas if Matthew had been around! Brenda tried not to laugh.

The British and Irish public speaking finals were held at Gatwick in early November, so we decided to drive down there on the Saturday night and stay until Sunday, bringing Matthew with us. My singing voice was in top form and I loved showing off my little son to all and sundry.

But on Sunday evening, back in Gordon Road, Brenda started up again.

'There we were,' she said. 'Didn't we look such a *nice* couple, showing them our baby and pretending everything was fine?'

'Well I don't see what's all that wrong. Anyway you don't ever seem to want to talk about any problems. So stop complaining and try and make the best of it!'

The result was a torrent of obscene abuse. The more I tried to get her to stop, the stronger and the louder it became. She was relishing it! Ignoring me, she sneered at my job, my accent, my income, my father and even my manhood.

Eventually something inside me snapped, and Brenda was staring at me silently. Then I realised I had just slapped her across her cheek with my left hand. She was not hurt but the shock had stopped her in mid-sentence. I marched out of the room angry with her and with myself for losing control. Stopping to run upstairs to check that Matthew was okay (mercifully, he was sound asleep) I ran down to Gustav's away from the madhouse. Brenda was asleep when I came in.

The following day, Monday, after work Brenda spoke to me as if nothing had happened. But when I apologised for losing my temper, the contempt came back into her face and her voice as she started to abuse me again. Now however, I was prepared. There would be no losing my temper this time. Turning on my heel quickly I went out for a walk, but came back too soon and she started up again. So there was nothing for it but to leave her alone once more. A big circuit brought me outside Gustav's door after three-quarters of an hour. After one quick pint and I arrived home for the third time that day. This time Brenda said nothing.

On Tuesday evening she surprised me by bringing up the subject at the kitchen table.

'A big part of the problem, Owen, is that I hate living in this country. I'd like to go back to Ireland. Even a few days there, would make me feel a lot happier. Besides Dad is dying to see the baby'

'Well I'm glad that you're talking to me at last; I was getting really worried. When would you like to go?'

'Soon! Tomorrow if possible! But there's no money in my bank account.'

'What, again? I'm a bit low myself now after Dave Buckley, but anyway, we can use my credit card'

'Oh, do you think I could go for four or five days maybe?'

'How long would you like to stay? A week?'

'A week would be lovely!'

'Okay lets make it a week then, starting tomorrow if you like.'

So the flight was booked for the following day. The return flight was also on the Wednesday, one week exactly. My relief was enormous. At last she was talking! Now we would find a way out of the nightmare and create a proper home for our son. She was chatty in the morning. Her back was acting up because there was no proper place to change the baby. Maybe if there was some kind of worktop in the bathroom before she came back.... Glad to be seen to co-operate, I promised that it would be done.

On the way to the airport she looked unusually meek and mild. 'She is sorry for the rows too,' I thought. It seemed a very good time to bring up the subject.

'Brenda, we have to think seriously! Either these fights continue, or *we* continue,' I said.

She nodded twice, silently almost humbly, it appeared. Feeling confident that she had finally come to grips with the situation, I said no more. My mood was happy and optimistic as she and Matthew left me to go on the plane.

In spite of missing Matthew, over the next few days my feelings were mostly relief. It seemed like a load had been lifted from my mind. The house had become a tense unpleasant place, and now the spell was lifted. 'Time to relax again.'
The very next day I set to work on the bathroom with new energy, building a line of cupboards with a worktop along one wall. It made a perfect changing area for Matthew, and that evening on the way to Gustav's there was a spring in my step.
It wasn't until Saturday that she told me what she had done. When Seamus spoke to me on the phone, he seemed unusually distant, not angry, just cool and mildly sarcastic. My mind was elsewhere, so taking very little notice I asked to speak to Brenda.
'I had to tell them about our fights,' she said in the even tones of a lawyer, 'about you hitting me with the child in my arms.'
'About *what?*'
She hesitated. 'Well...I'm a mother with a young baby and you hit me.'
'Hang on a minute! We *both* gave one another slaps on the cheek, but never in a way that could possibly hurt. Anyway Matthew was upstairs at the time you're talking about.'
'Do you feel proud of yourself, using violence, hitting a woman?'
'Do *you* feel proud of yourself for hitting me? Or do you think that's different? Maybe you're sacred or something!' She was getting to me, making me angry again; this wouldn't do! - Time to take a deep breath!
Brenda took advantage of the pause. 'You have all the answers don't you? Well Dad wants to talk to you.'
'Fine! I want to talk to him. If you're determined to involve him in this, he'd better know the facts. Put him on!

He needs to be put straight about this "hitting you with the child in your arms" business, for a start.'

'You bastard! I suppose now you think you can win my dad over to your side. Well I have news for you! Mum said that if he doesn't put you in your place she'll never speak to him again.'

'Look Brenda there is no 'my side.' We have got to sort this out. I'm sick of telling you. What about some counselling? Don't you realise if we don't do something, Matthew won't have a home?'

'Matthew! Matthew! Is that all that concerns you, Matthew?'

'Well he's the innocent victim of all this isn't he?'

She had a point. It came as a surprise to me, to realise that I hadn't been thinking of Brenda - or of myself. My concern had been purely for Matthew. Well, damn it! Wasn't it just as well that *someone* was concerned about him the way things were going? The thing to do now was to patch things up, get some advice, and then maybe tackle some of the fundamental issues threatening the marriage. That made sense didn't it? Wasn't that the logical way to go? The habits of a lifetime die hard.

'What do you say if I make an appointment with the local marriage-counselling people whoever they are? I'll try and arrange it for Thursday, when you're back.'

'No! This must be kept to ourselves. You know we're a very private family. I want you to come over here and talk to Mum and Dad. You can bring your father too, if you like.'

'You want me to bring an eighty-year-old man to talk to two lawyers? About what?'

'Well we can deal with the issues if we talk about them. You're the one who always wants to talk.'

'What issues have you in mind?'

'Well...the violence for one.' She had not meant to say that; it was clear from the silence that followed.

'Now I see! You want to make it into a grand indictment, with me as the defendant, in front of your whole family.

Chapter 7

What in God's name do you hope to achieve by that? That's not going to stop the rows between us.

Silence.

Look! Let's go for the counselling! What do you say to next Thursday if we can get an appointment?'

'You must be joking! I have no intention of returning back to that house until you change your attitude.'

'What?'

'You heard me. I'm not coming home!'

'But you came to me all smiles and asked me for money to make the trip. Are you telling me it was all lies - that you had no intention of coming home?'

'That's right! And if you try to use the courts to bring Matthew back, I'll tell them we left in fear of you. You've admitted hitting me. Anyway it will take at least six months before the courts do anything.'

I put down the phone feeling weak, too weak to say any more! I had to sit down. The full weight of the situation was now becoming clear to me. It was almost too awful to think about. My wife and child were gone! They were away in Ireland. And I had been tricked into letting them go, not to mention paying for it! How could I have fallen for that? Why? Because I was out of touch with my feelings, relying too much on my intellect and not enough on my 'gut.' And because I wanted desperately to believe her. The answer came almost immediately. It was a simple intellectual question after all.

I couldn't eat; I couldn't sleep; it was difficult even to think. After drinking a few glasses of milk (comfort food), my mind at last managed to come to terms with what had happened. There was no point in telling my father. He had been so happy two weeks before and no doubt he was happy still. It would be wrong to upset him now. Matthew and Brenda must be brought back at all costs, so from now on, my way of handling things had to change. But how? What was I to do? My thinking was still too muddled to come up with anything. Sometime after four in the morning, sleep came.

It was almost lunchtime before I woke. A quick snack, and then after a few hours making wardrobes in our bedroom, a course of action began forming in my mind.

First of all I had to speak to Seamus and try to let him see the other side of the story. If he believed the stuff about hitting her with the child in her arms of course, he might not talk to me, but there was a very good chance that he had taken that with a grain of salt. Margaret, I felt instinctively, would be deaf and blind to anything I might have to say. Her daughter's word was good enough for her; anything else was 'twisting the facts'.

'Better leave it until tomorrow, in that case, ring him in his office,' I decided.

It was the right thing to do. I knew it instinctively. Perhaps there was hope for me after all. And my lifetime habits of logical, analytical thinking hadn't gone to waste either. Definitely hope! And my wardrobes were coming along well too. There was no doubt that my mood had perked up since the night before. But now that my worries were under control, I began to miss Matthew terribly. It was one thing to have him away for a few days; it was another not to know when I would see him again.

About three o' clock on Monday Seamus and I had our talk on the phone. Although there was tension there, he clearly believed me when I explained what the so-called 'violence' really was, and he promised he would see what he could do to patch things up.

'By the way, Seamus, there's no question of any legal action to bring Matthew back to London. I was always told that when people fight, so long as they don't go to law, they can always patch things up again. As a matter of fact it didn't even occur to me until Brenda mentioned it,' I added.

'Very wise advice, Owen!' he replied.

His tone was hardly friendly, but I got the distinct feeling that he had a degree of sympathy for me. Margaret and her two sisters were no easy women to live with. Spoilt and proud, the daughters of a prominent barrister, they had never done a day's work in their lives but expected the best of everything. A few years earlier Seamus had set up a business venture with a client. It had gone wrong; the family home had to be sold and they moved into a more modest house at the less expensive end of the road. Margaret had never forgiven him.

A few days later on the phone, Brenda's tone was different. The grand indictment idea gone but she still insisted on my coming over to Limerick 'to talk things over'. She had phoned Valerie, she said, and told her that she would not be coming back to her job.

I refused, saying that we should go to counselling in Wandsworth, our home. For the rest of November and most of December, I stayed in London taking any jobs that were available and working on the house when there were none.

Tim, Brenda's brother helped me with one of the jobs and he obviously had nothing against me. Either Brenda hadn't painted me as a total villain, or else her family hadn't believed her. Margaret was the exception. She never spoke a friendly word to me again.

Tim liked to have the radio on, and one day we heard a newsflash that The Prince and Princess of Wales were to separate. We exchanged looks, then got back to work without saying a word.

The house was coming on in Brenda's absence. The wardrobes were ready at last and a plasterer came and finished off the ceilings and the walls. By building two floor-to-ceiling cupboards opposite one another, I partially closed off the drawing room again. The effect was very pleasing and the finished product was a good advertisement for my skills. The place looked like a house at last.

We spoke on the telephone two or three times a week. Brenda's voice sounded less angry now, but she kept demanding a promise from me never to lose my temper again.

'No problem!' I told her. 'Provided you must promise to treat me better in return. I don't mind the odd 'clatter' but the constant verbal abuse, that has to stop!'

But there was no way! In a letter explaining how important it was, not to feel constantly threatened by verbal abuse, I mentioned slapping her face but not the slaps she gave me. I was to regret that later.

The week before Christmas found me still undecided about what to do. If Brenda had not kept insisting, my mind would probably have been made up earlier. But now I missed Matthew more than ever, and my father was expecting me too. So with Christmas just a few days away, I booked one of the last car-spaces on the ferry and set off.

CHAPTER 8

Salvage

My father's house on the hill was a low rambling affair with different sections added over the years. One of them was a small self-contained unit, built when my aunt came to live with us in the 1960's. It comprised a living room, a small kitchen, a bathroom and a big bedroom. This extension was in better condition than the rest of the house and now Brenda suggested that I make it habitable as a second home. When it was ready she would move out of her parents place and in with me - not before.

I hated asking my father but there was no choice. In fact he was delighted at the idea of seeing more of us, especially Matthew, so I went to work again.

The job was mainly fitting a new kitchen. After that, double-glazing had to be fixed on the four windows and a few jobs done in the little bathroom. Brenda offered to give me a hand with the cleaning at the end.

My credit card was taking a beating but there was still enough to buy the appliances and materials. The job was done in record time, and the place looked well. Frank Collins helped me with the pipework. It was his last job on Christmas Eve. At first he said he couldn't make it, but once I explained what was at stake he came willingly on his time off. So Brenda moved in with Matthew; six hours before midnight on Christmas Eve we were a family again.

It was Brenda who suggested we go for counselling in the New Year. We arranged a session with the Catholic Marriage Guidance Service in Limerick. The counsellor was a young man in his late twenties, clearly unmarried and innocent looking. Chivalrously he asked Brenda to speak first.

She started her story and then she began to cry softly. The young man was visibly moved. He looked at her with tenderness and compassion, then at me in incredulous disgust. What a brute! To make this innocent young woman cry like that! Brenda had the floor and she made the most of it. She turned the discussion to violence. When this subject is raised the common assumption is that it is the man who is violent towards the woman. Men, in general, believe in the notion of the innocent woman. The belief that women are somehow less knowing than men can lead in male dominated groups, such as courts of law, to women literally getting away with murder - as long as they only murder a man.

'Of course Owen believes,' Brenda went on, 'that the odd slap in the mouth isn't particularly important, especially in our marriage.'

'Okay, we'll let him answer that for himself,' the counsellor interrupted. 'Now Owen how important do you feel this matter of violence is, in your marriage?'

'Not very, to be honest. Look we have been having nasty rows, verbal rows I mean, for over a year. There is serious anger on Brenda's part. She won't ever allow any discussion about what's making her angry. That's what's causing the trouble. I don't think it's very important if we give one another a harmless slap on the cheek, once or twice a year.'

'Give *each other* a slap, you mean she has slapped you back?'

It was useless. I felt like shaking him to bring him into the real world. Brenda was enjoying herself thoroughly. She had seldom or never had the better of me in any discussion up to now, but this time she had an ally that she could wrap round her little finger. There was no need to talk about what really mattered while the counsellor was more than happy to examine all the red herrings she was throwing out one by one. Nevertheless I agreed to another appointment. Perhaps next time I could make sure we talked about the real issue, *perhaps*.

He saw us again at the same time the following week. This time at least I was ready with an incident that happened in the meantime. We had been cleaning up our new living room, emptying cupboards and tidying. Everything was going well until I went outside for half an hour to cut some timber for the fire. Coming back in, it was the same old story. The sour puss met me at the door and you could cut the atmosphere with a knife. No reason as usual.

'Well? Why the sour puss this time?'

'What will you do if I don't tell you, hit me?'

'Idiot! You're making such a big thing about the few slaps; you'll have yourself convinced you are a battered wife. What does that make me, a battered husband?'

My reply made me feel better. Now she had to know how unreasonable and ridiculous her thinking was. What I did not know, at the time was how much she could afford to be unreasonable; perhaps it was just as well.

When he heard about the incident the young counsellor turned to Brenda.

'Yes,' she said 'I do get angry sometimes, but I don't know whether we're living in Ireland or in London. We don't have a proper home. The house in London is a tip! There is a recession on and Owen is having trouble finding work.'

'So you take it all out on me! You make the atmosphere foul all the time and that's okay isn't it? If I took out all my troubles on you would it be okay then?' I couldn't stop myself interrupting. It made no difference anyway.

The counsellor went away. He returned a few moments later. 'I explained to you at the beginning,' he said in his slow careful manner, 'that we have more experienced counsellors listening in. Well, they feel as I do that Brenda has a perfect right to be angry.'

'Does that mean she has a right to be angry all the time, or at least on a daily basis,' I said, trying to be accurate. Also, it was news to me that there were people whom we couldn't see, listening in. But if the young man said that he told us I have no doubt that he did. He was not capable of making it up.

'We can discuss Brenda's anger at future sessions, but in the meantime you must remember it is no excuse for violence.' He was looking at me.

'Good God! Do you think that I'm slapping her around or something? What I want to know is, is Brenda's anger an excuse for mocking and sneering and picking fights? Is it an excuse for refusing to discuss what's making her angry in the first place and for creating an atmosphere that nobody could live in?'

I was in full flight, but the counsellor brought me back down to earth abruptly.

'Mr. Sheridan! You will get your chance to put your viewpoint at future sessions. In the meantime can we discuss the issues calmly without getting worked up? Now, about the next appointment. Can we say Friday week, nine days time?'

'That's too far away; I must get back to work. It's not practical to stay in Limerick that long.'

He looked at me in dismay, all his power gone.

Brenda cut in hastily. 'We'll discuss it between ourselves. We're considering staying in Ireland a while longer.'

'Well, think of all the progress we made,' he said. 'We can't let that go to waste. You'll have to make up your mind by tomorrow. These appointments get filled very quickly indeed, I'm sorry to say.' He was looking at her.

We had a cup of coffee nearby and the discussion was short and sweet.

'Look Brenda, I don't know what you want out of these sessions. You don't seem to want to discuss the real issues between us.'

'Oh it's all my fault I suppose, and you're just perfect!'

'Come on! You know this isn't about dust in the house or even the slaps we gave each other.' I could feel the resistance building up; she did not want to dig any deeper.

'Well, you decide what's important then and we can all talk about what you want.' She was not going to be pinned down. I knew that insisting would only make her angry; then she would walk off. It had happened so many times before. Nevertheless I gave it one more try.

'So are you saying then that if the house got a good clean-up and if we take care to avoid anything that might make us lose our tempers then you'd be happy in the marriage?'

'You're putting words into my mouth now.'

'Okay then, in your own words, what are the big things that you are unhappy with about in this marriage?'

'We'll talk about that in counselling. We're not able to discuss these things on our own; we just get angry all the time.'

'No! We're well able to discuss it. You just *refuse* to discuss it. That's the reason we get cross most of the time. You are not prepared to discuss it in there either; you're just wasting his time and mine.'

'So you're going to run away?'

'I need to go home and get back to work but I'll tell you what; if you can bring yourself to talk about the real issues, even for a few minutes, then I'll put off going back for as long as it takes.'

'You tell me what issues you want discussed, and we'll discuss these at the next session.'

'Brenda, I want to discuss where the hell these rows are coming from, because I'm sure they're not coming from me... Hang on a minute! You've just changed the subject again. I want to know what *you* think the issues are. If we can just talk about that now, then we won't be wasting our time talking all that Mickey Mouse stuff.'

Silence.

It was the closest I ever came to getting her to tell me what was going on. A long time afterwards I worked it out for myself, but by then it was too late.

I broke the silence after a minute or so. 'Well, what's it to be? Will we be staying around?'

Silence, this time even more tense and longer.

'Well, tell me! What do you want the counselling for? You keep avoiding the issues all the time.

Silence. She was hoping to provoke me into getting angry. Then she would have the usual excuse to end the discussion 'See! We can't discuss it.' But not this time, my guard was up. I let the silence continue.

The arrangements were made the same day. Because it was my decision, Brenda would lose face by coming with me – but she didn't want her parents to think she was holding out for no good reason either. The following day, her back took a turn. Was it psychosomatically induced because she did not want to return with me to Gordon Road? My brain was also playing tricks on me at the time. I was in denial. By now the writing on the wall was plain enough – except to someone who did not want to see.

Feeling something that had been strangely absent up to now - sadness - I dropped Matthew and Brenda to her parents' house on my way to the boat.

*

In London, I decided to go for some help on my own. It seemed to be my only hope of getting any answers. A phone call to the local marriage counselling service led to an appointment with Shirley. I imagined Shirley to be a young girl and was pleasantly surprised to encounter a mature woman of Asian extraction, thirty-nine or forty years old. Taking the bull by the horns I began by asking about Brenda's anger and what was going on. She said she would have to speak to Brenda about that, but how did I feel about the marriage?

Men usually find it difficult to open up about their feelings. We have been conditioned to keep them well hidden even from ourselves, but this woman made it easy to confide in her. Anxious to get to the bottom of the problem, I told her the marriage meant different things to me.

'How many different things?'

'Perhaps three,' I replied. There was sharing a home with somebody, there was parenthood, and there was the sex. Being a parent was great! The sharing was mostly bad, because the effects of the rows lingered. They were never made up. The sex was... well... unerotic to say the least. It came out slowly and almost reluctantly. Until then I had never realised how unerotic it was.

Then she asked me if I was coming for help expecting the marriage to continue or to break up.

'You know, I never really thought about breaking up. Break up Matthew's home? No! No way!'

'What about it's being so unerotic? Do you perhaps want these rows, so you would have an excuse to break up?'

'Well... I feel pleased and happy when the atmosphere between us is good. And my main reason for coming here is to get to the bottom of them. They make me feel helpless. There's no way of knowing when it's going to turn nasty and I honestly don't think this anger is coming from me.'

'I see' she said thoughtfully, 'I'm glad you came today but there's no point in more than one appointment on your own. If Brenda comes back we'll arrange for another as soon as we can.

It put me thinking. Being a man is not easy. Men, since the hunting and gathering days, have had to devote most of their waking hours to jobs that are essentially drudgery and tedium. Going to work in a factory or a mine every day meant that your feelings had to be suppressed, fighting in a war even more so. After all it would hardly do to be in touch with your feelings when you were expected to go 'over the top' into the machine-gun fire in Flanders.

Tuning into my emotions was new to me, but it did bring answers, at least to what was going on in my own mind. For one thing there was no anger at the sex being unexciting. Men in my generation looked upon sex as a favour given by the woman to the man, not something he was entitled to. If I felt anything it was guilt in finding other women more attractive. There was also a fear that, in spite of all the nasty things she said, Brenda would find out and that her feelings would be hurt. I know now that my feelings were typical of most men. At the time I was only learning.

Brenda did come back at the end of January. All of a sudden the anger and hostility died down as they had done before. It began when I told her about going for the counselling. Probably my being away and not phoning too often was the main thing influencing her, but why she always changed when we were away from one another, I still don't know.

At the airport, Matthew chuckled in delight at seeing me, and we all had a lovely evening. Brenda seemed genuinely pleased at the improvements to the house, especially the wardrobes in the bedroom.

We both saw Shirley soon afterwards. Brenda began once more. She spoke of some of her concerns in her lawyer's voice, calm and unemotional. Then all of a sudden the soft crying started again. I was astonished, then angry.

'Oh, for God's sake, not again! You do it the first day in Limerick; you do it first day in London. You never get a second chance to make a first impression; isn't that right?'

It is a phrase used in selling houses, but evidently it had its effect. Shirley looked sharply in Brenda's direction and Brenda, tears gone, looked daggers at me.

Shirley was not going to let her have her own way like the young man in Limerick, so now Brenda used a different tactic. She set the atmosphere for each session, carefully in advance.

Men in general are emotionally inept compared to women. A woman normally sets the atmosphere in a home. If the woman is happy the rest of the home is nearly always happy too.

Brenda had me on tenterhooks, desperately anxious to keep the atmosphere pleasant between us. So for at least a day before each appointment, she would be sweet and gentle. Even when I brought up the subject of the quarrels she always said something dismissive and soothing. I tried to pursue the matter but kept getting the feeling that I was upsetting things, doing something wrong. Reluctant to push things to the point of a quarrel, I gave way again and again. The result was a long series of meetings where we never discussed anything that mattered. Brenda even brought Matthew to the second session and the third, but here Shirley put her foot down, saying it was impossible to turn our attention to important issues with a small baby in the room, so a babysitter had to be found.

Why did Brenda go to such trouble, all to avoid discussing the one thing that could save our marriage? The answer is very simple but in my slow analytical way it took me years to work it out. Had I been more intuitive then, we should have been talking about very different things - but perhaps I didn't want to know. It just didn't occur to me that saving the marriage was not what she wanted from the counselling. She wanted the support, the justification to put the marriage to an end. Her family, following my telephone conversation with her father, was no help to her here. But if she could get just one counsellor to say 'this marriage is wrong for you' then she would have plucked up the courage to send the dreaded legal papers and haul me into court.

There was certainly no love between us by then. Long sickening, it had finally died when Matthew was born. Strangely enough though, there were still good times, pleasant friendly days, acts of kindness, chats with friends and a common fascination and delight in our little son. These were the times I lived for. But the other times lasted longer, when I hated to go home and the atmosphere was foul. There was only Matthew then.

Why, when the marriage was so abusive did I not want to end it myself? There were two reasons, one of them a very big one.

They say 'what you never had, you never miss'. Living without affection was not new to me. My poor mother always felt sorry about what happened, and from the age of four she attempted to make it up to me. But she was trying to compensate; the feeling was never there between us. We both felt badly about the coldness but accepted it in the knowledge that neither of us could change it, bar a miracle. It was too late.

She died in bed one Saturday morning when I was home in Limerick. My father found her. 'Owen! We have a tragedy in hands,' was what he said.

It was so final! There she was, a corpse lying on the bed. It was the only time I cried as an adult. I suppose I had been hoping for a miracle after all.

But it was another reason, that most of all, made me desperate to keep the marriage going.

I didn't want to lose Matthew.

The man does not get the child. It was too awful to think about, but in the back of my mind I knew that splitting up meant my child being taken from me, something to be prevented at all costs.

Brenda on the other hand knew better than anybody that she had nothing to lose. Faced with the loss of Matthew, there is no doubt that she would have worked hard at keeping us all together.

After ten or eleven sessions it became clear that we were getting nowhere. We never even got close to the real issue. At the last session the two women looked at each other knowingly; there was no love lost there. Presently Shirley suggested that it might be a good idea to take a break from the counselling 'to see how we got on.' She had done her best and got nowhere. We never saw her again.

CHAPTER 9

The year of conflict

M atthew thrived.
He grew from a strong smiling baby into a hearty curious toddler. Every parent thinks his own child is special, but Matthew's smiling ways seemed to attract attention wherever he went. In the library, at the shopping centre and all along Gordon Road, people knew him.

Brenda moved him into the next room and he would wake us up about half past seven every morning, by pulling the string on a musical toy which played a little tune. It made me uneasy, putting him into a room all by himself. What if he woke in the night? He might think that he was abandoned in another world. But I gave in for the sake of peace, on condition that we left the two doors open. There's nothing like meeting a small child first thing in the morning. Children are so joyful and full of life compared to adults. It sets you up for the whole day.

He began to understand simple words and even to utter the thrilling 'Dada.' Outdoors, sitting on my shoulders, he would look about eagerly, taking everything in with interest and zest. He learned to crawl, backwards at first, then forwards. His new mobility delighted him. He crawled everywhere, across the room, along the corridor, out in the garden, even up the stairs.

One day, as I opened the front door on my way in from work, Matthew was on the landing on his way down to meet me. He knew my step and the sound of the gate. Seeing me, he turned backwards and slid on his tummy, down the stairs

'Dod-dee!' his little face beamed. No words ever sounded sweeter.

He loved sitting on my back as I crawled about on my hands and knees. I made up a little song about it:

Climb up on Daddy's back and press on his back-bone, being

on his back is migh-ty craic, I'm on- ly twen- ty stone.

With Brenda, my strategy was to play things down as much as possible, but sensing my weakness she began to press harder. Now I became the one doing the evading. She picked quarrels about all sorts of things, but the house was the single biggest subject. It came up again and again, so I decided to make a serious attempt to finish all the major jobs. It was plain enough by now that this would not stop the rows but at least it would deflect one major charge against me and the jobs needed to done for their own sake anyway.

The problem was money. By 1993 the recession was with us in earnest. I was working three days a week on average and Brenda wasn't working at all.

An idea occurred to me. Two years before, when moving in, we had applied for a grant because the house was uninhabitable. The inspector from the borough had drawn up a list of works that had to be done. At the time we just couldn't afford to wait, but now that neither of us was working full time, perhaps we could go ahead with the works still undone and draw the grant for them.

We could and we did. The patched roof was replaced, and all the windows. Dave Buckley did the job. He even took me on as an employee, at a time when work was very scarce.

Chapter 9

The house now looked very well. There had been no skimping on materials. The windows were wooden, sliding-sash with a polished pine finish inside; the roof was slate, with a red ridge tile: very impressive! The achievement gave my spirits a boost that was badly needed. Hadn't I overcome all the odds? Transformed the house and got three weeks work into the bargain! Not bad at all!

But my satisfaction only made Brenda even more bitter and angry. There were no compliments or praise, not a word! In fact she stopped talking to me entirely, and even though she was not working, she made no effort to help me get my meals in the evenings.

The reason, she told me one day as I was about to back to work up on the roof, was that during the clearing up, I had burned an old chest of drawers from the attic and she was attached to it. It was a very cheap thing from the 1960's and badly broken.

In no mood for this I said to her from the scaffold 'If you really think that's why you're angry you'd better go to the doctor, because you are very sick.'

She marched off, wheeling Matthew with her in his buggy. Afterwards I learned that she went straight to the police station, and reported that I had threatened her. A bitter woman can be dangerous - especially when she's a solicitor.

Tom O' Hara phoned me the following week. He wanted me to install panelling in a basement flat that he owned. At the job he approached me with a twinkle in his eye.

'Oh a bit of news, Owen, I bought that flat' he said
'What flat Tom?'
'The studio, you know, in Ellis Road.'
'How do you mean you bought it?'
'Just that! I bought it on Tuesday.'
'But Tom, we fixed up that flat last September and the tenants moved in. It's now June! What do you mean you just bought it?'

He explained. British Rail owned the flat and was anxious to be rid of it because it was occupied by squatters. Tom made an offer, paid the squatters to move out and dragged out the negotiations for months.

'So I was able to rent the flat out for nine months with no mortgage to pay,' he told me gleefully.

'Hang on a minute! I still don't get it. You didn't own it, so how did you arrange for you and yours to occupy the flat and keep everyone else out?'

'Well, you should know! You changed the locks.'

For a split second I stood still, then burst out laughing. I had to sit down. It was the best laugh I had in months. It was badly needed.

After that there were only scraps of work. For two months there was no choice but to sign on the dole. Brenda made no secret of her contempt.

'I always felt I owed it to myself, never to be in the same financial difficulties as Poor Mum' she said.

'Poor Mum' arrived on a visit shortly afterwards and now showed herself in her true colours. The flattery and the pleasant manner were gone. I was the ne'er-do-well who had tricked her daughter into marrying him. And what a fine catch she was, *a solicitor* with a fine job, until she met *him*.

'You'll end up supporting him if you're not careful,' she told Brenda. The only thing was, she was Catholic, so divorce was taboo. Even separation was a disgrace. Men were there to provide support and social standing and of course it was their fault if life was less than happy and fulfilling. We were to blame for the high taxes and the bad weather, but still 'marriage was for life.' So Brenda still did not have the moral support she wanted. It was her conscience, I believe, that prevented her. If the 'right person' came along to persuade her that it was 'all for the best', then Matthew's home was gone.

I was on the defensive anyway. With two against one the best thing to do was to keep out of their way. As luck would have it I got a week's work with Roger Tait, an architect and it took up most of Margaret's visit. Most evenings, as soon as Matthew was asleep I made it my business to go out to

Gustav's for a pint. 'Men are so selfish! He has to have his pint, no matter how scarce money is!'

The night before she left however, things came to a head. Brenda had been reading some book, which said that it was bad training for a child to rush to his side if he cried in the night. 'We must leave him alone in future' she said ' in order to get him out of it.'

'You've got to be joking, Brenda! A room like that is another world to a baby. If we let him alone in the dark crying, he'll be terrified! I only agreed to his being put in there if we let him know we are close by.'

'Oh? So you know better than the book I suppose?' she sneered.

'I do - especially when there are as many books as opinions.' Scornfully she turned her back on me to walk out. It was the last straw. For months I had endured all kinds of insults and hurtful remarks. Now she was going to put me down in front of her mother.

'Hold it!' I shouted **Don't you dare turn your back on me while I'm talking to you!'** She froze.

'Turn around!' She turned sulkily. There were no sneering remarks now. Margaret opened her mouth to intervene but one look from me and she stayed silent.

'Now listen to me. I will not be treated with contempt in my own house! That goes for you too Margaret if you're not happy with that arrangement, there's good accommodation up the road. Has either of you got anything to say?'

They said nothing and when I looked at them their eyes dropped. For about a week afterwards Brenda was quite civil to me, then the abuse started again.

Amanda Russell was a frequent visitor to Gordon Road these days. In her late thirties, she was married to a stockbroker. He had been to one of the top public schools and they socialised with very wealthy people. When Amanda asked Brenda to join her pyramid selling group she was delighted and became convinced that she was going to earn a lot of money.

Succeeding in that business meant having a team of people selling under you, and there was no doubt that Amanda had a lot of people under her. They all seemed to have three things in common: they were all women; they were all a few rungs down the social ladder from Amanda; and they all wanted to be like her - including Brenda. In the weeks that followed I cringed as she phoned up every one of my friends and subjected them to an awful sales presentation. One of them was Roger the architect. He never gave me any work again.

It kept Brenda occupied and she grew less angry. Also the last thing I wanted to do was to start a fight; so I sat in silent mortification as Brenda abused friendship after friendship. Amanda cleverly gave me a few weeks work in her holiday home near Brighton. We needed it badly, so there was very little I could say to her, or to Brenda. I would go down there on Monday morning, spend the week there alone and come home on the Friday.

These weeks were better. There were no real arguments. Brenda was trying to get me to come in with her pyramid selling, saying we could retire in three years. Apparently 'husband and wife' teams were more effective than spouses on their own. She and Matthew joined me twice, coming down by train on Thursday and returning with me the following evening. One of the Fridays I finished early. We went for a walk and we stopped for a picnic on a wide grassy bank. Matthew loved the grass, crawling everywhere and rolling over on his back. His mood was infectious; we were happy too. Whenever I remember us as a family, that's the time I like to think of.

I was changing. During one of Brenda's selling trips with Amanda the film 'Holocaust' was shown on television. It was all about Jewish people in concentration camps. Previously I could watch films like that, and feel nothing but anger at what happened. Now the bonding with my little son brought me in touch with my feelings as never before, and the full horror of those events hit me like a sledgehammer. It made me feel numb! I had had no idea of the pain and joy of being a parent.

Matthew was changing too. By the end of July he could walk. He developed an attachment to a knitted green blanket that he called 'Blankie' and brought it with him everywhere he went. By August he had a small and distinctive vocabulary of phrases. 'Tuggles' meant to pull something, 'minis' were breakfast cereal. Young children tend to have strong personalities before they are crushed out of them by years of left-brain education and before long we were all speaking about 'minis' in the morning. That's what I still call it; I used to say 'birdseed' up to then.

He loved to climb. One day in late September Dave Buckley was re-roofing a house with me in Tooting and we were running out of materials. Jumping into the Volvo, I drove to the supplier and picked Matthew up on the way back. The week before, Brenda had started a new job as a temporary solicitor, and Matthew was now with a child minder. Luckily there was a parking space right in front of the house. I opened the tailgate of the station wagon and began unloading the various items and placing them along the garden wall, where they could be easily loaded into the tub for hoisting up to the roof.

From the baby-seat, the shrill cries of indignation grew louder and louder. Eventually, unable to endure any more, I unbuckled him, put him inside the garden with the scaffolding and closed the gate. Balancing a difficult armful, my head bowed under the tailgate, something made me suddenly look round. There was Matthew slowly climbing up the ladder.

'Oh Christ! Mustn't make a sound' I thought. Then creeping slowly behind him, in the gate and up the rungs I grabbed him just as he was putting his little foot on the first level of boarding above the bay window. He was not amused. He had just discovered a whole new world and then along comes this spoilsport of an adult who snatches him abruptly away from it all. He was a year and six days old.

The year of conflict

After five weeks Brenda hadn't convinced a single person to join the pyramid. She grew disillusioned and her temper deteriorated again. There were more rows including one shouting match, but now she was not put off by a shout; it just seemed to make her worse. This nightmare had to stop! In desperation I found a firm of solicitors in the yellow pages. Perhaps a solicitor's letter might make her see reason. She found the telephone book open and questioned me about what was going on.

I told her. 'Look, Brenda this abuse has to stop. One row a day isn't enough for you now; it must be two or three. Maybe I can get a court order or something to shut you up. God help me if you were stronger than I am! You'd have me beaten round the house.'

She said nothing. But half an hour later she called me saying she had something to show me. It was a written promise never to engage in verbal abuse again. If I didn't go to the solicitor she would sign it, she told me. I agreed and she signed her name. It helped.

Her new job helped even more. A firm in Dulwich needed a temporary solicitor for fourteen weeks starting in September. Brenda liked both the people and the work and her mood improved. She usually dropped Matthew to the childminder every morning. Samina was Urdu-speaking, born in Pakistan and a mother of four. Matthew even picked up a few words of Urdu while he was with her and her children. Occasionally I dropped him off but he would get very upset as I left, crying at the door.

'A lot of children are like that, very attached to their fathers,' Samina said with a smile.

Coming up to Christmas, about a week after her job ended, we had the nastiest quarrel of all. The days spent in the house had made Brenda bitter and angry again. She laid into me about putting away the hosepipe, about dirt on my clothes and several other things. It was the vehemence of her attacks that was unusual. One morning in the kitchen there was some other dispute and she slapped me hard across my

right cheek. Whatever my reaction was going to be it was quickly forgotten when Matthew suddenly began to throw up. I carried him up to the bathroom and laid him down on the changing area. Brenda began to undo his little babygrow and she snapped at me to get another from the cupboard. Hastily I bent down to open one of the doors.
'Not that door, the other one, you idiot!' she snarled.
At that, my temper snapped. Springing up I returned the 'clatter' from downstairs and roared: **'Don't you dare speak to me like that!'** She looked at me for a second and then looked down. Silently I went to the other cupboard, found the new babygrow, and handed it to her.
Five minutes later we were all down in the kitchen again and both of us were feeling sorry. Knowing better by now than to apologise, I spoke kindly to her and five minutes later in her inexplicable way she was behaving as if nothing had happened. We had a cup of tea and a chat. I went to work late. It was our last major row.
One day, early in the following week Brenda was buckling Matthew's little sandal as he lay on his back on the changing platform. Stretching his little legs he accidentally kicked her just above her jawbone. She told me what happened that evening when I came home. A bruise was now visible on her face in the area of her lower gums. It was unfortunate that the bruise was still there two days later when we drove to Limerick for Christmas. We called to Seamus and Margaret first on the way to my father's.
On Christmas Day I was aware of a distinct coolness when we went to visit them again. Inside nobody addressed a single remark to me; it was clear something must be seriously wrong.
On our way home in the car I finally put two and two together and mentioned it to Brenda. 'Would you mind bringing it up with your dad?' I said to her. 'They probably think I'm beating you up. Things are bad enough as they are.'
'Let my family think what they like!' she said. 'It's none of their business and they were precious little use to me when

I wanted their support.' However when I asked her to mention it again, she promised she would.

Perhaps she did, because when Seamus telephoned me two days later, and asked if he could discuss the rows, his manner had changed. He never mentioned the mark on her face and he was always friendly to me afterwards.

That was the last Christmas we spent in Limerick. Outwardly, at the time, we were a happy successful couple and even in private there was a sort of peace. We both knew that the major battles had been fought. It was good enough for me, more than I had hoped for. However in other quarters a major change was taking place. Separation was now becoming respectable and Margaret became converted to the idea. Worse, she advocated it to Brenda at every possible opportunity.

*

1994 was a long year. There was no quarrelling now. Instead a feeling of bitterness and resentment came to dominate Gordon Road. Brenda was seething at living in a relationship where she was unloved, even though she still had not made up her mind about what to do. I began to dread coming home to my little house in the evenings to be greeted with the inevitable scornful remark. Even though the abuse was milder now, it was more deliberate and relentless, enough to make me wince before putting my key in the door.

Matthew was my lifeline. Every day he grew livelier, sturdier and more interesting. There was no bitterness with him! Seeing me he would stretch out his arms to be lifted up with a chuckle and a big smile. 'Daddy!' He had it right now, 'Daddy.'

He got sick once in March and he had to be given antibiotics for the first time. He woke from his sleep around midnight and Brenda, true to her theory, was for leaving him cry. I got out of bed and picking him up in my arms, brought him downstairs to watch 'Babar' on video. He began to close his eyes shortly before two. This went on for three nights and I managed to get the walls of the kitchen tiled. His little body eventually got used to the antibiotics, and on the fourth night, he slept through.

Margaret was doing her work well. She telephoned Brenda two or three times a week and never failed to mention the subject of separation. Finally in March Brenda brought it up with me. We were brushing our teeth in the bathroom when she turned to me and said:

'I've been giving this marriage a lot of thought, and apart from Matthew, I'm getting no fulfilment out of it, nothing! It's time we spoke about separation.'

The unthinkable had arrived.

What was the best thing to do? Saying that I did not want the marriage to end, would probably only make her more determined than ever. No! Better to play for time.

'Can we discuss it tomorrow evening?'

'Why not now?'

'Because I'm not ready, that's why.'

Twenty-four hours later, Brenda brought up the subject once again. This time, she got her answer.

"Listen Brenda, I know this has been in your mind for a while. The thing is, *you* weren't thinking of giving Matthew up, so you must be expecting to take him away from me. You'll have to kill me first! Nobody is going to take away my child! I'd go to prison for him! I'd *die* for him! And I'd break every one of your bloody laws to get him back.'

It was enough. It was more than enough! The very intensity of my response shocked her. I saw something in her look that I had never seen before: *fear*. She *had* planned to take Matthew from me, but now she was afraid.

So for the present it was stalemate.

CHAPTER 10

In court and out

Bob Wilson's marriage had broken up a few years earlier. It had been bitter and unpleasant, but at least there were no children to fight over. We met at a day-course on accounting given by the local borough. He had been made redundant the same time as his marriage failed. Once his wife had been paid off, he decided to set up his own business, designing machinery. Bob was interesting company. He did not read newspapers or watch television; he only read the occasional book and saw the odd film. But he had a technical knowledge that was second to none. Shortly after meeting him, he explained the theory of relativity to me in clear simple sentences that I can still remember.

We often enjoyed a drink together in the evenings when I was not working late. I hated being in the house now, after Matthew had gone to bed. The atmosphere was horrible and we spoke very little. I slept in the bed in Matthew's room. The sound of Brenda picking up the phone usually accompanied me on my way out the door.

Work was scarce and uncertain. Tom O'Hara still had jobs to do on his flats and my reputation in the neighbourhood was growing. But most of the jobs were small, and very often they had to be done in the evenings.

Brenda, on the other hand, had had a stroke of luck. In February she heard of a vacancy with a local firm of solicitors. She did the interview and got the job. They were good employers and the job was only ten minutes walk from the house, a very big consideration in London. Marianne Loder, one of her bosses gave me a few days work on her house and Brenda even had a good prospect of partnership in the firm. We came to an arrangement with the Martins, a couple who lived around the corner from Brenda's work, sharing a nanny with them in their house. It was the kind of change in circumstances couples dream about and I was really pleased. Matthew's companion was a little girl called Susanna, six months younger than he was. She idolised him as he led her in all kinds of adventures and games and waited by the window for him to arrive every morning.

But Brenda was anything but pleased, in spite of her good fortune. There is no doubt that things were bleak at home. We did not love each other; we didn't even like each other. She could have changed the awful tension, of course, but that meant reconciling herself to a relationship where she was unloved for the rest of her life, something she was not prepared to do.

I wouldn't have minded, and brought it up in a very brief conversation in June.

'Can't you just lay off?' I said, 'and things would settle down.'

'But there's no *love* there.'

'Yes there is! We both love Matthew.'

It was the truth - but hardly the answer she wanted. Since our brief mention of separation in March the subject had been avoided. Brenda's anger had become worse since then, because now she *knew* she was trapped. With the aid of a good push from her mother she had finally brought herself to acknowledge what she wanted all along, to end our marriage. But the thought of giving Matthew up was as unthinkable to her as it was to me. Brenda understood the bond between us and was terrified of what I might do if she tried to take him away. So now, knowing what she wanted, she was afraid to try to get it. Her fear was to make her take quite desperate measures before long. In the meantime she set about furthering her career in family law.

With Brenda working, we were better off than before and my credit cards began to recover. But the recession in the building trade showed no signs of coming to an end and I began to look at alternatives to conventional carpentry.

Timber frame construction was becoming popular in London, and there was a four-week course in Springfield, Massachusetts, which would equip me for a foreman's job. I suggested doing the course to Brenda. She thought about it and then she agreed with me, saying, 'It would be no harm at all!'

My passport needed to be renewed and it was unfortunate that I was now in the middle of my only good job since Christmas. Brenda offered to help me. She telephoned the Irish Passport Office in Victoria even though they always kept people on hold for over half an hour. Then she made the journey to collect the passport herself on her day off. She was behaving differently now, being nicer to me again. The swing in mood was nothing unusual, so I made the most of it while it lasted. She even dropped me off at the airport on the day I left and she was very friendly. I said goodbye to her and Matthew promising to bring presents back to them both.

*

The course was excellent and the other students were interesting and friendly. Since money was still tight, my accommodation was a cabin with no electricity or water, but that didn't stop me enjoying it all. The first day, after class I found myself flinching as usual before opening the door.

'Hold on a minute!' I said aloud to myself. 'She can't abuse me now, she's not even here!' It worked; I grew fond of my little cabin.

On the telephone, Brenda had changed again. All the anger and hatred were in her voice once more. I dreaded going back.

During the last week she telephoned me at the college to ask me to move out; she wanted a divorce. I told her there was nowhere to go, but that we would talk about it in a week's time. The next time we spoke, there was no mention of divorce and her tone was friendly again. She remained pleasant the last time I called her, two days before the flight.

By now I was missing Matthew terribly and looking forward to the journey home. He had spoken to me only twice in the four weeks, because he seemed to be asleep every time I phoned. I couldn't wait to see him.

It was a night flight and it arrived in Heathrow Airport early in the morning. Brenda's friendly tone had left me half-expecting that they might be waiting for me there. It seemed a long trip by tube and train to Wandsworth on my own. My eyes scanned the crowd hopefully.

'Owen Sheridan!'

He was a young man, thickset, clearly not a lawyer, but with the dull eyes of the legal profession, eyes used to inflicting pain.

'I'm serving these documents on you!'

*

At first I didn't take it in.

Surprised and dazed from lack of sleep, my eyes turned to the wad of paper I had accepted mechanically from him. He had already backed away and was gone. I was summoned to court on Friday. 'What day is it now? Wednesday? Yes, Wednesday morning!'

Still feeling unreal, I found a seat and sat down. In slow motion I looked through the papers, page after page accusing me of violence and cruelty, of irresponsibility and even drunkenness. All but one of the 'instances of violence' referred to real quarrels that we had, but they were cleverly exaggerated and distorted beyond recognition. Her lawyer's training served her well. Our row that first Christmas in my father's place became 'He dragged me out onto the road *and punched me several times.*' Other incidents were treated the same way. She was *'afraid to be in the house with me as my temper had become worse in recent months'*. She knew what to say from dealing with it in her job every day.

The full extent of her bitterness came home to me at last. I don't remember the journey to Gordon Road and half-expected to find a policeman there to arrest me. After all wasn't Brenda a solicitor and an officer of the court? Too numb to care, I trudged to the front door. The Volvo was not parked outside and inside the house there was nobody; no sound and everything was turned off. There was no point in going to bed now, no point in making myself breakfast either. Unable to eat a bite, I drank a glass of milk and pored over the papers again in painful disbelief.

'Why?' I asked myself again and again. 'Why would she do that?' Before long the answer became clear enough. It was Matthew! My little speech in March had convinced Brenda only too well. Even without it, she would not really have expected me to hand Matthew over willingly. As it was, she had no doubts.

The solution as she saw it was that Matthew had to be taken from me by force. This was a relatively easy thing to achieve since she was a woman. She had only to tell a judge that she was afraid of me and give him one or two 'reasons'. Then I would be thrown out of the house and a whole series of restraining orders would go into place, effectively changing the matter from civil law to criminal. She would only have to pick up the telephone to have the police force at her beck and call at any time, night or day. She knew her stuff.

'Did she actually believe her stories?' I wondered. Maybe some of them? I looked at the language again. No! There was no way! She knew exactly what she was doing. But by now she probably hated me enough to believe that I deserved it all 'for the way she had been treated over the years.'

Among the pages was a small note; it fell to the ground. It was from Marianne Loder, Brenda's boss, asking me to telephone her. In desperation, I phoned. Her voice at the other end was motherly and soothing. As I began to protest about all the charges of violence she interrupted me gently.

'Of course Owen, we know that the fault is never completely on one side. The important thing, *for Matthew's sake*, is to settle things as quickly as possible, without a nasty legal battle, and that's up to you.'

There was a pause. She seemed to expect me to say something but I couldn't think of anything to say.

'You see Owen,' she went on confidingly, 'Brenda feels she just can't stay in the house with you right now; she's with friends at the moment. If you could agree to move out *for the time being,* then things can settle down and you both could come to whatever arrangement is best for Matthew.'

'Tell me,' I finally found my voice. 'Can she just haul me into court at that kind of notice? This summons is for Friday and I'm just off the plane. I need some time to think.'

'Yes she can Owen, anytime she wants, that's the way the law is. But the important thing is whether you two settle things peacefully or not. And as I was saying that's up to you. You must be tired from your journey, but you have to decide now. What's it to be?'

'I s...suppose it's for the best,' I said hesitantly.

'Well done! Can we say four o' clock?'

'What? Four o' clock *today?*'

'Yes! It's best if things can calm down as quickly as possible.'

'But where can I go?'

'Have you a friend you can phone? Anyone at all?'

'I don't think I can do anything today. I need to sleep. It's even hard to think.'

'Well yes! Yes of course! I'd forgotten how tired you are. I'll tell Brenda that you just aren't able to move until *tomorrow* at four o' clock. That's better isn't it?'

'Yes that's better, I repeated.

There was a silence. Then I heard the phone being put down at the other side and went to bed feeling vaguely uneasy. At least I could sleep now.

*

People who are analytical are often gullible. Their way for working things out is very slow and they rely too much on words. Also, intuitive thinking looks at whole concepts and can constantly double-check itself. One false conclusion on the other hand can spoil the whole reasoning process. It had been my weakness all my life.

It almost betrayed me now - almost. Was it the sleep or was it the trauma that put me in touch with my feelings? Whatever it was, as soon as my sleep was over I saw through her at once.

The anger burned in me. *It was up to me was it?* Who took out the legal proceedings and swore perjury to the court? Was I the one whose mood changed everything, who was picking fights for the past three years? No! But now they were trying to get me to pay the price for all the damage done by a spoilt angry woman. And not just me but also my little son! No! By Christ no! I would fight this to the last. There was nothing to lose anyway. Once out of that house, there would be no more sweet-talk and no mercy. I knew that now.

Picking up the phone, I spoke to the firm of solicitors I had contacted the year before. When they heard that there was a hearing on Friday, they agreed to see me right away.

An hour later I was sitting at a large desk opposite a young man in a three-piece suit. He introduced himself as Bernard Timson. I decided to be candid with him, telling everything and describing the rows in detail. He telephoned a barrister and briefed him, there and then. Then he took out a notebook and began to compose an affidavit for the court.

'One sentence has to go in there,' I told him: 'There was no violence such as my wife described in her statement.'

'Mr. Sheridan, we have only two days to prepare this case. We must work together. Please let me do my job. It would be very difficult to persuade the court that a solicitor is lying.' His tone was pompous. I noticed he was speaking with an affected RP.

'Now,' he continued. Where did you say your wife works?'

Leaving his office, I felt tired again.

*

Chapter 10

The barrister's name was George Adams. 'Not *Gerry* Adams,' he smiled, as he met me in the courthouse building. With very little sleep and nothing to eat for two days, it was an effort to return the smile politely, before coming straight to the point.

'We must sell Gordon Road,' my voice was despondent. 'Then we can each get a place to stay and share the time with Matthew.'

'Yes, yes' he said. 'Look! Here's the other side now! Better have a word.'

Brenda was with Marianne Loder and another buxom woman in her mid-forties, the other barrister no doubt; she was evidently on very good terms with George Adams. Marianne Loder avoided meeting my eyes.

Presently he joined me again.

'Now what was it you were saying?' he asked.

'We must sell Gordon Road, buy or rent two smaller places and share residency of Matthew. It would be best if I could get two or three weeks to get the place fit to sell it. She and Matthew are quite welcome to come back in the meantime.'

'I see. Well I'll put it to them and see what they say.'

This time he was away for longer.

'It's no harm to have a fallback position ready,' he said on coming back, 'in case they don't agree.'

'The fallback position is this! She goes up into the witness box to talk about some of those things she's accused me of,' I said, looking at him suspiciously.

'Oh I see! Do you feel that strongly about it? You have to consider the long-term effects of a hard-line approach, you know.'

'The hard line approach was dragging me into court in the first place'

He squirmed, but eventually walked back over again to the other side. They were around a corner but something very like Brenda's suit was moving among them. 'What was going on?' I wondered. He was on his way back.

'Fiona Carter, their counsel is worried about how long it's going to take. Can we say two weeks?'

'It isn't in Brenda's interest if we do; the list of the jobs is too long. We have to try and sell for as much as we can.'

'Ye.... es! It does make sense, what about the costs? Can we say we are prepared to meet them in order to clinch the deal?'

'You mean reward her for all the lies?' my tone was incredulous. 'There is no way!'

Shortly afterwards he brought me a hand-written document. 'Sign here!' he said 'Fiona said the costs will have to be settled by the judge.' He looked at me questioningly but all I said was 'Fine.'

Within five minutes we were in court. The clerk called 'All rise!' and the judge came in. He was in his fifties and I noticed his face was kind. I was learning.

Fiona Carter was on her feet. 'We have a consent-order in this case, my lord, between the defendant Mr. Sheridan, a carpenter and Mrs. Sheridan, a solicitor.'

'A solicitor?' the judge repeated, looking suspiciously at Brenda. 'I thought there was to be an adjournment in this case as Mr. Sheridan could not be served with the summons.'

'We served the summons on him as he came off the plane, my lord, on Wednesday morning.'

'That was clever!' The judge's eyes cut through her and I saw Brenda's face fall.

She went on, 'We have been able to reach agreement except in the matter of costs.'

'Costs to be determined in the course of the proceeding!'

'All rise!' and we were through. George Adams was having tête-à-tête with Fiona Carter as I left the building quietly. There was no reason to disturb them.

I slept soundly that night; so did the judge.

*

Chapter 10

Matthew beamed when he saw me the following day. We were in McDonalds. I picked him up and threw him in the air catching him again, the way he loved. He had to be dropped back there again at six o' clock.

'What was I now, a McDonalds dad? No longer a parent but a visitor to my child's life, seeing him by appointment for a few hours?' That has got to change!' I thought, 'Whatever it takes.'

A few days later Brenda drove by Gordon Road. She got out of the Volvo and I asked her in.

'You don't seem to be making much headway, doing up the house,' she said.

'I've been feeling a bit down lately. Can't imagine why!'

'Well you'd want to hurry up! We're moving in, in two weeks'

'What? How are we to sell the property if you move in?'

'We aren't!'

'Oh yes we are, that's the agreement we made.'

'You were saying something like that in McDonalds; that's why I'm here, You had better look at the agreement again.' There was a note of triumph in her voice.

The phone in Bernard Timson's office was ringing before she reached the garden gate. He tried to put me off, but I told him to have a photocopy of the agreement ready because I was on my way up there right now to collect it. His secretary had the document ready for me - and an excuse. 'Mr. Timson has just gone out,' she said.

Brenda was correct of course. There was no mention of selling the house anywhere in the document. I was compelled by law to move out in two weeks time – and then she was perfectly entitled to move in and stay there. Meanwhile being still liable for the mortgage payments, I couldn't buy another home or even rent a decent place to bring Matthew to stay. I had been led by the nose into the grim world of dispossessed dads - and by the very lawyers who were supposed to be fighting for me.

My mind was full of questions. Do the lawyers acting for the dad not take his part the way the mother's lawyers do?

My own solicitor and barrister seemed more anxious than anybody to get me out of my home. Are the outcomes of these proceedings pre-arranged? Why did my lawyers not want to put Brenda into the witness box? Are family lawyers so accountable to one another that they cannot afford to alienate one of their own? Do they have important secrets to hide? Where does the judge stand? Above all else, what was I to do now? It took me a long time to get the answers to these questions - all except one.

When Brenda dropped Matthew off at McDonalds the next day, she arrived early. They were both sitting at a table waiting for me. She clearly wanted to talk; so did I.
'Well, did you read the agreement?'
'I read the document, yes! But that's not the agreement I made!'
Pulling her copy from her handbag, she placed it on the table in front of me, clearly enjoying her triumph. 'Well that's not what it says here,' she said.
'It doesn't matter what it says there. I didn't agree to it and I have no notion of going anywhere!'
'We can get the police to throw you out and you'll be charged with contempt of court.'
'Go right ahead! It will take another hearing in any case and I'm quite happy to tell the judge that I would never agree to that. He was quite suspicious too about the way you went about it. This time, you're going into a witness box - and I'll cross-examine you myself about perjury and things like that.'
The confidence drained from her face. 'We'll get you sooner or later,' she hissed at me as she left the table.
'Lift up!' said Matthew smiling at me. I lifted him up.

Marianne Loder phoned me almost as soon as we reached home.
'If you are not prepared to comply with the court order we will have to get the police to enforce it,' she threatened. There was no motherly tone now.

'You'll have to have another hearing. As a matter of fact I think I'll save you the trouble and apply to the court myself.'

'No! We can evict you without any more court hearings if you are not prepared to vacate the property voluntarily.'

'You lying bitch! Do you think I'm going to believe the same lies twice? You go to your court. Right now there's nothing I'd like more!'

She put down the phone. It was the last time we spoke to one another.

Early next morning a short phonecall to an agency got me a job in a large house in Chelsea, but it was difficult to keep my mind on the work. What was going to happen now? Were they going to throw me out of my house? Was a policeman already waiting for me at home?

Shortly after lunch, while shooting some French doors with my small block plane I suddenly felt a burning pain in my right thumb. Looking down gingerly I could see the nail standing up from the red flesh of the nail bed. A huge splinter had worked its way up as far as the joint and the root of the nail was exposed at one corner where it had been torn out.

At the first aid box, the foreman asked me what was wrong. Then, spotting my thumb, he made a grimace and turned his face away. It took all my will power to keep it under the running water. Then I took a good look at it; I had lost the nail.

'Is there anything I can do?' the foreman asked.

'Do you have a pair of pliers? I didn't bring mine.'

Gripping the nail with the pliers I closed my eyes and jerked. 'UUUHH!' It came off in one go. The pain wasn't much worse.

'Some trouble at home,' I explained.

He nodded understandingly. It's not uncommon in the building trade. We went back to work.

For the rest of the week Brenda tried a mixture of persuasion and threats to get me out of Gordon Road. She began by asking me if I wanted to leave my young son homeless. My reply was that he would always have a home as long as I had one - and I was going to make sure of that. She scowled.

By the weekend I had worked out a proposal and on Sunday I put it to her as she came to collect Matthew. She would sell her share of the house to me. My valuation was £110,000 but she was welcome to get an independent report. That left £39,000 in equity. Forgetting the fact that I had already spent £25,000 and two thousand hours of my time on it. I would pay her £20,000 for signing her interest over.

Brenda didn't take long to think about it. She had never liked the house anyway. On Tuesday she brought Matthew over again 'because he was missing me.' She also agreed to wait a few months for the last £10,000 if I threw in the Volvo. We shook hands on it in the front drawing room where Stephen Clarke had pulled down the partition with me, and Matthew stayed with me overnight. The following morning I dropped him off at the Martins' where Susanna was delighted to see him as usual.

*

Brenda rented a maisonette, part of a new development in Earlsfield. She also insisted on enrolling Matthew in a playschool nearby, saying that Gail, the nanny, 'didn't stimulate him enough.'

Poor little Susanna was heartbroken. Ignoring Gail, she moved her toys near the window and kept looking for him all day until evening. She even tried again the following morning before she finally gave up.

CHAPTER 11

Silver lining

Driving over Wandsworth Bridge, on my way to see Matthew in Earlsfield, I was conscious that something was different. It made me feel vaguely uneasy at first, distracting me from thinking of his bedtime story.

It was almost eight o' clock. So far, the journey had taken just over ten minutes, not bad for London! I had left Bob Wilson as soon as we had installed a shower for Tom O' Hara in Fulham. All day we had been rushing to finish before the tenants arrived home, so there was very little time to talk or even think. Now however, there was no doubt that something was out of place, unusual.

What was it? Nothing was wrong with the job and I was really looking forward to seeing Matthew in a few minutes time.

Brenda's maisonette was part of a small development close to the River Wandle. Everything was new and shiny with a lot of plush carpet and chrome. She was very pleased with it.

Turning into the little cul-de-sac, I realised what it was, a huge sense of relief. I was happy! Happier in fact than I had been for a long time and aware of it all of a sudden. It felt like a great weight had been lifted from me. Life was good again!

There is no doubt that happiness comes in strange ways and none more unexpected than this one. After the summons had been thrust at me getting off the aeroplane my mind went numb; any feelings were of pure humiliation. I hated these divorce proceedings, being hauled up in front of a judge, being accused of horrible things and being treated like a criminal. Worse than that is the sense of failure. A marriage is not like any other project that goes wrong. It throws your whole life into confusion and despair. All of a sudden there is no reason to get up in the morning. Moreover, being on the receiving end of the proceedings without expecting it is not unlike being rejected by a parent. It hurts. For weeks I had avoided meeting my neighbours in case they might see my disgrace, my pain.

But the situation had its good side. There is nothing so degrading as being in an abusive relationship. The constant wearing down of your confidence destroys self-worth. I had dreaded coming home to Gordon Road, to the inevitable scorn and abuse waiting for me there. Making money became difficult, impossible at times and the small debts kept increasing. At the end I even lost the ability to sing; my voice became hoarse.

Now at last the abuse was over. Gradually my nervousness about going home disappeared, and it was good to be in my house again. Even more encouraging was the knowledge that the nasty little pile of debt was rapidly getting smaller. I had taken a carpentry job working nights on the London Underground, replacing doors and other structures in order to bring them up to the new fire regulations. We could only work for five hours, while the trains were not running, but because it was night work our wages were good. That left me plenty of time for working during the day. So Bob and I started a building company and already it was showing signs of doing well. I would get home at about six in the morning, then sleep for seven hours before working from two until eight with Bob. Then there was usually time for something to eat between visiting Matthew and going to work again at half past eleven. My customer list was quite long and when added to Bob's we had a reasonable client base to work with - and it was growing.

Also, two rooms in Gordon Road were now let out to lodgers. On a very tight budget I had given the rooms a lick of paint, bought two mattresses and physically made two beds with some wood that was lying around. Then I put an ad in Loot, the London free ads paper and waited for replies.

The thought of the tenants made me quite apprehensive. What would they ask me on the telephone? Above all, what would they think of the rooms? Brenda's attitude to the house had convinced that they were not really acceptable. 'But at least they are clean and the house has character,' I reasoned. 'There must be two people who like them in all of Wandsworth.' Nevertheless, when it came to placing the ad, it only mentioned one room, the better finished of the two. 'No point in showing the other, not without doing some more work on it,' I thought. 'May as well be realistic about it.'

The day came for people to view the room. Eight people had said they would turn up and to my surprise, eight people arrived. More surprising still, eight people said they wanted the room. A teacher called Richard even arrived early, and saw me painting the room that was not advertised. He took one look at it and paid his deposit on the spot, so by the evening, the two rooms were rented. I was really thrilled. Being a man, I had instinctively deferred to the woman's opinion about a home; so when everybody else liked it so much, it came as quite a shock. But what an agreeable shock! Years of work and thought were suddenly justified - and by eight people out of eight! They had all liked my house! They had even wanted to live there. My confidence began to recover.

The two jobs and the rent brought me an income of over seven hundred a week and my expenses were just over two, so my finances were under control. When Bob spotted a red pick-up truck with '4 sale' written on it, the bank was happy to loan me the money. It was old, but in good condition and in many ways more useful to me than a car.

Best of all was seeing Matthew every day. He was less than a mile away, so every evening I would drive to the apartment after work. He was now just over two and he looked forward to my visits. We (he mostly) developed a routine where I would play with him each night before putting him to bed with a story.

It had not started out that way. Brenda, as an efficient solicitor had devised an elaborate access plan where I saw Matthew three times a week and he stayed overnight every second weekend. She would drop him to Gordon Road in the Volvo and then collect him in time for bed. The first time I carried him out and strapped him into his child-seat he announced 'Daddy in car!' and again firmly 'Daddy in car!'

Brenda was embarrassed. 'He'll get over that,' she said unconvincingly.

But he didn't; he repeated it faithfully every time, so that she couldn't meet my eyes. She began to hate collecting him and a change in the pattern was likely even if Matthew hadn't brought it about.

What happened was Brenda wanted some built-in furniture and a washer-drier fitted in the apartment. Prior to this she had warned me to stay away from there. Being a solicitor she knew very well that having me inside would not add credibility to her claims of violence or that she was afraid of me. However one estimate from a local property management agency was enough to change her mind. After three visits I had the apartment as she wanted it. My payment was time spent with Matthew and I got into the routine of putting him to bed. Brenda got the added bonus of not having to take him away from Gordon Road on those evenings.

One Saturday evening, on my way out for a drink with Bob and Richard, the telephone rang. It was Brenda; she had a terrible flu and needed some parecetomol so she could get to sleep? Matthew's voice could be heard in the background. My two friends looked at me incredulously as I agreed to go down to her. They had heard all the things she had accused me of doing, and now she had me once more at her beck and call. Nevertheless Richard gave me some tablets.

At the apartment Matthew was wide-awake, so handing Brenda the tablets, I put him to bed with a story. What she hadn't told me was that she had found it impossible to get him to sleep without me; that was the main reason she had phoned. After that, it was the same routine every evening except when he stayed over in Gordon Road. I never needed to call Brenda.

The hardest thing had been telling my father. He was now eighty-one years old and for him it was unthinkable to break up a marriage. It took all my will power to pick up the phone and blurt out the story quickly in case my courage failed. He went very quiet. His was a generation used to accepting hardship of all kinds. A few days later, I phoned him again and explained things in a bit more detail.

One of his worries was seeing Matthew, now that he was not living with me. Since I had not been to Ireland since Christmas it was time to take a short break in October and go over to see him. Brenda had no objection about taking Matthew. We travelled over on the ferry, so there was no set time to return. Our visit lasted ten days and we had a great time. Matthew never once asked for his mother but she phoned quite frequently towards the end.

Sadly, there was one other reason for my happiness. In spite of all that had happened, my mind would not accept that the marriage was really over. I was still in denial, believing that Brenda would 'come to her senses' and Matthew would have a proper home again.

Back in London, Brenda to my surprise, made one or two remarks about 'couples who split up and later got back together again' - almost as if she was thinking the same way. At first I did not respond but after about a week she became more specific. One evening having invited me to have a cup of tea after Matthew went to sleep she said that one of the main reasons that 'things were so bad between us' was that she hated living in London. If she was back in Ireland, then she would feel a lot happier. 'Since there is no divorce culture in Ireland it wouldn't be fair to him to live in a one-parent family,' was what she said.

At first, my reaction was suspicion, but it was what I wanted to believe. She was looking for work in Cork and Dublin, she told me, mentioning the names of two well-known Dublin law practices to which she had applied. I didn't know what to think. Once or twice she had seemed upset when she had phoned me in Limerick. Was she genuinely feeling remorse?

It was time now to pay her the money. My savings account had £10,400 (the last of the £50,000). We agreed that I would pay her the remaining £9600 when the deeds of Gordon Road were in my sole name, or else when she needed it to buy a house - whichever came sooner.

A week later she hit me with the bombshell. Burgess and White, the huge firm of Dublin solicitors was expanding its family law section, and had offered her a job. It was what she wanted and she was going to accept. My first reaction was to panic. What was she going to do? Go away, and take Matthew with her? Taking out my notebook, I wrote a short message refusing to allow her to take Matthew away, and marched out to the truck.

'Owen! It's not like that! I want us to get together as a family again. Just come back and discuss it. You're the one who always wanted to talk things over.'

The ringing of the phone had reached me coming in the front gate of Gordon Road.

'Well we're talking about them, aren't we? I had calmed down somewhat.

'Okay then! Now you don't have to take my word for this but I can get permission to take Matthew to Dublin. The court will give it to me because I'm his mother. Ask your own solicitor! He'll tell you. If you fight me in court you may stall things but I'll win in the end. The thing is, if we go fighting legal battles then Matthew will never have a home. Now you have to make up your mind! Do you want us to get back together or not? You don't have to answer me straight away just tell me tomorrow!' Then she said goodbye and put the phone down.

Chapter 11

The following night when Matthew was in bed, the cup of tea appeared again on the table. Brenda explained what she had in mind. She would take Matthew to Dublin *without permission from the court.* Then she would be at my mercy for a certain amount of time. I would come over at Christmas and we would be together again *as a family* and if we got on, then we could make our plans for the coming year.

'Hang on a minute! Getting on is not up to me; it's up to you! You can say anything you like, but it wasn't me who was picking the fights! Getting on means whether you lay off - or not.'

'We - ell, I suppose I was more unhappy than you were,' she said slowly. 'But if we don't get on, you can always take Matthew back with you to London in the New Year. That's the law! It's only four weeks to Christmas and this is our only chance to become a family again. I will never be happy in this country. I want to live in Ireland!'

Over the next two days, I thought it over. She had tricked me in the past but she really did seem to be telling the truth when she said she wanted me over at Christmas. Matthew could always be brought back to London if it was all lies. There didn't seem a lot to lose, except Matthew for four weeks. And there was everything to gain. When the choice was put before me, there was no question of what I wanted. Perhaps I was a fool but it was what Matthew wanted too when he said 'Daddy in car' - his home back again.

So they left, one cold Saturday morning and I braced myself for the coming weeks. Two things made them bearable. Firstly, Brenda was as good as her word phoning me two or three times every week and letting me talk to Matthew. The other was that Bob Wilson and I were busy; we were getting plenty of work. By the end of November the night work was no longer necessary and we began planning an advertising campaign for the New Year. Brenda also lived up to her promise about Christmas and suggested that I come over to her house on the twenty-third. When the morning arrived I threw my things in the truck and barely made the ferry at Holyhead.

Silver lining

Christmas in Dublin was the most relaxed in years. Brenda said that it was the presence of her family that made her tense and uptight and when she brought up the subject of 'uniting us again as a family' I could not have been happier. All the old anger, the bitterness seemed to be gone. 'Right!' I thought. 'If she can put the past behind her, then so can I! I'm going to call it quits and wipe the slate clean! Now we can start again!'

It was Matthew and the delight on his face when he saw me that made my resolve so easy. He just couldn't get enough of me. He wanted me to play with him all day and then to put him to bed at night. I noticed changes in him since he had left London. He had more to say, more questions to ask, and he had developed a delightful sense of self-parody that is very rare in a small child. The days flew by.

Brenda was happy to let him come to Limerick with me to visit my father. She would travel down and take him to her parents after a week. The house was cold but we all had a great time. Two days before she arrived, the telephone rang. It was Brenda! Even before she said a single word I knew that something was wrong. Her voice made my heart sink, my worst suspicions confirmed.

'What's wrong?' I asked. 'You sound angry.'

'Maybe it's about time I started getting angry!'

'Christ! It's about time you started getting anything else!'

But it was no good. She had destroyed everything again. The foul mood was back; nothing had changed. Of all my disappointments, this one hurt me the most. It really caught me by surprise. Her assurances seemed so real, and I had clung to them, hoping we could make a good home for Matthew in spite of all that had happened. Now my hopes were shattered, leaving me thoroughly shaken. The following day was very long. Still upset, and irritable, I knew in the back of my mind that I would probably still try, if given the opportunity, to make the marriage work but never again in the same spirit. Something had finally died.

Chapter 11

That was the evening of Dan Hurley's funeral. The Hurleys were neighbours for generations and there was no question of not going. But when Matthew heard he was to be left behind, he would have none of it. He was becoming quite sensible now and it was getting late - perhaps it would be all right to bring him along.

In the church I warned him that he must be quiet and for a time he was reasonably well behaved. But he eventually became bored and let out a high-pitched yell that echoed round the whole building.

'Stop squeaking!' I whispered. It was a familiar command, and Matthew was normally very good to do what he was told. He stayed silent for a minute or so, then yelled again and some of the Hurley family were looking round from the front of the church.

'Matthew! Stop squeaking!' This time it was a hiss. A few seconds later he opened his mouth to shout again, so I put my finger to his mouth saying 'sshhh!' This was no good; he had to be taken outside. There was a crowd standing round the doorway. They couldn't get seats because the little church was full. Whispering tensely 'be quiet!' I joined them with Matthew in my arms. All of a sudden he started up again, so I brought him quickly down the steps and into the truck.

'Matthew stop squeaking!' My voice was loud now, with the door closed. His response was to give another loud cry.

'MATTHEW STOP SQUEAKING!' It was a snarl! I noticed my two hands holding him by the shoulders were trembling in anger. For a moment there was silence. Then Matthew looked forward, away from my eyes and stammered 'M-Matoo's h-h-happy!'

My God! What had I done? My little son was terrified! I was losing control and he had sensed my anger. It had scared the life out of him! Christ! Was I capable of hurting him? I had to act quickly.

Picking him up in my arms I held him close. 'It's all right pet! It's okay now! You're a good boy! A very good boy.' He was calming down. I brought him out of the truck. 'My poor helpless little boy!' I soothed, rocking him gently in my arms.

It was working - better than I dared hope. He was relaxing already. He put his arms round my neck and very soon he even smiled. Thanks be to God! Feeling weak, but keeping up the talk, I walked him up and down the road.

The crowd was now coming out of the church. Anxious to pay my respects to the Hurleys I said 'Matthew, we must go into the church again. I'm only going to say hello, then we'll go out again. It's very important that you make no noise in a church. Can you be quiet for a few minutes?'

'Yes Daddy.' He didn't seem to mind, and inside he was as good as gold!

The Hurleys invited us back to the house and Matthew was in great form. When he saw the bottles of lemonade he asked me for a bottle of 'fizzy.' A little boy called Bobby made friends with him and they had a great time, happy and smiling as they played. Everyone could see the bond of affection between us. I saw the smiles of approval and even overheard a few remarks about what a fine father I was.

All the time I felt nothing but self-disgust. Nothing had ever made me feel so ashamed in my life. *I had almost lost control.* I had taken my anger out on my innocent little boy. What kind of a parent was I at all?

It was unfortunate for Matthew and for me that Brenda came to take him away the following day. I let him go without a word.

CHAPTER 12

Grasping at straws

'You see Owen it was the *violence* that was making me angry. I just couldn't put it out of my mind.'
'Is that so?'
'It's different for a woman. It's not the same thing hitting a man.'
'Why not?'
'It's so *humiliating* for a woman. A man doesn't get hurt that way - not so much at least.'
'I see. So how does a man get hurt?'
'Well I don't know, but the thing is we shouldn't give up yet. Matthew is very happy, by the way.'
 'May I have a word with him?'
'Well, he's asleep now. I thought we could have a talk ourselves.'

It was the third time in two days that Brenda had phoned me at Gordon Road. After she left with Matthew I had gone straight back to London, feeling miserable and not eating or sleeping at night. Should I demand that Matthew be brought back home at once? Would the court order his return or would they just give Brenda permission to take him to Dublin? She was 'one of the club' after all. The incident at the funeral still made me shudder. Maybe he was better off with Brenda.

I didn't want to talk to her. It had been a huge effort to put the hurts and wrongs behind me, and she had thrown it all back in my face. Also, I blamed Brenda as much as myself for what happened at the funeral. It was her about-turn that shattered my hopes and put my nerves on edge. Ever since

Matthew was born I had been at her mercy. Now the thought of her filled me with revulsion.

What was all the self-pity about? Was she genuinely feeling guilty about what happened? Or was she just trying to prevent me from taking legal proceedings to bring Matthew back? Her legal training? At that moment I didn't care.

Why did she keep talking about violence? Was she trying to make me feel guilty or to justify her own anger? Bernard Timson had made me realise that my slapping Brenda on the cheek was very different from Brenda's slapping me - at least as far as a judge was concerned. But she was not likely to make me feel guilty, not for that anyway. No, it had to be the other, an excuse for breaking up Matthew's home.

Realising that she was getting nowhere, she said goodbye before long. It was the same for the next month. During this time Matthew spoke to me seldom. I hated the thought of phoning Brenda and she deliberately called when he was in bed. She was hoping I would give in and call her. But I was punishing myself for what had happened. Even in my distraught state I partly realised that Matthew was suffering too, that it was up to me to contact him. But my feelings of disgust at Brenda were so strong that I couldn't pick up the phone.

During February, Brenda played the Matthew card for all it was worth and I flew over to see him. We went for a drive round Avondale, Charles Stuart Parnell's home in County Wicklow. Matthew enjoyed the woods and the freedom.

But when we were on our own, things quickly turned nasty again. Strangely, it was Brenda who started it, even though she was the one who arranged the visit in the first place. Seeing a history book in my bag, a biography of Eamon De Valera, she made a big issue about wasting my time and energy. I said nothing.

On Saturday we had lunch with Peter Tierney and his wife Celia. Peter is an extremely successful barrister who became a senior counsel at the age of thirty-five. We were in school together. Peter's air of success probably irritated her

Chapter 12

and she made several comparisons on the way home. It was time to put an end to the visit. I spent a few days in Limerick with my father before returning home.

Brenda moved house in mid-March, without giving me an address or phone number. That made up my mind. I wrote to Colman Kelly, her solicitor, telling him that I was about to take out proceedings for the return of my son.

His reply was very diplomatic. The letter mentioned the £9600 and suggested that the money was now due. (So Brenda had bought a place of her own!) There was also an offer of a weekend visit with Matthew. Peter Tierney was only too happy to offer me hospitality for the weekend.

'Would you go back and live with her again?' It was a perceptive question from Peter on the Saturday morning. By now, my mind was made up. Analytical thinking wasn't always a liability.

'Yes I would, Peter! For Matthew's sake, but not with the kind of emotional commitment as before.'

Was it coincidence that Brenda phoned me later in the week using all my own language about 'responsibility to our son?' She offered to come over to visit me - and this time Matthew was awake. 'When am I seeing you Daddy?' he said.

I met them in Shrewsbury. They were in the Volvo and picked me up from the train. For three days we drove around North Wales and took Matthew on a two-foot gauge steam railway. By chance the engine was blue and he loved it saying 'Thomas the Tank Engine' over and over again.

Brenda had not bought the place where she was living. She was still renting, she told me, so there was no need to borrow the £9600 right away.

In May the public speaking finals were held in Galway and Brenda invited me to visit her and Matthew on the way, so I flew to Dublin late on the Thursday evening. They were staying on the third floor of an ugly 1950's apartment complex that Matthew called 'the blockhouse.' Still, it had a swimming pool and a large lawn where he could play. He was now going to playschool and both his knowledge and vocabulary were growing very quickly. As I took him along to school he asked me 'Will you come again soon, Daddy? How many sleeps?'

'Two sleeps Matthew, then we're going to see Grand Dad on the train.' He chuckled happily.

That was the end of my resistance. But this time it was different. I was harder, far less inclined to talk, and under no illusions.

In Galway two women were discussing marriage. Eileen Davis was about twenty-five and single; Diana Cooper was in her forties and still attractive. She had been widowed, then divorced.

'Oh I'd love to be married,' Eileen was saying. 'To be able to come home to someone every evening.'

'For heaven's sake Eileen!' - I couldn't avoid butting in. 'Marriage is about the most unerotic place on earth!'

'*Owen*!' Diana cried in mock rebuke 'You're not supposed to say that to the *uninitiated*!'

We had a 'family holiday' in Rhodes. Matthew slept with me in one room, Brenda in the other. But at least we didn't fight and had a pleasant time. Matthew's mind was growing rapidly. This was the time I began telling him the stories. They came from mythology or from books I had read as a child. Wherever they came from, Matthew devoured them. He had to have a story at least twice a day. It didn't matter if he had heard the story before. Eventually towards the end of the holiday *he* even told *me* a story. There is a lovely photo of him absorbed in his little drama while I am listening intently. They left me in Gatwick on the way back to Dublin.

It was my father's news in July that brought me back to Ireland. He had been offered seventy thousand pounds for his house and half an acre of land, an offer he could not afford to turn down. Anne, my sister, and her husband invited him to move into town with them and he accepted. He was now eighty-two. He was going to sign over the yard and the fields to me, he said as I had done a lot of work on them over the years. I travelled over in the truck and cleared my things out of the house.

At the same time Bob and I had decided to close our building company. It was making money, but it was still 'more of a job than a business' as Bob put it. Anyway it was impossible to keep it going now that I was spending so much time in Ireland.

With Matthew on the phone to me regularly, it was a foregone conclusion that my trip would be via Dublin and 'the blockhouse.' He travelled down with me to Limerick. I stayed in Ireland the whole month of August, alternating between 'the blockhouse' and my father's. Matthew accompanied me most of the time. Was it because I was more detached that I never once lost my temper with Brenda, or even raised my voice? When she 'acted up' I just threw my things in a bag and went down to Limerick. Matthew usually insisted on coming too.

In the beginning of September my father moved out; my refuge was gone. Sadly, I packed some of my personal things in the truck and drove up to Dublin. Brenda had agreed to store them for me while I went back to Gordon Road to tidy things up. Even Matthew lent a hand carrying the clothes and tools up the stairs. He was fascinated by my father's old shotgun, now licensed in my name. 'I'd better take care of that, in case he might get his hands on it' Brenda said disapprovingly. She hid it in the back of the wardrobe, while I put the ammunition (far more dangerous!) on top of a tall cupboard out of his reach.

I had decided to rent out my room in Gordon Road, go to Dublin and make one final attempt to make the marriage work. There was some work to be done on my bedroom and Bob Wilson gave me a hand. So by the end of September both my homes were gone. It was a strange feeling, being a displaced person but Bob promised me that if things didn't work out, he would let me stay with him. I drove to the ferry with mixed feelings.

It lasted three weeks.

She probably couldn't help herself; it was a variation of the snapping. She began to criticise me sharply several times a day, hurling the rebukes without mercy and on small provocation; soon we stopped talking entirely. Finally I telephoned Joe Healy in Limerick, and asked him for a bed for a few days in order to get a few jobs done on the yard. He was happy to oblige.

She called me the next day, announced that the marriage was over, and suggested that we get some counselling about splitting up. She would give me permission to stay in her flat while visiting Matthew in Dublin.

'You mean *you* can stay in Gordon Road when you visit him in London,' I countered.

'We'll see about that!' she said.

We did go to counselling but it was useless. Brenda had very little to say and sat there looking more and more angry. She did not turn up for the next session and the counsellor said there was no point in talking to me on my own.

'Well! *When* are you leaving?'

'Ask Matthew that!'

'Very clever! But this is *my* flat, and you can see it isn't working. So why don't you just go?'

'Like I said, ask Matthew! Tell you what, we'll *both* ask him. Better again, let's see does he want to come with me if I go?'

'Don't you dare! He's just a three-year-old. He doesn't know what he wants.'

'I think he knows very well. He knows what you want too and he doesn't like a bit of it.'

'Look! Are you going to move out or not?'

'There's one simple way to get me out.'

'What's that?'

'Help me to pack Matthew's stuff and we'll be out as soon as we can.'

She was silent; her face became harder.

I was in limbo, no longer welcome at the apartment, but with nowhere else to go. The last time Brenda and I lived in an apartment together, things could not have been more different. Balham had been such a happy place. Now the angry mood was there all the time, like Brenda's last days at Gordon Road.

What had gone wrong? What had gone right in the beginning? What was the best thing to do now? Once a woman has decided that a relationship is over, is there *anything* a man can do? It seemed to me that from the time of my very first relationship, I had had very little control over what happened. Jimmy Nagle's words came back to me, 'Men don't even initiate sex...' 'Scoring' with a woman was not a mystery now.

The only thing I could think of was a last desperate appeal to save Matthew's home. But at the mention of the subject, she walked out of the room. I had no other ideas, so I waited.

Matthew however had ideas of his own. He may have overheard Brenda and me, or it may have been his uncanny intuition but he became very watchful. He hated parting from me, even when I took him to playschool in the mornings. At home he did not want me to leave the apartment for any reason.

But spending an entire evening in an atmosphere like that was impossible. I usually arranged to go out for something to eat and sometimes stopped for a pint on the way home. Matthew always came with me. He would sit quietly while I was eating and since I couldn't take him into a pub, we would go to The Mayfair Hotel, up the road from the blockhouse. I slept on the futon in the living room. Matthew came in to me every morning as soon as he woke.

The days were long! It was unusual for me to be hanging around, but it gave me the chance to look squarely at my marriage for the first time. All along I had been too involved, too worried to see things clearly. Now they were all too plain!

We had made a mistake. When we met, there was an instant physical attraction. This had blossomed into an exciting romance and we admired certain qualities in each other, but that was all. There was no affection, no meeting of minds and no mutual respect. We saw things very differently - and when we got married, my bank account held fifty thousand pounds.

The holiday romance became worn out and finally died. It had happened while we were rebuilding Gordon Road. I had been too wrapped up in the project to notice. It was not until the time Matthew arrived that it occurred to me that there was no longer any magic there. My outlook, like my father's has always been philosophical, and it never occurred to me to do anything other than make the best of it. I went for walks with her, brought home videos to watch and tried to make the most of the things we still enjoyed doing together. At the same time I lived my own life, going for a pint with my mates, reading my own books, thinking my own thoughts. So what if we did not love each other? Neither did most couples! Looking at other people's marriages, didn't we have more going for us than most? I was not unhappy.

Not so Brenda! Once she realised that it was not what she thought, she reacted in disbelief and rage. The spoilt daughter of a spoilt daughter, she was used to having what she wanted. Now she had a marriage that she didn't want at all, and *she* had known it from very early on. It was not her way to accept things; so she began to lash out at me. When she became pregnant she felt trapped. There was going to be no easy way out now and her anger hardened into bitterness and hatred.

There was no other way to explain all the sneers, the hurts, and the quarrels. Above all it explained why she had always refused to make up after each row. She didn't want the marriage to work; she wanted the resolve to finish it for good! But she didn't have the strength! She was held back by the expectations of her family and by her own conscience, especially when Matthew came along. No wonder she didn't want to be pregnant!

Hatred is helpless anger, anger that cannot be expressed, so that it festers and boils. The dirty tricks, the false allegations of violence, the friendly chat on the phone while she was preparing the summons at the airport, the fear of me that conveniently disappeared after the hearing in London; they made sense now, all of them.

It occurred to me that if the pattern of the last few years was anything to go by, one of the 'dirty tricks' was due very soon. She was feeling very angry now and very helpless. But what could she do? I was her husband and had not even raised my voice to her, so she couldn't have me barred from the flat. What was going to happen next?

I soon found out. A few days later she announced that she would like to take Matthew to school the following morning but I could pick him up in the afternoon as usual. Next day, he had barely waved goodbye when there was a knock at the door. A middle-aged man in a trench coat was standing in the corridor. Brenda must have let him into the building. He looked guilty handing me the documents, new to the job.

Opening the big brown envelope, my mood was more curious than angry. Inside was a summons to an emergency hearing in one week, to have me barred. There was also a protection order.

'Protecting her from what?' I wondered, getting angry now. Finally there was an application for sole custody of Matthew. This was what I had been dreading for years. It had to be fought!

Minutes later the doorbell rang. This time it was a Garda sergeant in plain clothes. He gave his name as 'Hyland' and asked me if he could come up to the flat. Inside, he told me that he had come 'to investigate a firearm'. His tone was apologetic; he seemed even uneasier than the man with the summons. When he saw the licence, he didn't even bother to look at the gun before going away.

A solicitor had to be found. One of my friends gave me the name of Kieran McGinley who had offices in the centre of Dublin. He agreed to meet me the following day after Matthew had been collected from school. The two of us walked to his office.

'She can't just take him away from me like this can she?' I asked.

'Don't worry, Owen! We'll look after it,' he said.

CHAPTER 13

A gun to my head

Lawyers are the legal clergy; they operate the courts. Like the religious clergy, they are good at justifying what they do. For solicitors and barristers practising family law, this is especially important - because the main part of their job is taking children away from parents. Sole custody means that the one parent has to pack his bags and leave, while the other parent is given the children and the home. The victim-parent is almost always the dad.

It could easily be seen as unjust and cruel, discrediting the whole legal process; so an elaborate set of beliefs had to be constructed round the whole subject of violence in the home.

Domestic violence has to be seen as serious enough and widespread enough to justify the ending of a basic right, the right to our homes and our children. And it needs to be firmly identified with men. The violent acts of women, the slaps and the kicks, the stabbings and the burning pans, these are played down as much as possible. So *domestic violence is seen as something that men do to women.* It is from men that children are taken away; they must appear to deserve it.

In family law, allegations by clients against their spouses are common. Hard evidence, however is a different matter. Where it exists, it is seized upon and passed along the lawyers' grapevine almost reverently. This is the stuff their careers depend on.

Now at last they had something they could trust. These were not the self-serving complaints of some unreasonable, demanding client. Here was one of their own circle; someone they could meet socially or in court. The story justified everything they were doing, and it spread like wildfire. *A good mother and an abused wife, she had fled London in terror of her violent husband. She had even taken him back for a time, until he started terrorising her again.* The poor thing deserved all the help she could get.

And she was going to get it! Any system is an abstract concept; it is the people who operate it who are real. These at the time, were the sixty or seventy solicitors and barristers in Ireland who specialised in family law. They were mostly women and Brenda was one of them. Perhaps it was inevitable that Brenda came to personify what they all wanted to believe.

A consensus was quickly established that she must be looked after, and her brute of a husband must get what he deserved! It is a brave judge who would go against such a consensus. He would find himself isolated, and his wife embarrassed in front of her friends.

Kieran McGinley was friendly and optimistic that first day in his office. 'She has no grounds for this barring order, Owen,' he said. 'Are you sure that you never had a fight?'

'There was nothing! Not as much as a shout and I'll go into any witness box and say so! - Oh! We did have rows at Gordon Road though.'

'They don't matter. She isn't trying to get you barred from Gordon Road.' It was reassuring.

At the second meeting, he was not so friendly and there seemed to be a lot more questions, but perhaps it was just that he had a bad day. It was the third meeting that worried me.

'The problem with you Owen, is that you are such a nomadic character. You never seem to stay in the one place what with Limerick, Canada, America, Australia, London and now Dublin.'

'That was all years ago. I'm not nomadic now, I live in London, so does Matthew for that matter.'

'I'm afraid not. He's been here over a year now. My guess is that's why she left the proceedings until now. She's very clever and her advice is good. I think she has outmanoeuvred us here.' He seemed very happy to be outmanoeuvred.

'How do you mean?'

'I mean she is likely to get sole custody, if this goes into court. But perhaps we can negotiate a better deal by staying out.'

'How can she have sole custody if I'm still in the flat?'

'Well, she can get you out, you *are* separated and it's her flat after all. That's why she has taken out these barring proceedings.'

'But she has no grounds for having me barred.'

'It doesn't work like that Owen. A woman gets a barring order for the asking. Anyway she has your past record to go on.' I wished he wouldn't keep repeating my name.

'What are you talking about? What past record?'

'Well you do have a record of violence.'

'Not that I know of! We gave one another slaps on the cheek but neither of us ever struck the other in a way that could hurt. She did swing a metal dustpan at me once, but I don't think she really meant that either.'

'Well there seems to be a lot of written material...'

'Hang on a minute! Where are you getting all this stuff from anyway?'

He was silent, so I continued, 'You've been talking to the other side and they've convinced you of something, haven't they? Well there's only one thing to do now; go up in that box to put the record straight, and it's about time Brenda went up there too.'

'Oh I see... Okay!' He was anything but happy now. Neither was I.

*

The same evening, I phoned Bob Wilson and a few of my contacts in London. Things were slowly picking up and work was available in Wimbledon or Fulham; Bob was as good as his word about a room. Brenda heard me make the calls; she seemed displeased but said nothing.

Two days later we were in court, a big brick building called Dolphin House, which could have been pretty if a little more thought had been put into it. As it was there was very little to break the smear of red brick against brick all across the front façade. It occurred to me that very few dads who went in there would have noticed the architecture. There is no place more hated by fathers all over Ireland. It is called 'the childsnatchery' by most of the dads who have been through its doors.

The childsnatchery, the place where they take away our children.

My mind was racing. What was I to do? Could my solicitor be trusted this time? He seemed so sure of his ground! And I was only learning to trust my feelings. My surroundings were very intimidating; I felt very alone.

We went up some stairs and came to an L shaped corridor. Kieran McGinley was leading, leaving me trailing behind.

'You wait here Owen,' he said. 'I'll have a word with the other side, see the lie of the land.' He was trying to be friendly again. It was a long wait nearly half an hour, and not made any shorter by a tense uneasy feeling that something was wrong.

Eventually he came back. He looked uneasy. 'They say they have some letters where you *admitted* striking her.' He was trying to sound grim, but he only succeeded in sounding puzzled, which he clearly was.

'Did you say letter or letters?'

'Well I'm not sure, but one letter is enough. If you admitted slapping her then we can't go into court. We *have* to make a deal! I've been talking to the other side and they don't seem too unreasonable. They're talking about mediation.'

'If they're talking about mediation, then what are we doing here? Are they prepared to call the proceedings off?'

As if to answer my question a disembodied voice came along the corridor 'Your case is called,' it said. He was like a man reprieved from the gallows as he beckoned me to follow him. We went round the corner and then round a second one where the corridor widened at the entrance to the court.

Brenda was there with her father and mother. There was also a person holding a sheaf of papers with her back to me. From behind, it was hard to tell whether it was a man or a woman.

'That's Jill Keegan,' Kieran whispered in respectful tones.
'Who?'
'Jill Keegan, the barrister' he sounded a little surprised. She looked over forty at first glance, but a second look (and my farming background) told me she was probably in her mid-thirties. Her face was lined and thin, and her dark hair was cut very short. She was wearing horn-rimmed spectacles and a suit cut like a man's. Quite unusual! She advanced half a step towards me like a watchdog protecting a young child, then turned and gave Brenda a motherly look.

What happened next took everyone by surprise. Seamus Newman stepped forward, walked up to me and shook me by the hand. 'Hello Owen!' he said. 'We'll talk later.'

There was no time to think about it as we were ushered into court. Our case was called along with several others while the judge asked whether each case was to be adjourned or whether it was going ahead. When our case was called Jill Keegan answered 'Going ahead' in a loud voice. She was clearly personally involved. Then we were outside again and Kieran McGinley led me back to where we were standing before, then disappeared. 'Was he negotiating with Jill Keegan alone or were they all together?' I wondered.

This time he wasn't so long. He approached me with a determined stride. 'Owen! We must be realistic about this. All you can hope to gain today, if you're stubborn, is to delay things. You will lose your chance to negotiate and you'll be lucky to see Matthew once a week in McDonalds.'

'So what is being stubborn?'

'Staying in the flat when you both know it's hers. She'll get you out anyway, sooner or later. Why don't you just go now and at least we can negotiate terms in exchange.'

The way he was putting it, it seemed the wise thing to do, but there was something nagging in the back of my head that couldn't be put into words.

'Hold on a while! What are we going to do about Matthew,' I said after a pause.

'She says she'll give you all the access you want.'

'You mean she gets custody? No way! I'm not having that!'

'Owen, custody only means who the child is living with. The other parent has access. Custody and access are only words. It's the time you spend with your child that matters.'

'Well if they're only words, give me the 'custody' word. She can have access!'

'Didn't you hear what I was saying? She *has* custody. The child is living with her and you have nowhere to take it.'

It irritated me to hear Matthew being referred to as 'it.' But I had no argument against what he was saying.

'Well it must be understood that this is a temporary arrangement. Then perhaps...'

'We'll have to hurry up if we're going to settle it. We'll be going in, in a minute. Will I go back and tell them that we might be able to work things out?'

'I suppose so.'

Thinking was becoming difficult. I was in a strange world and feeling hot and confused; he was my only guide.

He disappeared and came back very soon. 'Well they've agreed to only *interim* sole custody and you can have all the access you want.' He sounded very cheerful. 'But' he added 'they want maintenance for Matthew and they're insisting that the protection order is to continue.'

'In that case we're going in!' I said firmly. 'There was no violence to justify this protection order, no threats, nothing! I never once raised my voice in that flat. If she wants a protection order she is going to have to go up in the witness box. And that's final!'

He was somewhat taken aback. His face changed, then settled into *comprehension*, like he had made his mind up at last. He turned away again.

Presently he was back. 'They've agreed!' he said. 'We'd better get it wrapped up quickly before we have to go into court.'

'Whatever,' I replied.

My body was shaking and things were starting to blur in front of my eyes but I pulled myself together when Kieran came back. He seemed triumphant. 'It's going to be settled by mediation,' he said. 'That's the best news of all. You had no business going into court. In there a man will get destroyed. Here! We'd better get this signed.'

He handed me a hand-written sheet of paper and I looked at it stupidly, half taking in words like 'interim sole custody', 'access' and 'mediation.'

'Well, sign it!' he said, – 'if you're happy.'

I signed.

*

It was just as well that his grandparents distracted Matthew, that evening, because I couldn't talk to him when I called to the flat to collect my things. Feeling bewildered and very, very tired. I resolved to telephone him next morning. Peter Tierney had agreed to put me up for two nights before my journey back to London. I went to bed early.

Looking at my watch the following morning, I was surprised to see that it was ten o' clock. Twelve hours! Feeling better, but still puzzled, I took out the court document before going downstairs.

Celia was waiting for me below. 'Owen, I didn't like to wake you. You seemed out for the count.'

'Thanks Celia! Is there any chance I might use your phone?'

At the playschool his teacher told me that Matthew was 'off for the day'. Surprised, I telephoned the blockhouse only to hear the answering machine. Nobody home! Perhaps they would be back later. Celia had made breakfast for me; she couldn't have been kinder.

After breakfast the machine answered me once more. What was going on? Celia tried to make conversation. The divorce referendum was held in Ireland that day and she asked me how I was going to vote.

'I don't know, Celia,' I said. 'As far as I can see it makes very little difference. It's the rules about separation that matter.'

It occurred to me that Margaret and Seamus might have gone down to Limerick to vote, so I asked Celia to use her phone again.

To my surprise it was Brenda who answered.

'What are you doing down there?' I demanded.

'We're down for a few days, my vote is here and I'm going to use it. Which way are you voting?'

'I don't think I have any vote over here. Is Matthew down there too?'

'Of course he is! Don't you remember? You agreed to this yesterday.'

'There's no way! Not this weekend!'

'That's the agreement you made.'

'You mean it's written down here?' I pulled out the document apprehensively.

'Well...no! But you agreed that I could take him down this weekend.'

'Why should I agree to your taking him away the only weekend I would be in Ireland? And you say that it's not written down here at all?'

'We made that arrangement orally.'

'No we didn't! Anyway will you please put Matthew on to me?'

'He's asleep right now, he's had a tiring journey. I don't want to wake him. Can you call back later?'

The first thing I did was to unfold the 'agreement' and read it through. Celia poured me another cup of tea silently, a look of concern on her face. The agreement was brief enough; I had to leave the blockhouse, Brenda got interim sole custody of Matthew - and two hundred pounds a month from me for taking him. We both agreed to go to mediation.

But looking at the part that laid out the access arrangements, I realised that something was wrong. Instead of 'as much access as I wanted' there was a schedule of daily visits between half past four and six every afternoon. Matthew was to be picked up from playschool and delivered to the blockhouse. The problem was, *I was not living in Dublin* and these were *working hours*. I had been tricked again.

But why?

There had to be some kind of explanation. It was exactly what had happened outside the court in London. Both times the whole process seemed geared towards one objective – to get me out of the family home. And each time, it was the lawyers who were acting for me and taking my money who put the pressure on. Why?

It was time to have a word with Kieran McGinley, but he was out and Brenda in Limerick had gone out too, taking Matthew with her. Back in the kitchen, I sat down heavily. Poor Celia was now looking very worried indeed.

'Don't worry about me,' I said. 'Is it alright to use the phone to sort this out?'

'There's no problem, Owen,' she said.

Kieran McGinley's secretary wasn't sure when he would be back in the office, so I told her to expect a call every half-hour until he spoke to me. Half an hour later we were speaking on the phone.

'Do you remember agreeing to anything besides what was written down?' I asked him.

'I don't think so, Owen. No! Definitely not!'

'Well she has taken him down to Limerick and He's supposed to be with me today. And I want to know what we're going to do about it.'

'Well...You know, it's important not to inflame the situation.'

'What the hell do you mean?'

'I mean it's best not to make matters worse. You're both just out of court. It's better to let things calm down for the moment and maybe we can work things out peacefully. I'll speak to the other side.'

'Look, Kieran!' I was speaking through my teeth. 'She has just taken my son a hundred miles away and you're talking about *not inflaming the situation.* What's more, this is my last chance to see him before I go home. She won't even let me speak to him on the phone. What I want to know is what legal procedure is open to me to make sure this won't happen again.'

'Take it easy, Owen. It may be just a mistake. Do you want to see your son?'

'Of course I want to see my son and I want to *continue* seeing him! That's why we must go back to court and have that so-called access order changed. The thing is meaningless when I don't live in Dublin.'

'Okay, Okay! One thing at a time! If you want to see your son, your best bet is to go down to Limerick. It's not too far. You can sail from Rosslare instead. I'm sure she didn't mean to obstruct your access. I have a feeling that when you get down you'll have no trouble seeing him.'

'But if I do, what options are open to me?'

'We'll discuss that next time' his tone was soothing. 'It's a long drawn out business and it takes months. Anyway I'm sure it won't come to that!'

I made up my mind. 'Right! 'I'll cancel the sailing but we need to talk about this access order.'

'No problem Owen but right now you need to get going and there's a client waiting. Ring me the next chance you get. Thanks for calling!'

*

It was after four when I finally got going, in a kind of daze. There was a traffic jam all the way down to Portlaoise; it didn't matter. At the outskirts of Limerick the truck seemed to turn left automatically for my father's place. The cut shrubbery and the strange cars reminded me that it was sold and I took the back lane into the yard. Pulling the truck into the hayshed I just sat there behind the wheel for over an hour. Then a glance at my watch told me it was after eleven o' clock.

The thing to do was to use the phone in the workshop and book myself into a guesthouse but it was too much for me just then. My efforts to sleep in the truck caused me to wake, feeling cramped and stiff after less than an hour. Finally I made myself a bed out of some bales of straw and stacked a few more to provide a shelter against the wind. There was a sleeping bag in the truck and a coat for a pillow.

I woke just after eight feeling sticky and dirty. A blowlamp came in handy for heating some water in order to shave. That felt better! Then, picking up the phone I demanded to speak to Brenda.

'Where is my son?' I growled. She agreed to meet me in Cruises Hotel at ten o' clock, sounding guilty and apologetic - very different from the day before.

It was when she left Matthew and me together that it occurred to me that I was without a home. The weather was cold, even for November and now we couldn't play cards, watch a video or even draw pictures together. We spent the morning in the park and had lunch in a restaurant nearby. After that I instinctively drove out to my father's place (now of course *my* place) because we had nowhere else to go.

As soon as the truck stopped, Matthew opened the door and made straight for his grandfather's house as he had done many times before. With a pang I realised he had to be told that Grand Dad was no longer there. The place was deserted. Apparently the new family were still only staying the odd night which was just as well. Matthew didn't seem to take it in because he insisted on trying all three doors and looking through every window convinced that sooner or later he was going to see his grandfather inside. I trailed behind him not wanting to see the disappointment on his face.

When he heard that we would see Grand Dad in his new house later, he became cheerful again, and we had a very enjoyable afternoon playing and chasing one another among the bales of hay and straw in the shed. The time seemed to fly. Eventually it began to get dark, so I phoned Brenda and told her that Matthew wanted to see his grandfather in the town. Afterwards, she could meet me in the car park of The Travellers Rest on the main road to Limerick.

She was standing outside her car when we arrived. Maybe it was the sight of her bearing down on me to take him away but suddenly I panicked. This could not, *must not,* be allowed to happen. Shoving the truck into gear I revved up the engine and drove straight for the exit. The nose of the truck was half way out on the road when reality took over. I could not take on the power of the state. My only hope was some kind of legal victory, Slowly I reversed back into the car park again. Brenda marched towards us in triumph, flung open the door and took Matthew away in her arms. Neither of us said goodbye.

CHAPTER 14

The dark days

*'The white plum blossoms in the spring,
And is gone in the spring.'*
Chiyozuru-Korehide

Days were passing by, all the same; the pain would not go away.

The strange thing is, outwardly my behaviour was quite normal, going to work, having a pint with my friends, even dressing up to go to the Speakers' Christmas party in Hammersmith. Maybe going through the motions was the easiest thing to do.

But inside, the pain was always there; like part of me had been torn away leaving a burning hole behind. Everything looked different - dark, hostile and ugly. My child had been taken from me and I was helpless to do anything about it. How could one person fight the law? Worse, I could sense Matthew's suffering too; it merged with my own. It prevented me from sleeping properly even after working thirteen hours a day. The hurt and rage burned in me so much that after drifting off into unconsciousness I would wake an hour or so later beating the pillow.

My last two nights in Limerick were spent in Jury's Hotel and all day Sunday there seemed no reason to leave my room. On Monday I loaded the truck and drove out to say goodbye to my father on the way to the ferry.

I don't remember the journey, only arriving at Bob Wilson's house on Tuesday afternoon. He led me up to a small room on the second floor, which was to be my home for the best part of a year. That evening we went for a drink. At least it broke the ice and helped me socialise again. Next day a phone call to Duffy and Carr got me work in Wimbledon. An old building was being turned into a pub called 'The Pitcher and Piano' and there was plenty of work. The night shift started at six in the evening and finishing the following morning at seven. My only regret was that the hours weren't even longer.

The job got me into something like a routine. Playing some books on tape helped me to drift off to sleep after getting back to Bob's each morning. When the job was finished, Duffy and Carr sent me to do some repairs to girls' school nearby. The girls were on holiday, they said. I hadn't realised it was nearly Christmas.

The hardest thing was phoning Matthew. He just couldn't understand why he couldn't see me; his three-year-old intelligence struggled to make sense of it all. After several attempts to explain, he suddenly interrupted saying 'Mummy is cross with Daddy!' It was like he said 'Eureka!' His tone was triumphant, suddenly knowing, and he sounded happier, no longer bewildered.

'That's right Matthew! Mummy is cross with Daddy.'

On Christmas Eve, Bob left to be with his parents in Carlisle, leaving me alone with myself at last. To my surprise, the thoughts I had been dreading brought me understanding and some comfort. There is a kind of strength in depression - a strange wisdom.

More and more, things were making sense; no one was going to tell me the rules, especially the solicitor who was taking my money. The marriage was over for good; it had been over a long time ago. Brenda wanted to finish it on her terms and she knew the rules only too well. What she wanted now was clear enough. She wanted me to be a visitor to Matthew's life but not a parent. *She was trying to break the bond between my son and me.*

And so far she was succeeding. She, or her lawyer, had seen my state of mind on the day of the hearing and cleverly devised an access plan that looked very generous on paper, but which in practice was meaningless because I was not living in Dublin. They had guessed it would not be read. Her plan was to break the contact between us for a time and then allow me to see Matthew occasionally *by her permission*. It was a risk, taking him to Limerick after the hearing, but she did not expect to answer for it in court. Why was that? Because she knew that I would be in London and that my solicitor would be reluctant to bring proceedings.

At least I knew what to do now: protect the bond with Matthew. The telephone was our only chance of speaking to one another; he must get a call regularly, every night if possible. Also my solicitor must be contacted immediately after the holidays and finally there would have to be a visit to Dublin.

The first turned out to be the most difficult. Brenda and Matthew were always 'out' and couldn't take any of my calls. But I persisted and perhaps Seamus was on my side, because when Matthew finally spoke to me (two days after Christmas) Brenda was quick to arrange a schedule of telephone access. My son and I could now speak to one another three times a week.

Christmas Day was spent on my own. It was just as well; I needed the time to myself. Two days before the New Year, a letter came from the court. It said that the protection order was to continue.

*

'What's going on, Kieran? The protection order was to be dropped. Now there's this letter saying that it's to continue until further notice. Tell me what's going on!'

'It's just a mistake; I wouldn't worry about it.'

'I think there's good reason to worry. First the access order is different to what I thought, and now this protection order is to continue. You must arrange for me to get a letter saying it is *not* to continue. It's that simple!'

'Don't you think that it's a waste of your time and energy, especially since you are living in London.'

'That reminds me, my access order must be straightened out. What I agreed to was *unlimited access*, not what's written down here. It's *meaningless*! And this protection order is a slur on my character. It's got to be withdrawn as soon as possible!'

'Owen, this could be expensive and remember it's only for a few months. The mediation will change everything. That's what you should be thinking about!'

'So what's your advice?'

'My advice is, think about it!' And if you really want to go to the expense and the trouble then get back to me and we'll decide on a course of action. Happy New Year!'

*

Tom Cooke my accountant told me about an organisation called Families Need Fathers. He had several clients in the same boat as myself. A person called Tim spoke to me on the phone and he put me in touch with Barry whose child had also been taken to Ireland.

'Is it unusual for a mother to try to break the bond with the father?' I asked hesitantly.

'Commonest problem we have!' Barry replied. It made me feel better; at least I was not on my own.

'But why would a mother want to do that?'

'One of three reasons usually. She may hate the father's guts, pure and simple, and it's her way of hurting him. Or she may have a new man in her life and she wants *him* to be the dad. Or maybe she's just insecure, worried that the children prefer their dad and afraid of losing them. Any of those ring a bell?'

'Yes! The last one, it makes a lot of sense.'

Barry explained to me that 'custody' is now called 'residency' in the U.K. but that it amounts to exactly the same thing. He also told me that 'interim' sole custody means permanent sole custody for all practical purposes, because it establishes a status quo. Once a status quo is established judges are reluctant to change it - except when the child has been with the father.

'Why didn't you try for joint-custody?' he asked.
'Nobody told me that it existed,' I replied.
'I thought as much,' he said.

*

That was the end of Kieran McGinley. I wrote to him to say that I would be coming to Dublin shortly - to collect my files. Next I made out a cheque to Families Need Fathers. At least there was somebody who could be trusted. My last letter was to the judge who issued the protection order. It read:

> Dear Judge C____,
>
> My name is Owen Sheridan. In November you issued a Protection Order against me when I was not present. Since I did not use or threaten violence during the period I lived with my wife I should like to know what she said to influence you to make the order. Did she say it under oath?
> Yours sincerely,
> Owen Sheridan

I posted all three letters together.

*

'You can come up now!'
'What's that, Matthew?'
'It's okay Daddy! Mummy is cross with me too, so you can come up now!'

Because they were on the second floor of the 'blockhouse' Matthew always spoke about 'coming up' to see him. The poor little fellow reasoned that if his mummy was cross with him and he could be in the flat, then so could I. He was desperately trying to find the formula that would bring me back. But I still felt very weak and vulnerable and had a fear of going back to Ireland. It was doubtful if she would let me 'come up' in any case, even if I went.

The judge replied to my letter. Apparently Brenda had told him there was a shotgun in the flat and that there was a danger of its being used. She also said that I was barred from the family home in London. I kept his letter carefully. A week later a letter came from Kieran McGinley saying he could no longer act as my solicitor because of my letter to the judge 'without his knowledge'. It was a clever move to hide the fact that he had been dismissed already, two weeks before.

It was the end of January before I made the trip, feeling nervous and apprehensive. But the thought of seeing Matthew kept me going and I arrived at the blockhouse early one Thursday evening. To my surprise, Brenda did invite me in, because when Matthew said to 'come up' she did not want to be seen to refuse. My Christmas present was a racing-car game and now we put it together and got it going. Picking a toy car each, and with control switches in hand, we played for about an hour. Matthew eventually fell asleep and Brenda put him to bed.

Then she delivered her bombshell. 'We're going to Limerick tomorrow,' she said, 'so Matthew can see his grandparents.'

'No you're not! My access visit is tomorrow.'

'I'm afraid it's been arranged.'

'You just forgot to mention it I suppose?'

'Did I really? Oh sorry! I thought I did.'

'Strange it's the only two weekends I'm in Dublin that you choose to go down to Limerick. You'll pay for it when he gets older. Mark my words!'

Chapter 14

I went down the stairs quickly, anxious not to lose my temper just before a court hearing. And some court hearing it was going to be! All the lies and false allegations were going to be sorted out once and for all and I was finally going to get joint custody and win back my rights as a parent.

Because of the time of year, it was easy to book a room for a week. If she expected me to go back to London after one short visit, then she was mistaken! She would not be rid of me that easily! The following morning my first job was to go to Dolphin House and apply for a new access order. My second was to pick up my files at Kieran McGinley's office; he was conveniently out. Then, feeling better, I telephoned a few friends and arranged to meet them over the weekend.

The three days passed quickly - because I was getting used to being without him, I realised with a pang. Only Monday dragged. Would it ever be half past four? At a quarter to, my patience gave out and I went to the playschool collect him.

Outside the blockhouse at six o' clock, Brenda was very angry. 'How dare you take him out of school without telling me!' She spat the words out.

'Now you know what it feels like,' I taunted.

'What are you doing tomorrow?'

'The same as today of course. Can't you read your own court order?'

'Come on Daddy!' Matthew never liked to hear us quarrel. He led me by the hand up the stairs, while Brenda looked on in disbelief.

We were barely inside the flat when Brenda recovered her composure. 'You have to go or I'm calling the police,' she said. I shuffled uneasily.

'No!' It came from Matthew **'I want my daddy!'** and he wrapped his two small arms round my leg holding on tightly. My little warrior! One three year old boy against the whole power of the state! My magnificent little son!

'Let him go!' from Brenda

'Look again! I'm not holding him!'

Grimly she marched over and then catching him under the arms she began to drag him away.

'*You* let him...' but it was too late. He was gone from me sobbing. He gave me one incredulous look. Why hadn't I come to his aid? For a moment, my impulse was to knock her senseless and take my son away - but the awful consequences prevented me. I would be taking on, not just Brenda, but the police force, the armed power of the state. It was my first time realising how helpless I really was. Turning on my heel I went out the door.

We saw each other every day that week. By Thursday she began to panic. This was not what she had in mind at all and on Friday when I called to the playschool, he was not there.

Margaret answered the phone in the flat. 'No! She couldn't put Matthew on at the moment; it was not convenient. Perhaps tomorrow would be better.' Hurrying to another phonebox round the corner I tried again. This time Matthew picked the phone up; he was delighted that I was coming round to see him.

At the entrance to the building I pressed the buzzer. This time it was Brenda and she told me to go away and put the entryphone down. The buzzer makes a loud noise and I continued to press until at last they responded.

'We're calling the police,' Brenda said.

'Go right ahead!' I had expected it, wanted it even.

A blue-uniformed Garda[1] arrived within five minutes. As he marched up the steps towards me, he hesitated. 'Are you going away?' he asked hopefully.

'Just as soon as I've collected my son. There's a court order; my access is being denied.' He pressed the buzzer and disappeared up the stairs. Ten minutes later he came down again at the head of a procession. Matthew was next looking very happy. Brenda and Margaret brought up the rear; they didn't look happy at all. At that moment Seamus came in from the street. His look, especially at the Garda, was clearly one of dismay. Matthew and I enjoyed our time together.

---

[1] policeman

There was work to do in Limerick. For years a plan had been forming in my mind about building stables in my father's yard. First, the site needed to be levelled and Joe Healy offered me a good discount, if he could get started right away. February is a slack time for him, so we arranged to start on Monday. He had relatives coming on Sunday but there was a room free on Saturday night. I got in the truck and drove down.

On Sunday, my father's old tractor and trailer had to be got ready to draw the rubble away from Joe's digger. The tractor is 'a gravity start' since the battery hadn't been changed for years.

There was enough diesel left in drums to do the job and I filled the tank, sat on the seat and let it off down the hill. It started first go! 'Yahoo!'

On my way into town for a take-away meal that afternoon, a shout from the pavement made me look through the open window. It was Frank Collins and he was glad to see me. The windows in his house needed replacing and he wanted some advice. He offered me a week's accommodation at a very reasonable rent. I had very nearly driven into Limerick and eaten there. Luck was with me again.

It was good to get my teeth into a project. The site was on the side of a hill, so we had to make a 'terrace' wide enough for the stables and the walkway. In order to get enough broken concrete and rubble, some old buildings had to be demolished and two concrete slabs dug out. I threw myself into it with all I had. The job lasted all week and by Friday we had built an impressive bank of earth and rubble nearly a hundred feet long. There was nothing to do now except wait for it to settle, before starting to build on top.

My plan was to go to London the following Monday and come back in the autumn to lay the foundations. Earlier in the week, I had booked an appointment with Gerry Nolan, a solicitor in Limerick, for Friday afternoon. Gerry was another old schoolmate, so maybe he would give me some answers. He was helpful but for some reason it was difficult to concentrate on what he was saying. He asked me who her solicitor was, and I gave him the name of Colman Kelly, explaining that there seemed to be no solicitor acting for her in November.

'Do you want to see your son tomorrow?' He asked.

'Yes! Of course I do!'

'Hang on a while!' he said 'We'll see what we can do.' He got on the phone and asked me to call back to his office in an hour. When I returned, he was very pleased with himself.

'Ten o' clock tomorrow morning,' he said as I looked at him in amazement. He refused to take any money.

Dragging myself out of bed just before six, it surprised me how tired I felt, and how cold. Nevertheless Matthew and I had a good day together in Dublin and he was pleased with my present, a helium balloon.

Driving down, I stopped for a coffee but didn't eat any food, unusual for me. The journey seemed very long and at Frank's house it came as a relief to find he wasn't in. Glad to be spared the effort of talking to anyone, I went to bed exhausted and shivering, and slept for nearly twelve hours.

Next day I woke still feeling cold but not hungry, even though it was mid morning. What was wrong?

Of course! It was a chill - picked up while working on the yard. I had been sweating a lot moving things about, and hadn't taken much care to wrap myself up against the February weather. The best thing to do was to put my ferry ticket back for a few days and take a rest. Then I would be right as rain!

I wasn't. The cold would not go away. It seemed to go right inside me and the shivering got worse. 'Perhaps a holiday to some warm place like The Canaries mightn't be too expensive,' I thought. I had an irrational fear of never being warm again.

On Tuesday Frank took one look at me. 'You're going to the doctor!' he said.

'I'm not able to drive, Frank. Besides, I don't have a doctor over here.'

'Both easily remedied!' he replied. 'We'll go to my doctor in my car.' I didn't argue.

The doctor put me through some tests and asked me if I had been working exceptionally hard or if I was under any unusual strain. I told him. He diagnosed nervous fatigue as well as pneumonia in the left lung.

Frank brought me home to bed.

CHAPTER 15

Access

During the next three weeks Frank was my only contact with the world. He was a good friend, especially as he was under strict instructions to tell nobody about my illness. I didn't want to see anyone. Every morning I fed myself on toast and boiled eggs, and in the evening Frank brought a takeaway on his way home from work. Books like Nelson Mandela's 'The Long Walk to Freedom' made it tolerable and distracted me during the day. Television programmes like 'The Bill' helped to fill in the evenings. By the third week the books seemed to be more interesting and Frank's bits of news more entertaining. I was getting better.

It was time to make a few telephone calls. The first was to Gerry Nolan. Since working the miracle and enabling me to see Matthew he was giving me second thoughts about fighting the legal battles on my own. He seemed to be very familiar with the mysteries of the legal system and to be genuinely interested in helping me. We had been friends at school. Perhaps he would treat me differently than the other solicitors. They were strangers, after all.

He arranged to meet me in his office one Friday afternoon. I got out of bed and went into Limerick in the truck without telling Frank. He would have insisted on driving me. My access hearing was listed for the following week. Now it would have to be adjourned, until I was able to travel to Dublin.

'Look Owen! I want you to drop this hearing entirely,' he said. 'It will achieve nothing and I can get you an access order, no problem. What you need is a flat or a permanent residence here in Ireland.'

'You mean move to Ireland? That's a pretty big step.'

'Well, you're going to have to spend a lot of time here anyway when you're building your stables and you'll need somewhere to stay. Why not make the most of your time here by building a relationship with your son?'

'I can't do any more building until the autumn and it would be a lot cheaper to stay with Frank.'

'You're not going to get any overnight access staying with a male friend and it's not much good complaining to the judge about what Brenda did in the past. Judges see that as vindictive. It won't help you at all!'

'But she deliberately broke the order of the court and she is a solicitor. That must count for something.' He looked uneasy.

'All he's going to do is reprimand her. What good is that to you? Do you want Brenda punished or do you want to see your son?'

'I want to see my son; I want the *right* to see him and to know that she can't break court orders anytime she feels like it!' He looked even more uneasy.

'Well Owen, do you want to give my way a try? If you do we'll drop the motion for access and then I'm going to arrange a meeting of solicitors to sort this thing out once and for all. What do you say?'

This meeting of solicitors idea took me by surprise. It *did* sound sensible. And he was so clear and positive about it! Perhaps it would achieve my objective, protect my relationship with my son? And it didn't matter to me whether Brenda was punished or not. My mind was made up quickly; this was not something to turn down.

'Go for it, Gerry! But the only sole custody I'll agree to, is sole custody with me. I've had enough of access orders!'

'Okay! Okay! We'll discuss all that coming up to the meeting. Do I have your permission to drop the access hearing because of the negotiations?' I nodded. 'Oh and there's one small thing. I'll do this at cost of course since we know each other so long but....'

'Gerry! I don't want any favours. Do it at your normal rate! How much do you want?'

'I realise you're not working. How much can you afford?'

'Is four hundred all right?'

'Well... it may cost a bit more than that, but four hundred is fine for now.'

He phoned me on the Tuesday. 'Are you feeling better Owen? And could you come in to the office later in the week? There's something we need to discuss,' He sounded quieter than usual.

The following morning, Gerry was waiting for me. He told me to sit down.

'Brenda has served us with proceedings for a High Court separation,' he said solemnly. 'She has set down in a sworn affidavit her grounds for the petition, Owen! It's horrendous stuff!' He handed me the papers. She had repeated word for word the accusations of two years before.

'Horrendous or not it isn't true. Anyway I don't see what she wants a separation for. We're separated already.'

'There's more. She has put a caution on your father's place; she has a claim in on your property.'

'The bitch! That land has been in the Sheridan family for generations. And she signed a separation agreement two years ago, a full and final settlement.'

'Yes! Yes I know! We need counsel's opinion here. Can you come back in the afternoon? Say three o' clock?'

'Okay! But there's one thing I want you to do.'

'What's that?'

'Take out proceedings against her for obtaining a protection order under false pretences. We'll talk about it in the afternoon.' Leaving his office, I thought he looked worried.

Fergus Cronin was in his mid forties, tall and wearing a beard. He spent most of the interview trying to frighten me.

He began reading parts of Brenda's statement out with emphasis. *'Punched* me several times,' he intoned, *'several* acts of cruelty,' *Bohemian* lifestyle!' Shaking his head he went on. 'Then when you're in a hole you seem determined to dig yourself in deeper. Writing letters to your wife, *writing to the judge!* Your best bet is to act like the Galbally pig and keep your mouth shut except when you're eating.'

'Is it alright to call you Fergus?' I asked innocently.

'Yes! Of course it is!' Gerry interrupted. Fergus Cronin said nothing.

'Well *Fergus* I don't seem to have done myself any harm by writing to anybody. My so-called solicitor in Dublin used one of my letters as an excuse not to go into court, but he'd have found another - and my letter to the judge has given me bargaining power.'

Gerry squirmed in his seat, but it was his own colleague who was being offensive. Fergus Cronin went on to ask me a few more meaningless questions before announcing it was time for him to go - a little too hastily. He left Gerry and me alone.

'Now we must go ahead with the proceedings for the false protection order' I said firmly. 'There was no violence and no previous barring order. And I want my access this week again. I'm well enough now!'

'Can you ring her yourself? An ordinary access visit should not be a matter for solicitors to negotiate.' He sounded very unhappy.

Brenda refused point blank to let me see him that weekend. She had planned to go to County Clare, she said and Matthew was coming with her. When I told her she was breaking the court order she put down the phone.

The following morning I telephoned Gerry at nine o' clock. 'She's deliberately breaking the court order,' I told him. He said to meet him in his office at two.

'The first thing is, Owen,' he said. 'These proceedings about the protection order can't go ahead.'

'Why not?'

'I've looked over your files and you signed an agreement to move out of Gordon Road. That's the same as a barring order.'

'What? How can it be the same?'

'She applied to have you ordered out because of your violence and you agreed to go. For all practical purposes that's a barring order.'

'Hmmm! What about this access on Friday?'

'Well! Perhaps it is a bit unreasonable to demand access at that kind of notice.'

'Unreasonable! I see my son one day a month and you call that unreasonable! Who the hell are you working for anyway?'

'Take it easy, Owen! Look! We can work out an access order if you come back to Limerick. You'll have to spend a few bob and rent a flat that's all.'

'The thing is if I use my money to rent a flat I won't have enough credit left to build the stables.'

'Well, it's your only chance of a decent access order.'

'Talking about access orders; according to this one here, Matthew is supposed to be with me on Saturday. Now that she has stated plainly that she is going to break the court order, what is the procedure?'

'Yes... we can take her to court of course, but I wouldn't recommend that.'

'Why not? And what *do* you recommend.'

'I recommend that we work an access schedule out by negotiation.'

'Your meeting of solicitors idea again. Brenda gave us her answer to that. You can't negotiate with Brenda unless you first show her you mean business. Now why don't you recommend taking her to court?'

'Because it will cost you a lot of money, maybe seven or eight hundred pounds. Then all that happens is she gets a warning from the judge and we all go home.'

'So is there any way to get an access order enforced?'

'Only the way I just told you and....'

'...That's not enforcement at all,' I finished.

He was silent, so I went on 'And now you want me to move country and spend thousands of pounds on a flat, all to get an access order that won't even be enforced. Is that it?'
He was silent.
A few days later I went back to London.

*

'Gerry!'
'Yes! Oh hello Owen.'
'Is she even entitled to sue me over there? After all I don't even *live* in the jurisdiction. Doesn't she have to sue me over here?'
'No, Owen! Put that idea out of your head. She can sue in whichever jurisdiction she likes. Anyway we've accepted service of the proceedings now, so it has to go ahead. See you when you get back!'

*

In May I decided to take a break, a long weekend. My plan was to drive through the Cotswolds into Wales, and then visit the Centre for Alternative Technology before coming back to London on the Sunday evening.
On the Thursday, I started out early and climbed up to the top of Bredon Hill in the warm May afternoon. The hill is lovely, just 1000 feet high, a mixture of pasture and woodland on the border of Gloucester and Worcester. And the view from the top is magnificent! They say you can see into five counties including parts of Wales. True or not the view was a nice bonus to the walk, which was very pleasant in itself.
On Friday I explored the old city of Gloucester and bought a rabbit for Matthew. He has always been fond of cuddly toys. Then I drove through Herefordshire - one of the prettiest counties in England. In Leominster, the evening

passed quickly, thanks to an elderly Irishman and a retired police inspector who were having a drink at my hotel. It felt like my travelling days again, nearly ten years before.

After an early breakfast on Saturday I telephoned Brenda in Dublin and asked to speak to Matthew; his voice could be heard in the background.

'Let me talk to my Daddy,' he said.

Silently she let him come to the phone. He did not beat around the bush. 'Why do you always talk to me on the phone?' he said.

'W - why, what do you want me to do?' I asked him.

'Come and see me!' he said, as only a three year old can.

There and then my mind was made up.

'Okay, I'm coming to see you tomorrow morning.'

'I miss you Daddy.'

'I miss you too but I'll see you after one sleep. Okay?'

'Okay Daddy.'

That was it. Two quick telephone calls got me a booking on the ferry to Dublin and a night's accommodation in a hostel not far from 'the blockhouse.' All my arrangements were made in ten minutes.

It was a happy day. The Centre for Alternative Technology is very interesting and it was fun walking round examining the different ideas for taking care of the planet. Best of all, was knowing that Matthew would be with me in a matter of hours. There was plenty of time to make the ferry and park my truck in Holyhead before collecting my ticket, a special twenty-four hour return. On the phone, Matthew's babysitter took the message to expect me next morning. Brenda was out.

The ferry arrived in Dublin at one o' clock, and a taxi brought me to the hostel in twenty minutes. I slept very well.

The following morning, too excited to eat breakfast, I phoned Brenda and told her that I was on my way to see Matthew as arranged.

'No!' she said. 'You can't see him! We didn't know you were coming.'

'Well, Matthew knows; strange he didn't tell you.'

'I'm sorry, we have our plans made!' Click! She put down the phone.

My worry now, was that she would put him into the car and take him somewhere for the day. The blockhouse was only fifteen minutes walk away, so grabbing my bag, I half-walked, half-ran for ten minutes to a phonebox and dialled the number again. It rang out. Were they home? Or did they leave in such a hurry that they forgot to turn on the answering machine? No time to waste. I ran the distance to the telephone box round the corner from 'the blockhouse.'

My hand shook picking up the phone. Ring! Ring! Ring! Ring! Then the recording interrupted me. They were there! What luck! I shouted for joy. Just as well there was nobody waiting for the phone. Thank God for Sunday morning!

But I had to make sure. She could have put on the answering machine and hurried out the door immediately after my second call so I ran around the corner and looked into the car park. Yes! The Volvo was still there.

The flats are built around an open courtyard, comprising a car park and a lawn. A low wall and a hedge surround the whole complex, ideal for watching without being seen. Within five minutes Matthew came skipping down the steps into the courtyard. Brenda followed close behind him and last of all came Margaret. That explained a lot.

Yelling 'Matthew!' I ran down the driveway. He spun on his heel and before anyone could catch him he was running towards me. He gave a shout and jumped straight into my arms.

'I knew you'd come, Daddy.' He gave me a huge hug, delight written all over his little face. I hugged him back. It was so good to see him, to touch him and to hear his voice again.

Brenda was livid. She marched up to me with her mother at her heel, looking grim. Matthew gripped my neck more tightly. The anger was welling up inside me. I was a bull elephant protecting his young.

Somehow, I sensed that the real hatred was coming from Margaret and turned to face her. Our eyes met head on. She is a strong determined woman but her face fell under my glare. Then I turned to Brenda. She had her hand on Matthew's shoulder but the look of fury in Matthew's eyes made her freeze. She looked to her mother for support but Margaret's head was down. Brenda faltered. She was still angry but unsure of what to do.

'You'd better be careful,' she said in a threatening tone.

'I'm going with Daddy!' Matthew announced and Brenda knew she was beaten.

There was a long pause. Matthew stayed up in my arms with his hands around my neck. All the time, I hadn't spoken a word.

Eventually Brenda broke the silence. 'Okay, you can see him. But I'm warning you! Have him back here by half past one!'

'No problem,' I replied, and walked up the driveway holding Matthew by the hand.

The time flew by. We had breakfast together and then went to the park. At one o'clock neither of us wanted to be parted from the other so I phoned Brenda again and let Matthew speak to her.

'I want a full day with my daddy, not a bit of a day,' he said.

They had a short talk and then Matthew handed the phone to me. We settled for half past six that evening.

When the time came to take Matthew back, we were both tired but happy. At the blockhouse he climbed back into the taxi and gave me a last big hug.

The sailing was at eight o' clock and the truck is not fast on the road; so it took me until four in the morning to get back to London.

But I didn't notice the journey.

CHAPTER 16

'I want my daddy!'

Fathers' Day was Sunday the 16th of June. I was determined to see Matthew again and it was going to be on Father's Day! My first idea was to contact Gerry Nolan in Limerick, to see if he could arrange it, but with less than a week to go he still had no news. However I had been telephoning Matthew every day for the previous week and he was expecting to see me. For once his mother's insecurity worked in my favour. Matthew knew very well that if he didn't get to see me, it was Brenda who was preventing it.

On Wednesday she announced that he could take the Friday off playschool ('the boys and girls') and we could spend it together. Father's day was out of the question as she had her plans made. It was her way of keeping control.

'OK,' I said, 'I'll be there.'

A few frantic phone calls got me a reasonably priced flight to Dublin on Thursday evening and a night's accommodation in the same hostel again. A short walk would have me at the blockhouse on Friday morning.

I woke before seven. It's hard to explain the thrill a parent feels on seeing his child after a long absence. But my excitement about meeting my little three year old after a month was more than enough to have me out of bed, washed, dressed and finished my breakfast in record time.

At the flats, Matthew waved at me from his second floor window even though it was fifteen minutes early. He was uncanny! How did he know?

In a matter of minutes he was down to meet me and we headed off for Herbert Park where he always loved the swings and the slide. We had a great time playing chasing, and then he had a go on the various kinds of swings such as the one made up of old car tyres hanging from diagonal poles.

There was a tall slide he was particularly fond of. Once when he had climbed the steps at the back and was ready to slide down I called up to him jokingly and said, 'Matthew! Will we go to the boys and girls now?'

For a second he looked at me in total indignation. Then smiling, I said, 'I was only pulling your leg.' He didn't know the expression but he understood that I wasn't serious and his little face beamed again.

More goes on the swings, a chase and back to the slide. Then, reaching the top of the steps he stopped and said 'Well Daddy, are we going to the boys and girls now?'

'Oh no!' I almost groaned aloud. 'Two hours and he is sick of me already. I've flown over from London and he's had enough of me.' My dismay was overpowering.

'Well Matthew... if you really want to, I suppose we can go along to them,' My voice had a despondent tone.

'Daddy, I was only pulling your leg.'

The little rascal! He fooled me completely. I hadn't been tricked so thoroughly in years. He was still chuckling as he let himself down the slide. I let out a huge belly laugh. Imagine it! Caught out by a three-year-old!

The day passed almost unnoticed. Six o'clock came all too quickly and once again it was time to hand over my son not knowing when next I'd see him.

A wave of bitterness came over me as he got into the car with Brenda.

'Daddy, when will I see you again?

'Brenda, I'd like to see him again on Monday,' I said.

'Sorry, we have our plans made,' was the reply. His little face kept looking at me through the car window as she drove away.

It made me shake with anger. It was all so unfair. My innocent little boy! Why should he have to pay for all Brenda's mistakes and mine? Something had to be done about it.

For the rest of the weekend I asked my friends to look out for any building work in or near Dublin.

A few weeks later, a message came from the manager of a block of flats. He wanted the roof repaired; so the following weekend found me in the truck on my way to the ferry once more.

In Dublin, an ad in a shop-window caught my attention: "Mobile home in Wicklow for sale". The owner was only too glad take me to see it the same day. My idea was to have Matthew down in Limerick for a good part of the summer and this little mobile home suited me perfectly. Small, not much bigger than a caravan, with a tiny bedroom and a toilet-cum-shower, in lovely condition. But it was going to be very difficult to move it from where it was situated. My offer of £1800 was accepted on the spot.

The following day, having hired a contractor to transport the mobile home to Limerick, I went back to Wicklow to get it ready to load on his truck. It was sitting on a base of concrete blocks and it had to be taken down and fitted with its little wheels for him to pull it up onto his wagon. Also the laneway into where it had sat for the last twelve years was now quite overgrown with heavy bushes and limbs of trees. I had to work like a demon with a chainsaw and a kango hammer.

When the driver came, the job wasn't quite finished. He looked at me admiringly. 'You're a mighty man,' he said without irony.

What he didn't know was that I was fighting for my son. It was a chance to give vent to all my frustration and rage that an innocent child and his father should be torn apart at the whim of a spoilt angry woman.

By seven o' clock the mobile home was out at the public road ready to be loaded onto the truck and taken to Limerick.

Two more days and I had a home with electricity, a telephone and even steps up to the front door. It was the August bank holiday in Ireland, and the residents of the flats didn't want to be disturbed on their long weekend so I waited until Monday evening before setting out for Dublin.

*

By Friday afternoon, the work was finished; allowing me to collect Matthew from playschool as my access order lay down. He was delighted to see me. We went for a burger and played in the park. He had to be back at Brenda's flat by six.

When we arrived at the blockhouse she came down the stairs to meet us looking furious. 'Why didn't you tell me you were collecting him today?' she demanded.

'It's there in the court order if you want to read it,' was my reply.

'Well, you haven't been working the court order up to now,' she tried again.

My retort 'no more than you intended' went unheard as Matthew piped in. 'I want my Daddy to come up and play with me now!'

'Come inside now Matthew! It's getting late.'

'I want my Daddy!' As he spoke he lifted up his two little arms, so I instinctively bent down and lifted him up.

He was now sitting on my right forearm with his two little hands firmly around my neck. As she advanced towards us I could feel the small hands getting tighter.

'Hand him over!'

Matthew turned and scowled in her direction and a wave of fury was building up inside me. My son was not going to be handed over to anyone against his wishes and this time nobody was going to tear him from me either!

'Hand him over!'

'You filthy unspeakable witch. You'll pay for this when Matthew gets older!' My eyes were burning; Matthew gave a little kick.

She hesitated, taken aback by the intensity of our response. 'Well, you're not coming in here,' she said eventually.

'So what do you want to do?'

'Have him back here by eight, at the latest!' She turned away fuming at the loss of face and anxious to put the situation behind her.

Two hours and fifteen minutes later Matthew was still reluctant to leave me. Perhaps Brenda might be willing to compromise. 'Promise me he can spend a few days down in Limerick with me and I'll ask him to go in,' I offered. She put it in writing and also agreed to my seeing Matthew the following morning as the access order lay down. She consented to this not because she was a solicitor and therefore respectful of the court order, but because Matthew refused point blank to leave me unless he had a guarantee that I would be in the car park outside his window when he woke up next day. 'You must stay there 'til I come back,' he said.

'There's nowhere to sleep here but I'll go somewhere close by and come back first thing in the morning.'

He went up the steps cheerfully and gave me one last look and a wave.

Next morning, Matthew was waiting at the window as my truck rolled in. After breakfast at McDonalds we went up to the Playland, an indoor arena full of bouncy castles, slides and children's amusements.

He loved it! A little reluctant at first to go on a particularly long tubular slide, he soon overcame his fears and emerged delighted at the other end. Then armed with new confidence he swung Tarzan-like across some suspended ropes and pulleys and finally he went up and slid down the 'vertical drop' along with some older children. He took two goes before he did the drop but the second time he marched up the steps, determination written all over his little face. 'You know Dad, this time I'm serious,' he said, his three-year-old earnestness colouring every word.

And he was. When he had finished I ran over to give him a hug. He was delighted with his achievement; it was a moment to remember.

It was when I went across to get a cup of tea that misfortune struck. The paper cup was in my hand when Matthew burst in the door crying loudly.

'What is it?' I asked.

'My foot!' he sobbed.

Under his sock, the front of his left foot was covered in blood. His big toe had caught under a glass door it as it was swinging closed. Now that he was with me, he calmed down and almost stopped crying. Getting his coat and shoes from the cloakroom we drove to the hospital.

Inside I held him in my arms while the doctor pierced his toenail with a red-hot pin and let the blood out. With the pain gone he relaxed and began to feel tired. It was half past two. Carrying him in my arms to the truck I suggested that we go to lunch in the pub across the road, but his face became anxious.

'No!' I said quickly. 'Lets go to the Kingston Hotel where we usually go.' He relaxed again.

We found a familiar seat and he immediately lay down and fell asleep. I had my lunch and phoned Brenda.

'Bring him home right now!' she demanded.

'Sorry Brenda, he's having a little sleep and it's better not to wake him. Why can't you come down here and see for yourself? You may want to do your thing and sue Playland for faulty doors or something.'

She didn't take long. My cup of tea was half full when she came in the door. It seemed wise to try the diplomatic approach.

'Sit down and have some tea while he's having his rest. I'll get an extra cup.'

It worked. She sat at the table casting concerned glances in Matthew's direction while she helped herself from the pot. The atmosphere was almost happy until Matthew began to stir on the seat. She was over to him in a second, sitting down beside him and trying to win him over.

Chapter 16

He was having none of it. He sat bolt upright on the seat and pointed with his finger. 'Sit over there!' he commanded.

Brenda got up and did exactly as she was told. It was hard to believe it. Brenda! Bold angry Brenda meekly bowing to the command of a three year old! I failed to suppress a grin and she saw me. The veneer of pleasantness slipped from Brenda's face like a mask to be replaced with a look of fury. At least it was familiar!

'He's coming home with me right now, your time is up,' she announced.

'If he's happy to go with you fine. But you won't take him by force.'

Her face changed as the helpless anger burned up inside her. Once again she decided to get out.

'Have him back by five o'clock at the latest!' she announced before turning away hastily to leave the scene of her humiliation behind.

Matthew had barely been clipped into his seat belt, when she appeared again at the window of the truck.

'You're like a couple of knackers in that old truck,' she began and followed up with a stream of filthy language and abuse in the window while Matthew and I both looked away in dislike.

'You'd better get out of the way or you'll get run down,' I said eventually, turning the window up.

We drove in the direction of her flat and stopped to buy Matthew a Coca-Cola on the way. The day had been rather hectic so far, and it wasn't over yet.

Something told me to go to the Garda station. There's nothing like a little trauma to get you in touch with your feelings. Sure enough, Brenda was there on her way out. We all went back in.

Inside the Sergeant turned to me. 'We were going to have every Garda in Dublin on the lookout for you,' he threatened.

'Did she tell you she gave me permission? I'll bet she didn't!'

'Well if she did she's withdrawn it again and the court order here says he's to be back at 2.00pm. Kidnapping a child is a very serious matter.'

Matthew at this time was sitting on the counter with his arms around my neck, his determination and anger slowly giving way to resentment and disbelief. He could sense my powerlessness.

'He's my own child and you can see that he doesn't want to go,' I said

'Look, the law is the law. If you don't let her have him, we'll have no choice but to take him from you and detain you for breach of the peace. I'll leave you all here to work it out for a while.'

He almost made me give up there and then, but Matthew clutching my neck strengthened my resolve. Brenda's 'Hand him over!' was ignored until she eventually got impatient and pressed the bell.

After a short time the Sergeant re-appeared. This time he changed tactic. His voice became friendlier. 'Listen!' he said, 'your best bet is to go to your solicitor. What are you going to do? You can't just put him in the truck and take him to Limerick. What's a judge going to think of that.'

He was right, but it made me feel sick inside. I was still hoping for joint custody at a court hearing.

Men can be their own worst enemies sometimes. Policemen, in marital disputes, frequently act as a bullyboy organisation for the wife - especially if she is good looking.

There was a Bean-Garda[2] looking on from behind who was not so easily influenced by Brenda's charms. She looked at us with sympathy and at Brenda with loathing.

I knew I was beaten. My grip on Matthew relaxed, and he, sensing my weakness allowed Brenda to take him in her arms and carry him out to her car. The sergeant came and shook me by the hand. I had failed my son. He had been snatched from my arms against his will, leaving me powerless to stop it. It filled me with bitterness and despair.

---

[2] policewoman

All of a sudden I hurried out to the car where she was fastening him in a child seat at the rear. 'He's going to hate you!' My voice was full of pain. 'Wait and see, he's going to hate you.'

*

The following week passed by like a kind of limbo. I could sense plainly Matthew's urge to make contact with me and tried phoning several times a day, but in vain. Brenda's phone was not answered at home and she was 'not available' at work.

On Monday afternoon there was a meeting with Gerry Nolan.

'We were doing so well,' he complained. 'Now you've set it all back again.'

'Doing well? In terms of what objective?'

He didn't answer. Instead he tried another approach. 'Things were starting to work,' he said.

'What was working? My son and I forced to live apart from one another? Who wants that to work.'

He was losing patience. 'Like it or not the system of custody and access works - and you'll have to accept it.'

'Slavery worked for thousands of years and it would be a lot better if it didn't. Slavery took children away from parents too and it worked for as long as people believed they had to accept it,' was my final thrust.

Apart from making me feel a little better, this was getting me nowhere. During the week there was an exchange of solicitors' letters, meaningless verbiage all costing money and achieving nothing.

There was one other event, which was more significant. On Monday Brenda went before a judge and got a safety order by swearing something or other, probably that I had threatened her outside her flat, or perhaps on the roadway outside the hotel - the only times we were alone together. Safety orders are quick and easy to obtain - if you are a woman. They are often given ex-parte, even though, strictly speaking the judge is not supposed to do so, which means that the person who is a victim of the order has no opportunity to defend himself. All a woman has to do is to ask to go before a judge. She is given a hearing immediately and it only takes a few minutes. Then she can have her husband arrested for coming near his family home. Mothers, trying to obstruct access to children apply for most safety orders.

The notice came by registered mail together with a solicitor's letter telling me there would be another court hearing in September and that my access to Matthew was going to be withheld pending the hearing.

Knowing that a solicitor's letter could not set a court order aside, that piece of legal bluff did not worry me. If I had known the contempt that judges have for access orders, then perhaps it would. As it was, I still trusted the law.

I began telephoning her at odd times, but always the answering machine. Then at midnight on Friday night by some miracle, she picked up the phone. Did she answer it automatically from bed or was she expecting someone else at that hour?

'Are you letting Matthew come down for his weekend tomorrow, or do you just want to operate the court order?' I asked, in an acid tone.

'Oh, we must be careful not to upset Matthew,' she said calmly, before putting the phone down, her training showing.

My alarm was set for twenty to six.

The following morning, at half past nine the Volvo could not be seen anywhere around the courtyard of the blockhouse, and there was no answer from the bell or the phone. I stayed for ten minutes and then went across the road to a café to have breakfast. After all, my access didn't start until ten. Maybe she had gone out with Matthew for something or other and she would be back in time for him to spend the day with me.

At ten o'clock, there was still no reply. Now I was getting worried. What had been an uneasy suspicion was becoming a certainty. She had taken him away; she was not going to let him see me.

For about twenty minutes a glimmer of hope remained and I still looked longingly toward the road, hoping to see the light coloured Volvo with my son on board and visualising the delight on his face as he recognised me. Then the hope faded and a surge of helpless anger passed through me. My son! Where was he? Was there nothing I could do?

The thought of the previous week brought me back to the Garda Station and to the threats of what would happen to me if I didn't return the child. 'What will happen now that the boot is on the other foot? When she is making off with the child on my time?' It was probably worth a try and there was nothing to lose. 'Anything is better than standing here!' I reasoned.

The only person in the station was the Bean-Garda who had been watching us the previous week. She was sympathetic, and honest!

'There's nothing we can really do,' she said.

'But what about all the stuff the Sergeant said last week that you were going to chase me all over Dublin?'

'Well, we weren't really...'

'But why make all the threats then?'

'Well it was just that she came in first and made the complaint.'

'And she is a solicitor and a woman,' I added bitterly. 'But I'm making the complaint now so what are you going to do?'

'Look, I'll make a phone call, I saw your little boy hanging onto you last week and I was sorry to see what happened.'

Picking up the phone she spoke to the sergeant who dealt with me the week before, then turned to me. 'He says "why don't you go back after an hour or so?" Maybe she's only getting you back for last week.'

Her tone was apologetic - and ashamed. She didn't like the system either but she couldn't do anything about it. Police have a directive that orders for contact are not to be enforced, which means that such orders are meaningless. All the poor dad can do is to arrange another court hearing, which takes months. At this hearing he gets another court order in place which again will not be enforced, his wife gets a vague warning and he is loaded with costs of several hundred pounds.

'Well at least you didn't say 'contact your solicitor,' I told her. 'If you did I had my answer ready.'

'What was it going to be?'

'Something like 'if you can't enforce one court order what's the point in going after another.'

'Not much.' She seemed genuinely sorry.

The bond between parent and child is powerful. Just as Matthew and I had sensed one another the previous week, now I could feel his presence and his distress at not seeing me. He was expecting me to be there; there was no question of his having forgotten, not with the retentive mind of a child. It was making me more and more upset.

A telephone call to Gerry Nolan in Limerick got me nowhere; he was away playing golf. Then I headed back to the 'blockhouse.' There was still no car but there were people in the apartment. I marched towards the door. A man in a suit leaned out a window and beckoned me in. He pressed the buzzer and the door opened before me. What was going on?

Upstairs, all was revealed. People were being shown around the flat and the man in the suit, an estate agent, was doing the showing. He asked me my name and it slipped out without thinking. 'Never mind the consequences,' I thought to myself.

So she was moving, taking my son away without telling me. Where? When? Had she gone already? These thoughts were racing through my mind when the agent approached me and asked me was I interested in renting the flat.

'There's no shower,' I answered, so he gave me his card and I walked downstairs to the courtyard again.

My mind was in a whirl. Walking to where the truck was parked I sat in it for some time wondering what to do next.

'Some food' I thought. Nearby was the Mayfair Hotel where I often had my midday meal. The chefs serving behind the counter knew my face and I responded half-heartedly to their good-natured banter as they filled my tray. It took me a long time to get down the delicious roast beef, often pausing between forkfuls for minutes on end.

What to do next? 'No use phoning Gerry again, he'll be golfing all day.' My mind was moving slowly and carefully with no trace of weariness or fatigue in spite of having had only four hours sleep the night before. My watch said half past three! Where was the time going? Two hours had passed in a daze.

Half mechanically I left the table and made my way back to the block of flats.

The Volvo was in the car park; my mind cleared with a start. So my son couldn't be far away; my feelings were right once more.

Looking around I suddenly became aware of my surroundings. A team of gardeners was tending the flowerbeds round the lawn. Elderly residents were sitting on the benches round the open area and some younger people were lying on the grass.

Press! No reply from the doorbell, Press! Then a third time; still no reply. Walking down the steps on my way to the telephone across the road I looked up and saw the window open.

'Matthew!' I cried, and the answer came unmistakably. 'Daddy!'

'I've come up to see you,' I called. Looking up at the window expecting to see his face at any moment but there was nothing except a single knock, like the sound of a chair falling over. It could only have been a few seconds but it seemed like an hour.

'Matthew,' I called again.

'I WANT MY DADDY!' It was a scream. It reached to the furthest ends of the grounds; people looked up from their benches and their seats on the grass. The yell he gave had a constrained note as if there was a struggle going on.

'Matthew, are you okay?'

'I WANT MY DADDY!' This time even louder. All the people round the lawn were now turned towards the building and the yells coming from inside.

'Matthew, are you okay?' I called again. 'Is she hurting you?'

'I WANT MY DADDY!' Matthew's scream had now become a shriek. It penetrated across the grounds, out on to the road and cut through the traffic noises outside. People all round the complex were looking in horror.

The younger gardener rushed over to me with the keys of the building in his hand. Oblivious to the crowd I rushed into the building, upstairs to Brenda's flat and banged on the door. 'Brenda, let me in!' I cried. 'There's a crowd coming in from the street.'

There was the sound of a struggle and the muffled thud of a chair falling on a carpeted floor.

'I WANT TO GO OUT TO MY DADDY!' It was not a scream now; it was a sob.

'Brenda! Let him out! What are you doing to him?' I shouted through the door.

'I WANT MY DADDY!' from Matthew again.

'Brenda! If you don't let the child go I'm calling the police,' I said. 'This is criminal abuse of a child.'

My mind was becoming cooler. It was very important to comfort Matthew and to calm him down.

'Matthew pet, she's going to let you out soon,' I told him.

Then came the sound of a telephone being dialled and Brenda's voice speaking to the police.

'Come quickly it's my husband!' she said convincingly. 'He's in the building outside the door and he's shouting and causing a disturbance. There's a safety order out on him and I'm terrified that he may hurt me - or the child. Please! Come as quickly as you can!'

Why hadn't Matthew spoken to me? Was she preventing him? It was more than likely that the Gardaí were going to arrest me, given their habit of taking the part of the woman in this kind of dispute, but I was hoping they would arrive as soon as possible because they would have to look in on Matthew.

There was no need to worry. A police car pulled up in a matter of moments, and four Gardaí walked out of it and marched towards me grimly.

'No dismissive indifference now,' I thought walking straight to them.

'Go up and see if my son is all right. He's been screaming his head off!' I demanded.

After a slight pause one of the Gardaí spoke. 'We've been called to deal with a disturbance; someone had been shouting and frightening a woman. Was that you?' he asked.

'The only one who has been shouting is my little son and I've about a hundred witnesses,' I responded. 'Now will you please go up and see if he's all right? Don't worry about me, I'm not going anywhere and two of you should be enough to mind me.'

The same Garda spoke again. He instructed the other three to look after me while he went up to speak to Brenda. He was taking no chances - and leaving me in no doubt whose side they were on. The three Gardaí soon relaxed when they saw that I had no intention of giving trouble. Still quite worried about Matthew, I called his name again. The Gardaí didn't interfere. He was at the window in a second. Obviously the Garda had come into the flat. She couldn't stop him now.

'Matthew, are you okay?'

'Yes Daddy.' The relief swept over me. It made me feel weak.

We spoke for about five minutes. I don't remember what we said except that he asked me 'Can I go out to you now Daddy?'

'Ask the Garda, he'll probably let you out.'

No such luck! After five or six minutes he emerged from the building and marched towards me aggressively. 'She said you were sent a solicitor's letter saying that the access was cancelled,' he said. 'So you shouldn't be here.'

Numb with confusion and relief, I couldn't think of anything to say for a time. Taking this to be a sign of guilt, he went on.

'There's a safety order out on you so you can be arrested anytime and criminally charged.'

'Well then arrest me!' Matthew was all right and I couldn't care less.

'Well, if you come around here disturbing the peace we'll have no choice but to arrest you especially when you have no right to be here.'

Slowly my mind began to clear. There was something wrong with what he was saying. 'Hang on a minute! She's not a court; she can't change a court order by solicitors letter,' I blurted out.

He stopped. 'Yes... that's true,' he said after a long pause.

Now sure of my ground I added 'And the court order says my access is every Saturday, so I'm quite entitled to be here.'

'Why didn't you report it at the Garda station that you came to see your son and that access was denied?' He was defensive now - and worried.

'I did! - At half past ten this morning, to a Bean Garda, but no one was going to do anything about it.' I drove my point home. 'But you turned out in force when you thought that *I* was breaking a court order.'

He was visibly embarrassed.

'She's a solicitor, and a very clever lady,' was my final shot.

He gritted his teeth, turned and marched into the building.

Matthew was still at the window. He caught my eyes. 'Can I come out now?' he said.

'We'll know in a minute, the Garda is going to speak to Mummy.'

We had another few words before the Garda came down the stairs again and out the door. He was walking quickly now, but in the direction of the car. He would not meet my eyes. Finally turning to me he said, 'Look! As regards seeing your son today, forget it! Go back home. But if you come up next Saturday you'll be able to see him, okay?'

'And you'll be able to enforce the order if I can't.' My tone was mocking.

Putting his seat belt on, he turned the window down. 'Your best bet is to see a solicitor,' he said, as the car pulled off.

CHAPTER 17

Aftermath

Looking up, I called goodbye to Matthew (he was still standing at the window) and told him he would see me soon. In fact it was several weeks before we saw one another again. Then, still feeling shaken, I walked back to the truck and started for Limerick. Before long, the enormity of what had happened began to take hold of me. The thought of Brenda made me seethe with anger but the picture of Matthew staring down at me from the window calmed me down again.

At the next phone box I pulled over; my mind was made up. Witch or no witch, Matthew must not be subjected to that ordeal again - ever. It was time to talk to her.

'Beep. Beep. Beep. Beep.' The new touch-tone phone sounded a free line. No reply. The answering machine came on.

'Brenda! I know you're there. Pick up the phone! We have to talk. We must work something out! If this is the best we can do for Matthew, we don't deserve to have him.'

Silence, from the other end. I appealed to her once more. Nothing! It was just like the rows in Gordon Road, total stonewalling and no hope of any communication. It was hopeless. I drove down to Limerick without stopping.

Gerry Nolan was beside himself. He was almost caught for words - almost. 'What were you trying to do?' he said, trying his best at a superior air. 'And we were making such progress.'

'You keep saying that, but progress towards what? Towards forcing my son to live where he doesn't want to, with a woman who is prepared to abuse him before she'll let him see his father? Is that what you mean by progress?'

He changed tone. 'I have a letter here from Colman Kelly accusing you of all kinds of *frightening and bizarre behaviour,*' he said.

'And you have my memo showing how she is guilty of criminal abuse of my son and how she is in plain breach of the court order. Now, what are you going to do about it?' I could sense his opposition.

'It's her word against yours and in court, a woman's word is worth far more than a man's. She is seen as innocent and truthful.'

'Not this time! There were dozens of witnesses. What about the gardener who gave me the key?'

My voice had a rough edge to it. Something was wrong. Gerry seemed to be working against me; he looked very worried. The legal profession is a tightly knit body everywhere, but in Ireland it is unthinkable to break ranks. Brenda, Brenda's father and Brenda's brother were all members of the club and Gerry would be accountable to them long after my case was over - as he knew very well.

'You could get six months, you know,' he went on.

'For what?'

'For harassing and intimidating a woman.' He could see he was getting somewhere and he played on it for all he was worth.

An awful thought had crossed my mind. 'The truth' was going to be decided at a secret hearing. Every person in the room was going to be a lawyer, apart from me. And if my own solicitor was not prepared to take my part, what could I expect from the judge? What if he didn't want to know about my evidence or my witnesses? In open court, at least justice would have to be seen to be done. But family cases are held 'in camera'; no one is allowed in the courtroom.

Brenda was already one step ahead of me through swearing God knows what, and obtaining a safety order. And she was a woman, in a forum where a woman's word is worth far more than a man's. Things were not looking good for me at all.

'I believe the law does tend to favour the mother but that's only natural. Can you imagine what would happen if it was the other way round?' Gerry went on.

'Why does it have to be any way round?'

But the words came out mechanically. The lie of the land was becoming all too clear. The people who operate the system were not going to let me win this round. Whatever happened to my son, they were not going to turn against one of their own, unless forced to do so by public opinion - and the public would not be allowed to see. I was learning the grim lesson of putting your trust in rules: rules are only people – and if the people are against you, nothing else makes any difference.

That was the end of the meeting. On Friday evening we met again to discuss a further complaint to the court that had been lodged by Brenda.

'What I don't understand Gerry, If there is a standard simple procedure for complaints, then why haven't we been using it all along for all the breaches of the court order?'

He shifted in his seat. I knew part of the answer, but only the minor part. This extraordinary accountability between solicitors again! For a solicitor who breaks a court order, the consequences could be more serious than for a lay person and the last thing he wanted to do was to get his colleague into trouble.

'Like I told you, the judge is unlikely to take any action and it would only lead to resentment,' he said, after a pause.

'And letting her do as she likes with me and my son won't? Or is it just that *my* resentment doesn't count and neither does Matthew's? Anyway, it's nearly five o'clock. May I use your phone?'

'Sure! There's the line.'

There was no reply from Brenda's office or from her flat, only the answering machine. Then I tried her father's house nearby, and Brenda answered. She got quite a shock and put the phone down quickly.

'Gerry, you'd better get me a copy of that court order,' I said. 'Otherwise they could arrest me again.'

Silently, he put the court order through the photocopier and handed me the duplicate. I ran out to the truck. It took me very little time to get to Seamus's house on the Ennis Road. The Volvo was there, the door open. loudly I rapped on the front door.

No answer. I tapped again.

'Come on Brenda!' I called. 'Matthew is supposed to be with me until six. Come on! Let him out!' There was still no reply but there seemed to be a scraping sound from inside. Was Matthew in there?

'Matthew!' I called, loudly. Was she forcing him to stay away from the door again? Was she holding his mouth so he couldn't cry out? This time I'd better find out.

At the back of the bungalow there were several open windows but nobody seemed to be inside.

'Matthew!' I called again, and a third time, 'Matthew.' My voice was loud enough for the neighbours to hear me. A few more attempts produced nothing. Then a police car rounded briskly into the drive and three Gardaí got out promptly.

'Not again?' I said marching over to them. 'Take a look at this!'

The court order stopped them in their tracks at the critical moment. A few seconds delay and they would have bundled me into the car leaving the facts of the situation to be explained later. Here was a man, and a woman had called them out. Normally it was more than enough.

Eventually the senior Garda spoke to me 'We were called here to investigate a disturbance.' He chose his words carefully.

'Well investigate it! You'll find that the nearest thing to a disturbance was myself calling out to my son. I'd be glad to see if he's all right.'

At that point the door opened and Brenda's face appeared outside. She made a motion with her hand and the Garda went over to her obediently. A few minutes later and walked towards to me slowly.

'She says you were outside shouting at her. She turned on the waterworks.' He was clearly not taken in.

'What about my son? Is he all right?'

'He's not inside. Now the best thing you could do is to is to go away from here.'

'Well, will you find out where he is and I'll be on my way right now. This court order says he is to be with me and he's being withheld from me illegally.'

'If you don't go we'll have no choice but to take you away - with us.'

'If you're so worried about enforcing the law, this is a piece of law here! How about enforcing that? Last Saturday, I got up at six o'clock and drove all the way to Dublin and I had to come away again because she held him kicking and screaming.'

'Your best bet is to...'

'To contact your solicitor. And if I'm lucky, in twelve months time they might give me another piece of paper just like this one and you won't enforce that either.'

But he wasn't ruffled. 'A careful man,' I thought. 'No mistakes here.'

'You obviously know the situation, now there's no point in staying here. The people living in this house are elderly; it's not fair to upset them.'

He was right and we both knew it. It was almost twenty to six and at six o'clock my access was over. They watched me drive away.

At the mobile home, I decided to telephone once more. Brenda's brother Cecil answered.

'Hello Cecil! Owen here! I'm trying to arrange to see my son, would you talk to Brenda,' I said.

'Owen, if you come near her, or him, or me you're going to be in the height of trouble, do you understand me?'

'No I don't understand, I don't understand at all. What has she being saying to you?'

'Well, that's it,' he replied and put the phone down.

Gerry couldn't be contacted over the weekend so it was late on Monday afternoon before he could see me. I was determined to go through the motions of a complaint to the court even though by now I didn't expect a lot by way of concrete change.

'Well, if you really feel that this is the way to go then I'll get it set up for you' he said.

Before the end of the week I was in Dublin sitting before a judge, the same judge who had issued the protection order in November and who replied to my letter asking for an explanation. If he remembered, he gave no indication. To my surprise, the document that they gave me mentioned only two breaches of the court order.

'There's nothing here about all the other breaches,' I said.

The court clerk intervened. 'These documents came from your solicitor and if they are not correct you'll have to sort it out with him. In the meantime, do you want to go ahead?'

'Yes I do!'

It was all over in less than five minutes. The judge agreed to shorten the time between the hearing and the serving of the summons in order to have the breaches of access dealt with along with Brenda's complaints. We would be in court on Tuesday week, eleven days time.

It took me some time to figure out what was going on. What Gerry had done was just enough to neutralise Brenda's complaints about my behaviour outside her flat. By showing a judge that I only showed up outside her door to visit my son and that any acrimony only arose out of my not being allowed to see him, he was doing enough to protect his client. To show a continuous pattern of breaking the court order on the part of a solicitor on the other hand would be to get a colleague into serious trouble - and that was professional taboo.

Judges hate it when one of their own bucks the court system. Being a woman Brenda would probably get away with a humble apology; a male solicitor would probably receive a short suspension from appearing in court, a serious matter for a lawyer.

Meeting the judge also enabled me to understand the main reason why solicitors like Gerry are so anxious to discourage fathers from complaining to the courts when their access orders are broken. It puts the judge in an embarrassing situation. The last thing he wants is to be confronted with a court order that he is not prepared to enforce. A solicitor who brings such a complaint does himself no favours at all.

For the next week Gerry kept me worried about getting six months in prison. Even though it seemed unlikely, being upset and new to the court system it was hard to be confident. What scared me was Matthew. If they put me in jail, would he think I had abandoned him? Would he ever trust me again? Would he ever trust anybody again? .

Gerry also told me that Brenda had bought a property in Dublin but he 'wasn't in a position to say where'.

'In that case, we must send £9,600 to Brenda immediately. That was the deal we made.'

'Ok!' he said. 'Will you make out the cheque?' I signed it and handed it to him.

'Now,' he said 'What about my own fees? Can you let me have, say £1,000 for the court hearing and for all the legwork I've been doing?'

'Here! - And I'd be glad if you'd remember who is paying who. I'd like some results for my money.'

Our relationship was becoming strained but we were still on fairly good terms. I handed over the money cheerfully. It was the least of my worries.

'By the way, if she has a new house, she has a phone, I'd like to speak to my son.'

'Her number is ex-directory, she says you were harassing her on the phone.'

'By trying to talk to my son? Can you arrange for him to ring me?'

'Well... I'll see what we can do.'

I wasn't holding out much hope.

Chapter 17

On the Monday night I got no sleep at all and couldn't eat a bite next morning on the way to Dublin. Gerry went with me on the seven-thirty train. The carriages were full of accountants and lawyers. Plump and oily, they exuded wealth and insincerity. They were very much at their ease and were mostly on first name terms with each other, apart from the women who looked grimmer and more determined. Conversation rebounded across the carriage in marked contrast to an English train.

Gerry joined comfortably in the conversation and they were happy to include me. I was dressed in a sports jacket with a woollen tie and a pocket watch and they took me for one of their own. I didn't mind. It helped to pass the time.

Colman Kelly and Brenda were in the courthouse ahead of us, but there didn't seem to be any barrister around. The solicitors immediately began to negotiate leaving me on my own for a long time. A Garda came over to me and started talking about unruly behaviour among teenagers at rock concerts. Clearly, he took me for a lawyer. Anyway it shortened the time for me; we chatted for about a quarter of an hour.

The lawyers eventually came up with a new access agreement where Matthew was to see me every two weeks, one visit in Dublin, the next visit in Limerick. He was to be picked up at the home of Sally Donnelly, a barrister-friend of Brenda's.

Towards the end of the negotiations Gerry came to me saying, 'They are demanding that you apologise to the court for your behaviour.'

'I'm not worried,' was my reply.

He was taken aback. The pattern was familiar to me by now. It was a standard ploy by solicitors on their clients: make the client feel insecure, settle out of court for less than he wants, then give him some meaningless gesture to console him at the end. I had been there before and just let him get on with it. He came back twice more and eventually announced, 'They've agreed to dispense with the apology.'

'Now can we go home?'

It didn't take long to sign all the papers. Gerry suggested that I shake hands with Brenda.

'How would you like to shake hands with someone who abused your child? - And who is still doing it?'

He let the matter drop.

When we were in front of the judge he made one significant remark. 'I'm glad that the two solicitors - no, *the three solicitors* - were able to settle matters among themselves,' he said pointedly. So there were weapons that could be used if only I knew what they were. But Gerry was not going to tell me. Still, I was getting familiar enough with the system to be able to read the signs.

As we came outside, the ugly brick building loomed ominously above me.

'How many children have been taken away from their fathers in there?' I thought, looking away in disgust.

By the time we reached the railway station Gerry still found it hard to make conversation with me. I was still too tense, so he suggested a drink. 'It would do you good,' he said.

For once it did. We had a pint before catching the train and a few more on the journey home. My capacity for drink is low, and it didn't help being exhausted from lack of sleep and nervous energy. So it went to my head; at least it got me to unwind completely.

Gerry wasn't a bad guy – one of the best in fact. It was just that as a pimply faced teenager he had been sucked into the system and he couldn't help what the system was or what he was. We were the best of friends when we got to Limerick.

CHAPTER 18

The dispossessed

Passing by Christine's flat, it seemed a good idea to call in on the way home. She made me some strong coffee while I told her the news.

Christine and I had first met in the spring, during my stay with Frank, and in spite of all my reservations I found myself getting closer and closer to her in the months that followed. It seemed clear to me that I was too odd and eccentric to live with any woman. And my habit of suppressing my feelings and analysing everything when things went wrong only seemed to make things worse. A girlfriend? Maybe. But she must keep firmly to her space and I to mine; otherwise it would lead to more trouble.

But for once I met someone as different as myself. Christine's space was important to her too. A member of Mensa, she had been isolated as a teenager because of not being interested in pop music or fashion, failing to make the connection between such things and her sexuality. She was unmoved by all the brainwashing of the market, either as a teenager or as an adult. During the tension and trauma that followed my coming to Ireland, she gave me constant advice and support.

My plan was to go back to London in September having spent the end of the summer building my relationship with Matthew. Now for a number of reasons, it seemed better to delay my return for a few months.

The first of these reasons was Matthew. He had not seen enough of me. At least there was a regular access order now, and one that Brenda was not likely to break. We had the chance of being together on a regular basis and it was important to make the most of it.

My second reason was Christine; I found myself reluctant to leave her and to go back to London on my own.

The third was the stable-building project on the land given to me by my father. The site had been levelled in the spring and now we were ready to go ahead with the foundations and the walls. The idea began to lift my spirits as they had once been lifted at Gordon Road.

The final reason arose out of my telephone conversations with Families Need Fathers earlier in the year. When they heard that my case would take place in Ireland, F.N.F. gave me the name of Liam Hogan and an organisation called Parental Equality in Dublin. The name struck such a cord with me that I repeated it over and over again 'Parental Equality.' It seemed to sum up all the injustices suffered by Matthew and me over the previous two years. 'Parental Equality' is a cry for justice, that strikes home in any fair minded person - and creates a guilty foreboding among the people who operate the present system of family law.

Liam gave me the name of Kevin Price and his telephone number. He met me one evening in 'The Travellers Rest'. That meeting was the beginning of our southern branch of Parental Equality, which was to give expression to so much of my energy and feelings in the months ahead. A week later, five or six of us met for the first time in a shabby little room. All dads at first, later on women began to join us as they realised that our fight was not against them but against taking children away from any parent.

The meetings began to evolve naturally from the beginning. Having first exchanged a promise of strict confidentiality, we began to tell our stories. Sharing our experiences was unforgettable. We could have been any bunch of dads thrown together at a children's outing - except that the children were not there. Instead there was a look of pain on every face. It was partly a kind of hunted look, seen on the faces of gypsies or on black teenagers talking to policemen; partly a look of loss that only a parent could understand. Loving dads, who cared very much about their children, they had been thrown out of their homes and their children taken from them by the horror called family law.

For the most part they were gentle, inoffensive men, shy about telling their stories and desperately trying to come to terms with what had happened to their lives.

My own experiences were put into perspective by accounts of systematic cruelty and injustice that seem to belong to another country or another age.

There was a case of Alan who moved out of Dublin and spent his life savings on buying a house in Limerick at the demand of his wife. Sharon was pretty, glamorous and interested in high living. She set up a business importing cosmetics with Alan's money and support. As soon as her business was up and running, she began seeing an ex-boyfriend and announced that 'the marriage was over.' They had a little son Rory and it was often remarked in the town that Rory was always seen with his father, never with his mother. In fact she took very little interest in the child, and whenever Alan could not look after Rory, her parents stepped in.

But that did not stop her demanding sole custody at the separation hearing, and being a mother the judge gave it to her automatically. When it comes to break-up, children are serious money - a house and a regular income. So Alan was given a few days to pack his bags and leave his home and his son. Sharon drafted in her father, her mother and even her brother to look after Rory. Alan even got a chance to be with him, when no one else was available. He had to stand outside his house one evening, while Sharon's brother was beating Rory inside. He called the Gardaí but the Garda on arriving, went into the house for tea. Alan was cautioned for breaching the peace. He has the child's cries recorded on tape.

Tony is a big teddybear of a man, partially disabled following a serious injury to his back. Nancy, his wife, became bitter and angry after the accident when Tony lost most of his earning power. When she lost her temper, she used to beat him with brushes and mops. Once Tony reported her at the local Garda station, but the Gardaí told him to 'go home and stand up for himself.' Later when she accused Tony of threatening her, they came round immediately.

We are told of course that the system is to protect 'all victims of violence, male or female.' Police spokesmen chant this like a mantra. But the fact is the domestic violence procedure was never intended for male victims; so when the victim is male and assailant is female the system simply shuts down. Violent mothers are not carted away in police cars nor are they issued with barring orders. It was never intended that they should be.

For a short time after separation Tony and Nancy shared their house and custody of their two little boys. Then one day a man arrived at the door and handed him a summons. Tony was accused of violence and rape. He immediately demanded a full police investigation. But it was not to be; no investigation took place. However a feminist social worker took Nancy's allegations on board and the judge acted as if they were proven. They put Tony out of his house and allowed him to see his boys once a month under supervision.

To this day he has never had a private talk with either of his sons. At the time of writing Nancy has broken the access order twenty nine times. She has constantly denied the children the love and support of their father. Tony, being disabled, is receiving legal aid and has therefore been able to bring his wife to court for breaches of the order more frequently than the rest of us. She has never received anything but a verbal warning from the judge about the 'dire consequences' if she was to appear before him again. She soon learned to laugh at the warnings. Tony laughs at them too.

Damien is a farmer living fifteen miles from Cork, a father of four. His wife began having an affair with a local double-glazing salesman. She told Damien that she was 'unfulfilled' and she wanted to end the marriage.

At the court hearing Damien was dumbfounded to find it was *he* who had to leave his home and his children. Since then, she has sold the house and moved away taking the children with her. By obstructing Damien's visits she was able to break the emotional bond between parent and child and convince three of the children that Damien did not want to see them. Hurt and angry, they still don't want to talk to their father. The fourth child ran away to live with Damien, and now they live in an old outhouse that had been partly converted into a dwelling.

Jimmy was a big country boy from West Limerick. He drives an excavator. His wife had moved in with a new boyfriend whom she wanted to assume the role of father. One year old Lisa had other ideas, however. She kicked and screamed every time her dad had to hand her back; so her mother swore an affidavit stating how she saw Jimmy putting his hand down Lisa's nappy. The mere hint of child abuse was enough for the judge to suspend all access and leave Lisa without her father.

Jimmy told us the story frankly. Big and innocent, he was no more capable of child abuse than the baby herself. The 'hand down the nappy' we were later to realise, is a standard formula among unscrupulous mothers who want to shut the father out of the lives of his children. His solicitor, who didn't want his own advice to come under scrutiny, eventually talked Jimmy out of coming to our meetings.

Stuart is an electrician. When he and his wife were married five years, she began going out 'with her friends' several times a week. One Sunday she was missing all day; it was one in the morning when she returned.

'Where were you?' Stuart demanded.

'In Ennis – with my new boyfriend' she taunted.

'Wait 'til I see him! I'll give him 'boyfriend! I'll kill him!'

The following day Stuart came home from work to find a Garda waiting for him at his front door – with a barring order. His wife had gone to the court saying that she was terrified. The judge gave her the order in ten minutes. The Garda gave Stuart the same amount of time to pack his bags and leave his home. Next day the boyfriend moved in.

Kevin Price's story was typical enough. After eight years of marriage, he noticed his wife Norma becoming irritable and distant. Before long he was told that 'it was not working' and 'would he agree to an *amicable* separation? There would be 'no problem with access to Hugh, their eight year old son'. His solicitor advised him to 'do the sensible thing', so he moved out of his home and signed over custody of Hugh to Norma.

Afterwards Kevin realised that she had had a boyfriend all along, and that was why 'it' was not working. No sooner had he agreed to leave his home than she moved Derek in. There was worse to come. Now Norma wanted Derek to become a *'father figure'* and began to make it difficult for Kevin to see Hugh. Kevin had been tricked out of his parenthood and his home. The solicitor charged him £850.00 plus VAT

There were many men like Alan and Tony and Damien and Jimmy. Some came and went, some stayed, so that the group now has over forty members. But that was hard to see in those early days when we would be lucky to have nine or ten at a meeting.

We looked like a darts club: eight or nine very ordinary looking men, a few approaching middle age. But to judge by the volumes of allegations made against us by our wives, we could easily be mistaken for followers of Al Capone or the Dirty Dozen. Altogether we were accused of every crime except murder, including assault, robbery, buggery, child abuse, drug trafficking, sadism and rape. Just to look at the faces and the ages of the dads was enough to make the accusations laughable and we did laugh a lot as we became more at ease with one another after a time.

But as we began to compare our experiences we began to realise that we were guilty of a far more serious crime than robbery or rape. Under the inquisition called 'family law' we were all guilty of the crime of being a dad. As in the Spanish

Inquisition, we could be denounced by someone who was interested in our property or by someone whose motive was simply hatred. No better 'proof' was needed than someone bringing a self-serving allegation. The punishment was swift and ruthless; we were thrown out of our homes and our children taken from us - often screaming like my little son.

It's a terrible thing for a parent to have his children taken away from him. All nature cries out against it. Timid animals like horses will seldom stand and fight, but they will fight to the death to protect their young. We dads welcome our sons and daughters into the world as babies. We bond with them and we love them. As they return our love the bond becomes a full parental relationship. Then one day the bond is suddenly torn apart as the parent is forced to leave the family home. The hurt never goes away for the parent or for the child.

Nevertheless, judges treat us like animals without feelings. To them a dad is just a provider, not a real parent. The guilty party in any break-up, he is lucky to be allowed to see his children in McDonalds on a Saturday afternoon.

Absent fathers, feckless fathers, irresponsible fathers, the phrases were coined, all very similar, all making it easier for the people who profit by our situation. We were outcasts, villains at a time when there was little sympathy for separated men and no emotional support. The common perception of marital break-up was that of the boss running away with his attractive young secretary or the feckless irresponsible husband leaving his wife and children to starve. The fact is that men initiate a tiny fraction of separations. It's not hard to see why, even where they have good reason. It's effectively saying to a judge 'evict me from my house and take away my children.' Judges are only too happy to oblige.

Men find it difficult to talk, and when they do they seldom have the vocabulary to express what they are feeling, so they suffer in silence. People in stable marriages caught up in day to day worries usually don't want to think about people whose homes are falling apart, and it's hard to blame them.

The dispossessed

A marriage that fails always raises questions for couples still together.

Where there is any sign of sympathy it is usually reserved for the mother. A woman is quick to seek help and to tell her side of the story. This is the story that finds it's way round the grapevine through single and married women; the story that reaches married men via their wives. 'How *could* he treat her like that? The brute!'

Married men, whose marriages are unhappy but still intact, tend to be the most unsympathetic of all. No man wants to believe he is effectively a guest *in his wife's house*. They tend to argue that it can only happen to *bad* fathers or husbands who *'did something wrong.'* Trying to find a formula to distance themselves from the victims is a universal reaction among members of any persecuted group. The last thing they want to believe is that it can happen to them.

At least we were outcasts together. Gradually as the weeks passed we all began to grow stronger, to heal. Some of us spilled out our stories quickly, others piecemeal. Still others said nothing at all for weeks, then it all came out in a gush.

Our discussions brought answers to several questions. We learned about the burly female court clerk who refuses to accept legal proceedings from a man, insisting that they had to come from a solicitor, but who regularly slips outside her desk to help a woman fill in the forms. There was also Judge M --- who gives barring orders for the asking (to a woman) and who invites the mother to make out the access schedule laying out when *she* allows the father to see *her* children.

Other questions took longer. Why do the solicitors acting for the dad put so much pressure on him to leave the family home? Why are they so reluctant to tell him about joint custody, or even to defend all the barring orders, safety orders and claims of violence? These things too, became clear in time. The problem for many of us was that time was running out.

Having someone to talk to is a rare experience for a man. Now we were all benefiting from it. We began to stop turning our anger and shame inward. Deep down many of us had an uneasy feeling that somehow we must be to blame. Men are programmed to feel guilty when it comes to women, and at school we were taught that punishment follows sin. Not understanding the process we had nowhere to turn our anger but against ourselves.

But we understood now. We were not absent parents but *dispossessed* parents. We did not abandon our children; they were taken from us. Now with all the facts together we realised that we were not untouchables or criminals, just victims of a cruel and inhuman system. The knowledge helped us to come to terms with what happened.

The sharing of pain brought out a spirit of comradeship and caring among us. We all began to grow as human beings. Groups like Alcoholics Anonymous produce very fine people. Now our group was having the same effect on us. The friendships forged under such circumstances are special; they last a lifetime.

We could not put our pain aside but we could grow bigger than it, see it in perspective - move away from our own injustices and identify with the greater hurt of other parents and children torn apart against their will. After about ten weeks we decided to make our case public. It would help all the others, and our own situation couldn't become much worse. When RTE, the Irish national television channel was contacted they interviewed us almost immediately. Three of us spoke: Kevin, Alan and myself and they put us on the air within a few days. Kevin was the informal chairman of our group and it was in his apartment that we all gathered to see how we did.

The programme took less than fifteen minutes, but it was at 7.00pm, peak viewing time. We were excited, sitting on the sofa or on the floor in front of the television. Kevin was very calm as he spoke about the exclusion of fathers from the lives their children. There was a lovely shot of Alan throwing his little son into the air. He spoke about the financial factors that limit a separated father from seeing his child. I said that in court, a child has no rights; the child's rights are taken away and given to the mother, and that the courts are guilty of appalling crimes against children and their fathers. The programme concluded with a film shot of each of us in our makeshift 'homes', the children's toys scattered around. It was very effective.

We were delighted! We went absolutely wild! Kevin had made a recording and played it again before we all went out to celebrate.

All the following day the phones kept ringing. Everybody seemed to have seen us. Liam Hogan called from Dundalk. He was in a hearty mood as he congratulated us on a job well done.

The plight of separated dads had been mentioned before in a few radio interviews and discussion shows. But nothing had touched the general consciousness like our short programme. No higher tribute can be paid to the members of our group than to say that in less than three months we had moved on from our own hurt, to address the pain of dispossessed parents in general, and to do something to confront the cause of that pain.

There was a long struggle ahead of course. Since then, the number of children and fathers split up by the courts has gone up, not down. New and even more draconian legislation has been enacted. Non-sexist in theory, in practise judges only use it against a man.

But now at least there was hope. From now on, it was not going to be all one way traffic; there was going to be a fight back.

And we had struck the first blow.

CHAPTER 19

Making a life

'I'm a dispossessed dad.'
'What?'
'A dispossessed dad!'
'What's that?'
'A dad who has had his children taken away from him.'
'What? Who is going to take away somebody's children for God's sake?'
'A judge will, if a marriage breaks down.'
'Oh I see. You left your wife and the children are with her.'
'I didn't leave anybody...'
'But you separated from her.'
'No I didn't! A man came to the door and shoved a pile of papers at me, so I had to go to court and now my son isn't there any more.'
'But that means you separated from her.'
'No! It means *she* separated from *me*.'
'What's the difference? Anyway you must have done something to make her want to leave you.'
'Well, we weren't getting on. But I wanted it to work out because of the little fellow.'
'I'll bet they all say that.'
'I don't know, but the last thing I wanted was to lose my son and see his home broken up.'
'But you haven't really lost him; he's with his mother.'
'A hundred and fifty miles away, behind a locked door!'
'But she lets you see him?'
'When it suits her. And she took him far enough away to make sure it doesn't happen too often.'

'Yes! But there must be two sides to the story. I mean, a court won't punish you unless you do something wrong. Anyway I'm sure things will settle down in time and you'll see more of him when he gets older.'

'Perhaps they will - settle down I mean. Must go now. Bye!'

'God! What's the use?' I thought. It was going to take a long time to change people's attitudes. For many people the word 'woman' means almost the same as 'victim' and they still think of *'women and children.'* This conversation took place early in my Parental Equality days A married man; his response was a healthy reminder that we weren't going to change the world overnight. If I wanted to be there to change anything I had better make plans to live in it as it was.

My first priority was my living space. The little mobile home was pretty, but it was designed for a week's holiday, not for a long stay. There was nothing like enough storage, no place for books or dirty boots or even for my clothes and belongings.

First the two tiny wardrobes had to be ripped out. Then, with half a sheet of plywood and two lengths of dowel I made a good-sized wardrobe with one hanging rail above the other, more than enough for all my clothes.

Next came the shoes. Shoes can clutter a large area when they are spread out on the floor. In my little place I could end up falling over them everywhere. My bedroom had two doors; it had been designed as two tiny 'sleeping cubicles.' One of these doorways was immediately inside the exterior door. Taking down the door, I made a floor-to-ceiling shoe cupboard in the doorway with the remainder of the sheet of plywood and divided it into several shelves about eight inches high. Twenty inches wide, it projected a foot into the corner of the bedroom. There was even enough space for visitors' shoes when they came in. My mobile home would be 'a shoe-free zone.'

The little bathroom had no cupboard. A few cuts through the discarded door with my power saw and then my cordless drill screwed everything together and fixed it on the wall. The bathroom door collided with the door of the bedroom when they were opened together, so I quickly took it off its hinges using the drill, and soon had it hanging again as a sliding door. An extension for the phone meant it could be answered from my bed. My total purchases came to eleven pounds.

There is a joy in building things; I hope Matthew knows it too one day.

Having somewhere to live, my next problem was earning a living. Apart from my credit cards, my money was gone. Joe Healy came to mind. After all we had been friends for many years and I had worked for him before. On the phone he told me he had just bought a large three-story house and he was converting it into flats. Did I want to start tomorrow? Yes! Yes I did!

It was good to be back at work, to have somewhere to go to every day and the company of the lads. It was what I was used to; it was comforting. Christine worked at the edge of the town, so I often collected her on my way home. My days became quite enjoyable.

Best of all was seeing Matthew again. The first Saturday morning I got up at 5:45 and drove to Dublin, arriving at Sally Donnelly's house at 9:45, fifteen minutes early.

Seeing the truck she came to the door, a grim look on her face. 'You're not to have him until ten o' clock,' she announced 'I can't hand him over to you until then.'

She didn't see Matthew running out the door behind her and before she could do anything he had jumped up into my arms.

'So what are you going to do, drag him off?' I said sarcastically. 'Better brush up on the laws about assault first.'

Carrying Matthew to the truck, I could feel the two eyes piercing my back. Even among the ranks of bitter spouses, Sally was notorious for the way she pursued her husband through the courts. A lady barrister, she knew how only too well.

The thought of picking him up had made me nervous for days because of my feeling of having failed him. Had I not allowed him to be taken out of my arms against his will? Would he blame me - the same way I was blaming myself?

There was no need to worry. He was delighted to see. I am convinced that children have a kind of telepathy. Adults do as well of course, but in children the faculty is far sharper. He could sense my thinking about him all the time.

His birthday present was on the seat of the truck. He was only three the last time we were together. Now he was four. I thought of my own fourth birthday, getting up early and making my way up to the stall to 'help' my father milk the cows, feeling big and happy and secure - a man like my dad. 'How would Matthew feel about his dad not being there on his birthday?

In his uncanny way he seemed to know what I was thinking. 'This is like a second birthday, Daddy,' he said.

The day passed all too quickly. Matthew left me cheerfully when he realised that he would see me first thing in the morning. I reached Peter Tierney's house very tired. Getting up at a quarter to six, driving to Dublin, and then spending the day running after a four-year-old had made me feel my age. Peter had insisted that I stay the night as soon as he heard about my visit to Dublin. At dinner, he assured me that since Brenda had now been paid the £9,600, there was nothing to fear from the High Court proceedings.

'Oh but she sent it back again. Gerry Nolan got the cheque in the post during the week.'

'That makes no difference once you paid the money,' he told me. It made me feel much better.

The following day, Matthew and I had breakfast in McDonalds before going to the park. On Sunday afternoons, with the help of the local Methodist Church, Parental Equality holds 'Fathers' Family Time': twenty or thirty children running around a hall with their dads looking on. Matthew joined in the play with enthusiasm.

In between games I read him stories from the children's books on the shelves. One of the stories was about a little teddy bear whose parents split up and so his daddy had to leave the family home. Daddy Bear would visit, take the little bear to the park to play and then leave him home again. When his dad had to leave, the little bear used to get angry and stamp his foot.

Matthew was fascinated with the story. It seemed to echo his feelings. He asked me to read the story again and then a third time. The idea of stamping his foot to give vent to his feelings stayed in Matthew's mind for the rest of the afternoon. For two years, he had been bewildered by forces which had torn his daddy away from him again and again. 'Do you stamp your foot too Daddy when I'm gone?' he asked.

'Always Matthew!' I answered. It wasn't really a lie, just an understatement.

The overnight visit came two weeks later. On the Friday morning I caught the train. Coming out of Dublin on a Friday afternoon is awful! We both had to stand all the way to Limerick junction and the books and games had to stay in the bag. Children in Matthew's situation can be older than their years and he didn't once cry or complain. He seemed to know there was nothing we could do.

We drove to Christine's flat in the truck and the two of them became friends at once. They stayed playing for over an hour while I watched from the sofa. It had been a long day.

On Saturday the three of us went for a walk up the hill and then for a run in the park. Where do children get their energy? It was just as well there were two adults around. On Sunday, there was very little time to do anything except to take him for a short visit to his grandfather before packing his bags and driving to the train. At least we got a seat this time and he seemed resigned to leaving me when we arrived in Dublin. He gave me a hug and left without saying a word.

It was a long journey back. The train was nearly empty and I had the carriage to myself. It was just as well; a conversation was the last thing I wanted. But it gave me a lot of time for thinking and my thoughts didn't exactly cheer me up. It was really my first experience of being an access parent, of seeing my child for a few specified hours a fortnight and then having to give him up again. It's an awful feeling handing over your own child and then seeing the door shut between you - and it does not get better 'in time' - not at all!

These 'weekends' really boiled down to one day; the rest of the time was all travelling. And it was expensive! The train fares alone came to seventy pounds and it cost me another sixty in pay to take Friday off. He still had to be fed, he had to be taken places and of course there was the fifty pounds, the so-called child maintenance to be handed over to his mother every week. It couldn't last. Every month found me deeper in debt. Before long all the travelling would have to stop. What was going to happen then? Back in London, would I just drift out of his life like so many other dads? 'That's what happens to over half of all visiting parents' I thought. 'And for long-distance dads like me the dropout rate must be even higher.'

It was the thought of joint custody that kept me going. This arrangement didn't need to last for much longer. In a few months things would be different; I would not be a visitor but a custodial parent. Matthew would have a home with me and we would be together for all the holidays and mid-term breaks. No longer crippled with 'maintenance' payments I could travel regularly to see him from London. In the meantime contact must be kept up by all possible means, so my credit cards suffered.

According to the agreement, there was to be a phone call from Matthew every Wednesday evening between seven and eight. As Brenda never rang at the same time, it meant sitting by the phone until she called. Whenever I couldn't answer immediately she put the phone down after four or five rings. She knew the courts would not be too bothered.

My response was to phone him at his playschool during the day. However after a few weeks, Sarah his teacher told me he was no longer there.

'He's well able for primary school,' she said cheerfully. 'He's a bright child. No doubt he's *a mensan* like his dad.'

'But he's barely *four!*'

'But his standard of learning is ahead of most five year olds.'

'That's hardly the point...But anyway I was very happy with Southgate School and I'm sorry he's leaving. Thanks for your help. Bye!'

The phone in Gerry Nolan's office was ringing within seconds. 'I'm not having this! Get her in front of a judge!' I told him. There was a long silence.

'My recommendation... is that we leave this until the High Court' he said slowly. It would only inflame matters now.'

'Leave it until it becomes established *for months*? Anyway it will be only a drop in the ocean then, in with all the other stuff. I'm a guardian of my son and I do not consent to his being removed from his school. What is guardianship supposed to mean anyway?'

'It means you have an interest in the life of your child and you are entitled to a say in his upbringing.'

'What does that mean? Anyway I don't care what it means. If we take this lying down she'll walk all over me. I want her in front of a judge and it's got to happen quickly! Can we get some kind of injunction?'

'Owen, Do calm down and think things over! There's a client with me at the moment. I only took your call because you said it was urgent. I'll get back to you.'

'Do, Gerry! And my mind is made up: Issue the summons! Bye!'

That was our last talk as solicitor and client. He did not return any of my calls. Of course no summons was ever issued. Gerry would have had to face Seamus Newman later. It would be no good saying 'Owen insisted' because solicitors are expected to control their clients. They generally live up to the expectation.

By this time Gerry was very anxious to be rid of me as a client. He had learned that there would be no compromise from the other side. Brenda and her feminist legal team were spoiling for a fight. She had very little to lose. Solicitors and barristers look after one another when it comes to legal fees. Moreover her firm was huge; she was in a position to give any barrister as much work as she wanted. In other words, Jill Keegan and Alice Campbell (her senior counsel) were almost certainly working for free, and Colman Kelly was charging very little as Brenda was doing a lot of the work herself. It was going to be a fight.

Solicitors live by negotiating. There is far more money in settling cases than in fighting them. For that reason and because there are so many tricks of the trade that need to be kept secret, they are extremely dependent on one another. Also from the time they begin studying law, they are taught to be loyal to their own colleagues. Gerry was caught between a client who was learning too much and a whole family of solicitors to whom he was accountable on a daily basis. He wanted to get out.

All he needed was an excuse to quit. He got it in the form of a stiff letter from me asking why no summons had been issued in spite of my instructions. He replied, saying that in view of my attitude, he didn't want to act for me any more. I was not surprised.

Brenda knew what she was doing. By establishing Matthew in a school where he might be expected to attend for the next eight years, she was helping her case for sole custody. Her lawyers could argue that it would be disruptive to move him away from his school and his friends. It also put an end to my phone calls.

Coming up to Christmas, her confidence boosted, she went on the offensive again. As she was visiting her parents that weekend, Matthew was at Seamus's house. When I came to collect him, she announced that she was reducing his stayover from two nights to one as 'he needed to spend time with his grandparents.'

'Have him here by five o' clock tomorrow,' she demanded, as he got into the truck.

Chapter 19

'No way!' I replied. 'He's staying with me tomorrow! Ever since you abducted him from the U.K. you seem to think you can do what you like.'

We didn't get back to the mobile home for over an hour as I had some shopping to do. On the way home I slowed down to pass a neighbour on the narrow road. He rolled down his window. 'The Gardaí are looking for you,' he said. 'They said you had kidnapped a child and taken him to England.' So Brenda was up to her tricks again!

On the phone to the local Garda station I said that Matthew was right beside me and I had no intention of taking him anywhere. Of course they insisted on coming over to check it out. Within ten minutes there was a police car in the yard.

'Satisfied?' I enquired; my tone was less than friendly. 'So now she can even report him missing on *my* time and you come running! When she hid him a few months ago when he was supposed to be with me, What did you do? Nothing!'

'He is to be back tomorrow night' said the Garda angrily.

'No! The court order says two nights with me' I told him.

'Well, we were instructed to see that he's back tomorrow night - or we'll have to speak to you again.'

'What I'd like to know is who is giving you your instructions?'

'Look! I have a job to do; it's nothing personal. If you're having problems why don't you go to a solicitor?'

'Good idea!'

Later that evening Brenda phoned me asking when she could collect him the following day. She was chatty and friendly on the phone, so it seemed best to compromise a little, especially as it was near to Christmas. We arranged to hand him over the following evening at six o' clock. Lifting him out of the truck, her father and brother appeared out of the shadows. They were dour and threatening as they took him away.

A week later a summons came ordering me to appear in court. Brenda had made an application to cancel all access.

Making a life was not going to be so easy after all.

CHAPTER 20

The professionals

Other things were running more smoothly. In December, we started building my stables.

They were being built on a bank of rubble, so the foundation had to be a continuous 'raft' of concrete and steel, twenty metres long by six metres wide. When the concrete had set and hardened, the walls could be built on top.

Frank Collins was working as an electrician on a site where there was a large amount of steel mesh left over. So one day after work he helped me to load it onto my pickup truck and we drove out to the yard. The next job was to construct a 'box' out of planks to hold the wet concrete in.

With the aid of an old 'dumpy level', I levelled up the box and nailed it together. Then Frank helped me to cut the steel mesh to shape and tie it together with wire. So far so good, but the concrete posed a problem. It was going to cost me well over a thousand pounds, and I was nearly broke.

Joe Healy came to the rescue. When I hesitantly brought up the subject he jumped in without further prompting. 'How much concrete do you need?'

'About 20 metres, three good loads.'

'Consider it done!' He ordered the concrete there and then, and it was all advanced to me on my wages. Some of my friends were superb.

The three loads were ordered for the following Saturday, so a gang had to be assembled. Frank, John Gildee a friend of his, and John's son all agreed to give me a hand. John, an expert at concrete and groundwork, had spent all his life working on building sites. At fifty years of age he moved like a far younger man; he naturally took command.

His first instruction was to untie the steel along most of the slab area and move it to one side in order to allow the trucks to reverse far enough to empty the concrete throughout the job.

'You might feel like barrowing all that concrete sixty or seventy feet,' he said, 'but I certainly don't.' His tone of voice implied that we should have known better and he was right, we should. Frank and I both have tanned features. It was just as well.

It was also Matthew's weekend to stay over with me, so Christine offered to come and take care of him. He held her hand, watching me untying mesh, while the lads moved it to the sides. There was a sound from the lane and a cab appeared. Matthew stood enthralled as the driver pulled his huge blue truck with it's shining drum up beyond the bank and then reversed until the wheels were about an inch away from the steel. Then he jumped out of his cab back to where John Gildee was already setting up the unloading chute. Matthew had never seen wet concrete before and his eyes were riveted on this grey delightful substance as the driver reversed the drum and the concrete began to pour out.

He could sense the excitement as we all set to work shovelling and tamping or working the vibrator, 'the poker' as it's called in the trade. All the concrete had to be vibrated thoroughly in order to get it to go down through the mesh. Running down to the mobile home, he came back with his toy shovel and he was soon up to the top of his little wellies in concrete, shovelling as hard as any of us.

It was a clear cold December morning but the sweat ran down our backs and faces as we shovelled and poked, tamped and fixed the mesh for the next load. We were half way down a cup of tea when the blue and white drum of the second truck could be seen above the bushes at the sides of the lane. The tea was gulped down as we got ready with our shovels a second time.

The professionals

This load went very smoothly. By now we were used to each other as a team and we instinctively knew what to do. Even Matthew never seemed to get in the way. The rest of the steel was tied a good twenty minutes before the third load and we all sat down to a cup of tea and a rest.

The job was going very well and we were in good spirits, sitting on concrete blocks, mugs in hand. I entertained them with the story of my first experience of using an angle grinder. I was nineteen, used to cutting metal with a hacksaw and hating it. One day, a large piece of steel needed to be cut for welding. My father didn't offer any sympathy. 'No harm to teach you young lads what work is like,' was his contribution. I thought of Joe Healy who had just bought an angle grinder and promptly got on the phone to him.

'I'm in the middle of a job, Owen,' he said. 'So I need it here, but you're welcome to drop over while I'm milking the cows and do the job.' He was still living with his parents at the time, and helping his father on the farm.

There was no need to tell me twice. Ten minutes later we were both standing in his yard.

'You know where the workshop is,' was his greeting before he disappeared into the milking parlour.

Soon my piece of steel was locked in Joe's vice and with goggles in place I lifted up the grinder with its nine-inch disc at the end. Pulling the trigger, I braced myself for the kick and applied the spinning disc to the pencil line on the steel. A shower of sparks told me something was happening and letting go of the trigger, I could see a line four inches long and about one eighth of an inch deep across my pencil mark. All in just over a second! Wonderful!

Confident now, I pulled the trigger and applied the disc again. Within moments the big spinning disc was eating through the metal like a knife going through butter! What a wonderful machine! Flushed with the power of it, I took no notice of the stream of bright sparks nor of the effect on my brown nylon trousers. No notice that is, until the sparks bit into my bare legs. By that time the brown nylon trousers had become brown nylon knickers - with the two leggings hanging down around my shoes!

The lads guffawed to hear how I ran for my car and made for home. Matthew joined in the hilarity too. He didn't understand the story but caught the general mood repeating the words 'nylon knickers' as we laughed out loud.

When the last of the concrete was spread and finished we were almost sorry, the work had gone so smoothly. It was the satisfaction of a job well done.

Now that the work was over, the lads lost no time packing up and driving away. Nobody in the building trade likes to linger on a Saturday. Matthew stood beside me and we both admired our gigantic concrete 'cake' in silence. Then picking him up in my arms, I put him into the wheelbarrow and wheeled him round the yard at a running pace while we both gave whoops of delight. Christine looked on in amusement. The three of us went for a pizza about 4.00 o'clock and stayed in for the evening.

*

Towards the end of December, with no hope of seeing Matthew and the mobile home becoming cold, I decided to return to London. Bob Wilson needed some work done on his new office, so there was work available.

Christine decided to come with me and to go back early in the New Year. Helen, a friend of hers invited us to stay for Christmas. Then I would make arrangements to move back into Gordon Road.

We drove over in the pick-up truck with my tools in the back. Helen was delighted to see us and we had a very enjoyable Christmas. She is a highly accomplished cook and we all did justice to her skills on Christmas day. It passed quickly, the only sour note being when I telephoned Seamus's house they would not let me speak to Matthew. As soon as Margaret heard my voice she slammed down the phone and it was off the hook for the rest of the day. Neither

Christine nor Helen said a word but they flashed me looks of sympathy; it helped. Over dinner we had a lively conversation, even some poetry, so I forgot about Matthew for a while. He came back into my mind with a sharp pang, shortly before going to sleep. The 'vibes' were becoming familiar by now; he was thinking about me.

It was good to be back in London with my friends again. Christine came with me to Gordon Road and we talked about smartening the place up in the New Year.

On the 30th of December my cousin in Harrow phoned me and even before he spoke, I knew something was wrong.

'It's Mother,' he said very quietly. 'She was killed yesterday evening in Limerick.'

My aunt had been struck by a car and died instantly. Aunt Jane, my godmother, was close to me since I was a baby. It was important to attend the funeral, so we 'rang in' the New Year, sound asleep on the ferry on my way to attend a very sad event indeed.

In Limerick, I spoke to a few blocklayers about building the walls of my stables. They promised to come on the third week in January, so I reluctantly abandoned my plans to go back to London for at least a month. Because of delays and frosty weather it was early February before the walls were built. Once they started, they got the job finished in two days and it was great to see my design taking shape before my eyes.

Gerry Nolan called to me in my mobile home. He brought out my files to spare me the ordeal of having to collect them at his office. It was kind of him, and typical. It reminded me of why I had always liked him when we were at school.

'What I can't understand, Owen, is why you didn't just accept that the marriage was over' he said. 'Then you could co-operate with Brenda and you would be seeing more of your son. That's what I'd do in your place.'

'I wonder, Gerry! Do you really know what it's like, having a locked door between yourself and your own flesh and blood, seeing your own child every couple of weeks *by permission?* You are operating a system and you don't want to look too closely at it. You're afraid of what you might see. Besides, there's no problem accepting that the marriage is over. What I can't accept is being a visitor to my child's life, standing outside the door with this access order in my hand that no judge is going to enforce. Matthew hasn't seen me *in a month.*'

'That's your own fault for antagonising Brenda. If you were a bit more diplomatic...'

'Diplomatic! What has my right to seeing my child got to do with being *diplomatic*? And what about his right to see me? But no! His mother is given all the rights by your colleagues; the right to snatch him away from me, the right to shut the door in my face every time she doesn't want us to be together. But of course I'm supposed to be diplomatic; then she'll let us see one another - when it suits her! And when she takes me to the High Court and puts a caution on my father's land, then am I still supposed to be diplomatic?'

'Why not? If it meant that Matthew would be able to see more of you?'

'Because I can only be so much of a hypocrite, that's why! And it's no good being at her mercy. The only way I'll see my son is to show her I'm prepared to fight. We had some very good weapons and you just threw them all away; you didn't want to use them against a colleague.'

'Hang on, Owen! What weapons are you talking about?'

'The protection order for a start, she had no grounds for that at all. If she was found to have obtained a dodgy court order it could be very serious for her as a solicitor. But you got me to drop the whole thing last March. You told me that my agreeing to leave Gordon Road is the same as a barring order. It's not is it? It's not the same thing at all!'

He reddened, but there was no stopping me now.

'There's more than that! In August she assaulted my child so she could break the court order. That's a lot more like the six months you kept talking about, frightening me - and she would never be allowed to practice again. Then what about changing his school without telling me? We could have joint custody ten times over if we showed her we meant business even once. But you prefer to talk down your own client while she hits us with everything she's got.'

Poor Gerry was now quite scarlet. There was a long pause. Eventually he said, 'Owen! You've got to remember that a solicitor's job in family law is to look after the interests of the child as well as those of his own client. That means advising the client to compromise in order to pacify the situation.'

'Bollocks, Gerry! I've spoken to enough dads to know that what you've just given me is the formula used by the dad's solicitor to justify getting him to sign away his children and his home. *"The best thing you can do John - for the children's sake - is to move out quietly. Why don't you get a nice little flat somewhere?"* Tell me Gerry! Of all the dads you advised to sign away custody of their kids, how many did you tell that access orders are not enforced?'

He was silent for over a minute. I felt sorry for him in spite of my anger. He had barely got a word in edgewise.

Eventually he said, 'I have another bit of news for you I've been on the phone to Colman Kelly. Brenda has agreed to drop the case for cancelling all access. Next weekend you can travel up to Dublin for Matthew as usual.'

Now I was silent.

Gerry went on, 'Look! I'm sorry that you aren't happy. I did my best. Here's your cheque for a thousand. I never cashed it. Maybe we can put this behind us with no hard feelings. He sounded very forlorn, hurt even.

We parted on good terms. He gave up family law.

*

By the end of January the spectre of the High Court was looming over me and I didn't have the confidence to do the case on my own.

Joe Healy came to my rescue again. 'I can arrange an interview with Carol Duggan of Murphy, Duggan and Bell' he said. 'See how you get on.'

She saw me in her office a few days later. The office was impressive, part of a large building owned by her firm. 'They certainly seem to be doing well by their clients,' I thought as she beckoned me into a room filled with chairs and a large table. She was low sized, reasonably good looking with dyed blond hair and an accent that had more of the country than the city in it. That at least was comforting. Her face looked shrewd.

'Too shrewd to be wise,' I thought. 'But maybe that's what I need right now.'

One of the first things she brought up was the question of money. That meant another trip to London to cash in the last of my savings.

'Consider it an investment in your property,' she told me.

'Well, well! No fear *she* is going to get personably involved!' I thought. 'This lady is very clear about the difference between her client's interests and her own. Well at least I don't have to pull any punches either.'

Looking across at her I replied, 'Fine - but I want to discuss my objectives regarding the case.'

'And what are they?' her voice got thinner. A client who knows his objectives is always more trouble. Most lawyers would prefer to tell a client what his objectives should be. Then there is no such thing as unsatisfactory service.

'To preserve the agreement of '94 and get joint custody of my son.'

'Well... I have to consider whether or not to take this case on' she said coldly. 'There's a large case load in front of me already and I don't know about taking on one more, especially as it's getting close to hearing.'

'Okay! Perhaps you'll let me know what's happening in some kind of reasonable time.'

She seemed to be bluffing, trying to conduct the case on her own terms. A solicitor-client relationship is normally a matter of the knowing against the unknowing, the powerful against the vulnerable. This is especially true when the client is a dad on the receiving end of a whole lot of terrifying summonses and legal documents. Of course the client is the one with the money but money is only one kind of power. Raw psychological power is far stronger and solicitors normally manipulate their clients as they please. A client who knows what he wants is not a solicitor's ideal. Nevertheless, money is money.

A few days later, I flew back to London and stayed in the loft at Gordon Road. It was like returning home after a long weary journey. There was a competition for the best controversial speech of the evening at the Speakers Club in Hammersmith and my speech got joint-first. My topic was the educational system and how it eats into a child's zest for living. For a while I forgot my situation, forgot that my child had been taken from me, and gave myself up the fun of entertaining my old friends. It was a good feeling.

The following morning, my first job was to telephone my answering machine in Limerick; there were two messages from Carol Duggan. So much for not being interested in me as a client. I had made up mind to stay in London but at the mention of this the anxiety in her voice came through.

'No, you must base your residency here in Ireland.'

'I don't see why.'

'It's your only chance to get joint custody of Matthew,' she answered glibly. 'You'll have to trust me here. Either I run this case my way or I won't have anything to do with it'

'What about the fact that she took Matthew illegally from this country? Isn't there a strong case for staying here and asking that he be brought back?'

'You haven't a hope, not after two years, your only chance is to set up a proper home in Ireland.'

She didn't quite convince me, but I didn't have the knowledge or the confidence to back my own judgement. 'What about this big compliment about taking my case at our meeting?' I wondered. 'Why has that suddenly disappeared?

Chapter 20

Was she ordering me back just to keep from losing a lucrative high court case?'

Brenda was now claiming that Gordon Road was still half hers even though she had not paid any of the mortgage payments since signing it over to me, so her estate agent had to be allowed to value the house. As soon as that was over and I had done a few jobs for Bob Wilson on his new premises I reluctantly boarded a flight to Shannon.

By now I was reconciled to staying until after the hearing, which was due in late April. Limerick did have some attractions: Christine was nearby and I could get on with building my stables. The stables were my lifeline during those few months. They kept my mind occupied and fulfilled; they doubled as a favourite project and a job to do during the day. They kept me physically and mentally occupied designing and fixing the roof, then making and hanging the doors. Looking at each day's achievement I felt far away from the lawyers and all their courts and summonses.

But they soon came nearer. A letter arrived from Carol Duggan instructing me to travel to Dublin to see a psychologist who would assess Brenda and me as parents. The psychologist was to be Alice Condon who was based in Limerick but it seemed that she was unavailable. Instead we were to see Pauline Maxwell at the Sandymount Clinic in Dublin.

'She trained with my uncle,' Carol Duggan assured me, so I took the train to Dublin one Monday morning and presented myself at the clinic at 11.00am. There seemed to be no clients present other than myself but the receptionist told me that Brenda was already inside with Dr Maxwell.

'Strange!' I thought. 'Shouldn't she be interviewing me first? After all this is all our doing, isn't it?' Anyway I was confident. At least we were moving; something was being done about Matthew. I had made up my mind not to concentrate on Brenda at the interview but to tell her about the relationship between Matthew and me and to give full details of the ill treatment of Matthew the previous year.

At last the door opened and Brenda came out looking guilty and a little uneasy. There was no time to puzzle over that. This was my first chance to get a hearing for all the wrong that had been done to my little son. I made straight for the door and into the room.

Pauline Maxwell was sitting at a desk facing the door. She was in her mid fifties with a gaunt slim look as though she was on a diet. Her manner was easy and pleasant; her voice was rural, West of Ireland.

There was no need for prompts. Starting with the time Matthew was dragged away by Brenda while he was holding on to my leg, I went on to describe the awful incident in August when Matthew was screaming 'I want my Daddy.' Brenda's anger at being in an unhappy marriage was mentioned, but only barely. Most of the interview was spent telling her of my relationship with Matthew; how he loved to be with me, of the stories I used to tell him, many of them from classical mythology.

Here she cut across me looking displeased. 'What's wrong with *Irish* mythology. Why don't you tell him stories of Ireland?' was what she said. It was as though she didn't want to hear any more. I changed tack, telling her of my own relationship with my father at Matthew's age; how he told me so much and developed my mind, of the bond between us and how Matthew had a very similar relationship with me. Here she seemed displeased once more, so coming straight to the point I told her that my main objective was joint custody of my son.

'Why not go for sole custody?' she responded in her sweetest tone.

'What? Well... sole custody is child abuse - taking away a parent I mean. Mind you, after all Matthew's ill treatment, I'm not so sure. But joint custody is the one to go for. They told me I hadn't a hope of getting sole custody anyway.'

'Who told you that?' Her tone was incredulous.

'Just about everybody! Gerry Nolan for one; he was my solicitor before Carol Duggan.'

We let the matter drop but the fact that she seemed to be urging me to go for sole custody was very encouraging. She must have been very impressed by me as a parent.

When she brought up the rows between Brenda and me when we were living together, I told her the truth. There was a lot of shouting and we each gave each other slaps on the cheek but that neither of us ever struck the other in a way that could hurt.

'Did your parents ever row like that?' she asked me.

'They never showed their feelings at all, let alone start shouting at one another,' was my reply.

It was time to break. Helpfully, she told me of a very good pub-lunch up the road. Afterwards she was to see Matthew first on his own, then Matthew and Brenda, next Matthew and me, finally all three of us together.

So Brenda was ahead of me again! This was our part of the battle, or was it? There was no one in the waiting room, not a soul! As the minutes ticked by there was nothing to do except read some silly magazine.

Finally the door opened and Brenda appeared, this time looking less uneasy. She told me that it was my turn to go in and I went, feeling a little worried. What if she had told Matthew that I was angry or something and he wouldn't be happy to see me? My mind was racing thinking the worst.

But Matthew was delighted to see me as usual, and ran straight into my arms. Holding him, I relaxed again, my confidence restored. Pauline Maxwell observed my interaction with Matthew for a while and then began to ask me some more questions. My answer to one question was that he would be better off out of Dublin 'where half his class would be on drugs.' Hyperbole is a standard form of expression among rural people like myself. I meant that there was a serious chance of a drug problem among his classmates if he went to a Dublin school, and she understood me perfectly. She spoke to Matthew for a few minutes after that and the interview was over.

Then it was time for all three of us to have a short interview together. This went off easily, with Matthew happy to have his parents together again. We both agreed to have one more mediation session together without Matthew a few days later. It surprised me that Brenda would agree to go to mediation with our side's psychologist but I was glad that she did.

At the next session, my first remark was that it was wrong for Matthew to live all the time with a parent who was in full time work, when there was another parent who was prepared to devote the time to taking care of him. Brenda and Pauline Maxwell exchanged looks; it made me very uneasy. Something wasn't right. Nevertheless I ploughed ahead outlining my plans for joint custody. During term time, one of us would have him during the week and the other would see him once a fortnight. The visiting parent during school time would be his main parent during mid-term breaks and holidays while the other parent could visit him every fortnight.

Brenda immediately said there was no way she would agree to that, offering instead a tiny amount of extra access. My reply was that Matthew was her son and *my* son and if we couldn't agree on some method of sharing residence there was no point in being there.

At this point Pauline Maxwell interrupted me to say that this meeting was to see what we could agree on - not what we couldn't! She went on to talk in terms of access visits for me, a train of thought that didn't please me at all. 'Access' is a hateful word for dispossessed dads. It seems to mock any chance of a parental relationship.

My trust and confidence were now turning to suspicion. I felt like an outsider in the room.

Brenda meanwhile was visibly relaxing. 'You know, sometimes Matthew says 'I'm going to my Daddy now.' She said with a little laugh as though she were a secure mother who would never in her life prevent her child from seeing his father.

It was a relief that the interview was over. Brenda allowed me to play with Matthew in the park before taking the train back to Limerick.

CHAPTER 21

Baptism of fire

Two weeks later the report came. I read it through and then read it again. Clearly, at the last session all was not well, but on the first day she couldn't have failed to get a good impression of me. I still had enough faith in 'professional integrity' to believe that Dr. Maxwell would convey this in her report.

My faith didn't last long; it was the most thorough whitewash job I had ever seen. Brenda came out of the report absolutely blameless. Everything said about her was positive and praiseworthy. She was the perfect parent: loving, enthusiastic, secure - and was more than happy to involve me, the father in bringing up *her* child.

Dr. Maxwell paraphrased Brenda's account as though she believed every word. *'Brenda described a happy home life, and how she went on to university and obtained a law degree'*, a clever mixture of a claim with an indisputable fact in order to give credibility to the claim.

My account, by contrast, was written so nobody would believe it. How did she do this?

First and foremost, she used an incredulous sneering tone, *'He describes himself as a builder - he lives in a mobile home.'* Secondly, everything she recounted was prefaced with 'he feels' or 'he believes', a very deliberate technique to isolate my version of events - noticeably absent from Brenda's. More blatantly, she put several of my remarks in inverted commas, *'He feels Mrs. Sheridan is insecure with Matthew'.* Inverted commas are a well-known literary device for disparagement and contempt. They do not occur once in Brenda's story.

Most important of all was what Dr. Maxwell left out. My side of the story was only half as long as Brenda's and what she left out was critical. The whole incident where Matthew was screaming out the window was ignored in my account, - but not in Brenda's. *'The police had to be called, as Mr Sheridan was outside her flat shouting at her.'* No mention of Matthew at all!

Finally Brenda's account was before mine, giving that vital first impression. That would put me at a disadvantage even if the language was neutral and impartial – and it was anything but that.

During the interview I had carefully explained how Brenda had obtained various safety orders by making allegations and how several of these allegations could not possibly be true. My explanation was dismissed in a half sentence *'court orders, which in his view were not based on reality.'*

The report was full of ambiguity and half-truths. *'Mr Sheridan admitted there were rows of a violent nature'*. For most of us, that phrase conjures up a picture of the man beating the woman; it's what we have been conditioned to think. My words were "some of our rows became shouting matches and once or twice we even slapped each other on the cheek, but neither of us ever struck the other in a way that would hurt."

Two sentences in the report helped me. One said that Matthew was happy to be with me and did not miss his mother even when he got tired; the other that Matthew expressed anger towards his mother. Maxwell included these items to protect herself in case another psychologist examined Matthew. A long paragraph followed. It described the *'playful, happy way'* that Matthew and his mother interacted *with one another, how well attuned Brenda was to his needs* and how *inevitable* it was that Matthew show anger toward her as *'she had the daily task of disciplining him'*.

I had no chance. The report was careful to avoid any mention of Brenda's being in full time work and my wish for joint custody was changed to one for sole custody. Joint custody might even (heaven forbid!) make me look reasonable.

The conclusion was that Brenda get sole custody of Matthew and my two-day visit to Dublin be changed to two one-day visits. In other words, she wanted to make seeing my son more expensive and time consuming, to bring me into line with the pathetic 'McDonalds access' of so many dads.

Eventually, I calmed down and put pen to paper detailing some of the more blatant examples of bias in a five-page document for Carol Duggan.

Leaving Matthew with his grandfather, I drove into Limerick and phoned Carol Duggan from a phonebox, hoping she would see me right away.

'What do you think of the report?' she asked me a little too casually.

'I think it stinks!'

'What do you mean?

'I mean the thing is a complete whitewash job, It takes Brenda's side from beginning to end. There isn't a bad word about her in it, or a good word about me.'

'Give me an example!'

'Well, take the time when Matthew was screaming "I want my Daddy" outside the flats. She completely ignored my side of the story; even though I told her there were about a hundred witnesses. What she wrote was "Mr Sheridan was outside her flat, shouting at her and the Gardaí had to be called." No mention of Matthew at all!

'How dare you badmouth Brenda in front of Matthew! That's appalling behaviour for a parent! I have to go now.'

'But wait, Matthew isn't....'

She had put the phone down. Walking to her office, I dropped in my five-page answer to the report and asked for an appointment as soon as possible.

It was now early April, so another psychologist's report had to be obtained very soon. To my relief, the telephone rang the same afternoon and Carol Duggan offered to see me the following day.

'One thing,' she added, 'You mustn't bring Matthew into the office during the consultation.'

Up to this Matthew had always come along with me when he was in Limerick. He played with the secretaries or amused the clients waiting in the lobby during my time in Carol Duggan's office. Every ten or fifteen minutes he would poke his head in the door to make sure I was still there and then he would go back playing again.

'Isn't that a bit sudden? Surely there's no need; it's not as if he can hear anything.'

'No! It wouldn't be ethical,' she announced. 'If you can't make arrangements we'll just have to make it another day.'

There was no choice but to 'make arrangements', and the following day I was in her office with the report in my hand.

'You must remember, Owen, Dr Maxwell is a *professional*! That's what you don't seem to realise.'

'Professional or not her report is biased and I know the reason.'

'Oh! What is it?'

'There wasn't a trace of another client in three visits to her office. Brenda's firm is huge, they can give her more work than she can possibly do. There's another reason too.'

'And what's that?'

'Both herself and Brenda are part of the system; they are accountable to one another and they are both women and mothers so they are likely to be in sympathy. And she was probably influenced by this "brutal husband story" that's doing the rounds, as well.'

'What are you saying? How dare you suggest that Dr Maxwell is not honest? She is a professional; she trained with my uncle in Dublin.'

'Well, she recommended sole custody of Matthew to Brenda and that is the opposite of what we want. And she was so nice to me at the interview and so helpful. She even suggested a place for me to have lunch... My god! She was probably expecting I'd have a pint, and then she could report the smell of drink from my breath. The place she recommended was a *pub*.' I gave a gasp.

Carol Duggan looked uneasy. Finally she said, 'Look! You're going to have to trust me. If you don't trust me I can't handle your case. The proceedings are coming up in a few weeks and how are you going to get someone to act for you at that kind of notice. I don't need your case. There are hundreds of them on my books right now. You'd better decide now. Do you trust me or not?'

I was worried and she knew it. I changed tack while trying to get my thoughts together.

'What about this matter of a barrister. We have only four weeks to go! Isn't it about time we saw someone? Brenda has been briefing her counsel for *over a year*.'

'Well... Fergus Cronin won't handle it, so we'll have to look elsewhere - but I'll have news for you soon.'

'Anyway, we must have another psychologist's report! We can always adjourn. Brenda's solicitor's name is on top of this report. I understood from you that this was our move, now if seems that Maxwell was her choice; so we can have ours.'

She didn't reply for a moment, then she said, 'First I need £400 from you, that's half the cost of this report. She must be paid.'

'You must be joking! Pay her for this pack of lies, for helping to steal my son. There's no way! Brenda can pay for her report and we'll pay for ours. That's only fair.'

'Also,' she went on ignoring me, 'I need more money to carry on with this case. Can you let me have another £3,000? You have to make up your mind to trust me if I'm to continue working for you.'

I wrote out a cheque for £2,000, handed it to her and walked out of the office feeling totally bewildered. After picking Matthew up at his grandfather's I turned my attention to him for the rest of the day and put it out of my mind.

The following morning a letter came from Carol Duggan berating me once again for daring to criticise 'a professional' and saying my comments were 'a bit daft.' I immediately got her on the phone.

'Carol, I want another psychologists report, is that clear? And you must arrange it as soon as possible. If that thing is the only expert opinion guiding the judge it will be a disaster. Have you got that?'

'I have but I've also had Colman Kelly on the phone. He has arranged for McCarthy, Quinn & Co. to value your property here in Limerick. When can you accommodate them?'

'Any time you like but please go ahead with the other psychologist, there's no time to waste.'

'Can you see me here this week?'

'Yes I can, but for what?'

'Let's say tomorrow at 3.00pm.'

The meeting brought another demand for money to pay Maxwell and another instruction from me to obtain another child psychologist. To my surprise she seemed to agree. 'I'll contact you during the week,' she told me.

She also brought up another matter, which she had mentioned once or twice before.

'My opinion is, you'll have to *buy* joint custody of your son,' was the line, which she was to keep repeating until the day of the hearing. 'It's the only way you are going to get it.'

That comment stayed with me; it made sense. The courts are notoriously biased against men and Brenda had had Matthew living with her for two years even if she broke the law to do it.

It also had the effect of increasing my trust in Carol Duggan again. I was a drowning man and she was the biggest straw.

With Matthew back in Dublin, it was time to make a burst to finish my stables. By now the roof was on and the doors made and hanging.

Next the electricity had to go in and the concrete path to the front had to be extended to meet government regulations. Even though Frank Collins was busy, he managed to give me two days work.

The first day we began to tackle the concrete. We had to erect a framework of planks on edge about two feet from the original path and parallel to it, then pour the concrete in.

One of the planks was already jammed in concrete. A lot of heaving and grunting only broke the plank leaving a jagged end crossing the site of our path.

There was nothing to do, but soak the jammed section of plank in petrol and burn it out. We had a four-gallon drum of petrol handy for the chainsaw and I poured some over the exposed part of the plank, then set it alight. It began to burn very slowly.

Frank was setting up the shutter at the other end of the building. I said something quickly to him and then turned back to the plank, holding the drum of petrol in my hand. Unthinkingly, my eyes on Frank, I opened the cap and sloshed some more petrol on the burning wood. The look of horror on his face made me turn my head. There was a continuous flame from the burning plank all the way to the drum and when the flames licked my hand my grip relaxed and the drum fell to the ground. Almost immediately it exploded, sending flames up to the timbers in the roof of the building.

'It's gone!' I said with a groan. Then I ran forward and began to kick frantically at the blazing drum in order to move it away from the stables. Frank yelled at me to move away.

The stables had been my lifeline for the previous five months. They had settled my mind and given me a project to do at a time when it was desperately needed. It was unthinkable to abandon them without a fight. Only vaguely conscious of Frank's yelling, I could see nothing but my beloved stables about to be burnt down.

My kicks had moved the burning drum a couple of feet when all of a sudden there was a tremendous pain in my right ankle. I was on fire! My synthetic sweatpants and white running shoes were ablaze. The flames bit deeper; I was yelling.

Throwing myself on the ground, I tried to smother the blaze - but the petrol-soaked nylon was not going to be extinguished so easily. Now both my legs were burning inside my trousers and the pain was unbearable causing me to roar at the top of my voice.

I was burning for perhaps ninety seconds before Frank succeeded in removing my trousers and the smouldering shoes. The pain seemed to vanish. Shock is wonderful! I stood in my underpants without shoes or socks with the skin gone from most of my lower legs and part of the flesh burnt away. In disbelief, Frank watched me hobble up to the blazing drum and push it away with a plank. It seemed like a dream - but my stables were safe!

We were nearly at the hospital when the pain came back. Frank pulled me out of the car and helped me in to the accident and emergency desk.

'My legs are burnt,' it was a whisper.

The last thing I remember is lying on my back with Christine standing beside me and getting a second dose of morphine, before drifting off the sleep.

CHAPTER 22

Countdown

I was in hospital and I couldn't walk.

It's strange the things we take for granted. An attendant had woken me up with a cup of tea and a boiled egg and my first conscious thought was that my bladder was about to burst. They had given me copious amounts of water to drink before putting me to sleep the night before. Pulling the covers away, I discovered both my lower legs wrapped in thick white bandages. Hospital beds are high, so even sitting on the side, my legs dangled above the ground. Gently easing my way down, I put the weight on my feet. The pain tore up my legs and along the side of my body. The solution was a 'pigeon' supplied by an understanding staff nurse; it came in very handy.

Later in the morning a young nurse came to change my bandages. She was about twenty and finishing her second year of training. Seeing my burns she winced. The huge blisters, the blood and the black holes in my flesh were not a pretty sight. Pulling the saturated gauze gingerly away from my flesh, she seemed to feel more pain than I did. It was as if I was the spectator and she had the injury. Her job done, she wheeled me back to the ward and helped me into bed.

This was probably the strangest turn of events at all. I was helpless. For the previous five years I had always been fighting in one way or another, to survive, to save my marriage, to save my house, to keep my son. Now here was something that could not be fought. There were two choices: kick and struggle or submit gently to the inevitable.

As the days passed by the routine of the hospital became familiar. So did the strict regime of Sister Barratt who was in charge of our ward. She was tough, but in the interests of the patients. There was no malice in the way she turned down my two requests to go out and see my stables and I did not resent it. She probably concluded that I might get caught up in the job and not come back - and she may have been right!

The nurses and staff were pleasant and genuinely caring as they went about their jobs. Seeing them hard at work every day, it was impossible to avoid a comparison with the grasping and deceit of the legal profession.

The surgeon cut an enormous swath of skin from my right thigh and wrapped it around the lower leg. It was amazing to think that they could 'flay' so much skin from my body and sew it on again somewhere else and yet there was no hurt, no pain. The wonders of anaesthetic, the art of touching the body without touching the mind!

A lot of visitors came and they were good company but best of all were the long periods by myself. Reading, writing and just thinking filled my days. Nurses, doctors, patients, the dimpled physiotherapist with the grip of iron and all the staff, these were the neighbours who greeted me every day in my wheelchair and the hospital was my home. Christine came every evening and she phoned me during the day. It felt like she was never far away.

Matthew eventually came down to see me accompanied by Brenda. The wheelchair fascinated him but he was gone in an hour.

The best thing about a long hospital stay is that it gives you time to think. Before long it became clear to me that the best thing for Matthew would be to offer Brenda a compromise. I wrote her a letter, and gave it to her as she left Matthew with me. It read:

Dear Brenda,
I have been thinking about a long-term compromise that will allow us to co-operate in parenting Matthew.

Here it is:
Firstly: We share residency/custody of Matthew.
Secondly: I agree that his primary residence will be with you; my home will be his secondary residence.
Thirdly: I agree to give this arrangement my full co-operation and support.
                Sincerely,
                Owen

After a few days I telephoned her in Dublin and asked her had she considered it.

'Oh, there's nothing in that for me,' was what she said.

'Nothing? What about my co-operation and support?'

'You have to talk to my solicitor, or, better still, put it in writing and send it to him.

'It's in writing already. Has your solicitor not seen it?'

Silence.

'Well? Has he seen the letter or not?'

'I refuse to discuss it! Now, do you want to speak to Matthew?'

'No, I'll speak to him later'

It was the same stonewalling ever since our first row. There was nothing to do, just grit my teeth and put up with it. In one way it's hard to blame her. With the courts completely on the side of the woman, it's hard to expect her to compromise, even for the sake of the child. So there would be no agreed settlement; we would have to have our day in court and that was that. I might have known.

My term in hospital lasted the whole month of May and the rest did me good. Towards the end, I could hobble about for short distances with the aid of a stick given to me by my father before the stabs of pain brought me back to bed. Outside the window, spring was turning into summer.

When the doctor came to see me one Friday, he found me quite reconciled to spending another week there. Nevertheless a thrill came over me when he allowed me to go home, like a child being let out of school on a Friday afternoon. He told me not to drive for a week but the same evening I got into the truck and took Christine out to dinner. There were no ill effects, but Sister Barratt knew her job.

Things began to happen very quickly after that. The case was to be heard in a few weeks and Carol Duggan agreed to see me the following day. At the meeting I felt somewhat unreal. It was as if years had passed since going into hospital. She seemed to sense my bewilderment and used it to her full advantage.

'What about the other psychologist's report?' I asked her, trying to sound determined and strong.

'Oh, there's no time for that now. Besides, they don't have to agree to it,' she answered.

'Well then, lets go on our own and have a report just on Matthew and me. Then we can cross-examine Maxwell at the hearing and their refusal will look suspicious.'

'I'm telling you there isn't time.'

'Well, adjourn the hearing.'

'They don't have to agree to that either.'

'Yes but can't we ask the judge since it's important?'

'Well, he may accuse us of stalling, it's being adjourned once already.'

'Because I wasn't able to walk into the courtroom, for God's sake! He can hardly blame us for that!'

'The thing is, Owen, another report is not going to get you joint custody. As I've being telling you before, you are going to have to *buy* joint custody from your wife. It's the only way you'll get it.'

She moved on to discuss financial matters but it was hard to give her my full attention. I found myself very weary. Even the trip in the truck and the walk across town to her office made me tired. Was my body so unused to exercise or was it the nature of the business? The second, probably. Hospital was a kind of escape, from the nightmare. Now that it was back again, part of me wanted to stay away. I felt weak and my leg began to throb. It was an effort to gather my thoughts for the matter at hand.

'When are we going to see a barrister?' I interrupted. She was taken aback. My question had cut across her in mid-sentence and the word 'barrister' was evidently causing her some discomfort.

'Sorry! I'm still not quite myself. What you were saying about buying joint custody? I'm very reluctant to abandon the '94 agreement, it seems to be the most solid ground we have.'

'Look Owen, you have to trust me to run this case. I've been handling family law for ten years and I'm good at my job. Now either we handle it my way or I don't handle it at all. You must understand that I don't need your case. There are an awful lot of cases on my books. If I pull out you'll just have to get an adjournment of the hearing. Otherwise you'll be on your own at the High Court, *unrepresented*. You'd better make up your mind between this and the next day what it's to be. Now I can see you're not feeling well; we'd better call it a day. Let's make it next Thursday. Phone me if you can't make it.'

The barrister was forgotten.

The next few days were spent in a quandary. What was the best thing to do? The interview had brought me back to reality and the realisation that my case was only four weeks away. I had an uneasy feeling that all wasn't well with Carol Duggan but in my upset state it was hard to know whether to trust my feelings or not.

*

'If you ask me Owen, you saved yourself some money, by not getting that other report.'

'Why?'

'It would have made no difference at all. These "caring professionals" are all the same; they know which side their bread is buttered on.'

Tony was talking to me one evening after a Parental Equality meeting. It was cold comfort. Was Carol Duggan right after all?

*

What was the best thing to do about Pauline Maxwell and her report? Carol Duggan was insisting on half the cost, so I reluctantly made up my mind to pay. However I composed a note to Dr. Maxwell, which read as follows:

> Dear Ms. Maxwell,
> I was appalled to read the report you made out concerning my family. I have never seen such a collection of bias and lies in my life. It is disgraceful coming from somebody who claims to be a professional person.
> Fortunately the bias is blatant and obvious and my barrister will have no problem exposing it in court.
> Owen Sheridan

At our next meeting I handed this note to Carol Duggan with the money due to Maxwell and instructed her to send it with the fee. As she read the note a look of fury came over her face. There was a pause. Finally she looked up at me.

'That's not true,' she said. 'That's a lie!'

'What's a lie?'

'Saying your barrister will have no problem. No barrister has seen it.'

'If he did, he wouldn't have a problem. I could tear that report to pieces myself.'

'She handed me the note. 'I can't send this,' she said. 'It would be unprofessional.'

'Okay then, I'll have to send it myself.'

'No! We have three weeks to the hearing, now you have to let me do this my own way otherwise I just can't act for you.'

'Well, what are you going to do about joint custody then?'

'I keep telling you; you'll have to buy joint custody from Brenda.'

'You mean do away with the '94 agreement?'

'Yes! I believe this case should be settled; its in your interest and Matthew's. Anyway, you should have paid her all the money.'

'I did pay her all the money; she sent back the last £9,600.'

'You should have paid her on time before she took out the High Court proceedings.'

'The High Court had nothing to so with it. She was paid as we agreed. We made a slight variation of the terns by word of mouth afterwards.'

'There is no documentary evidence of that.'

'Yes there is! She was paid more than the agreement and the letter from her solicitor asking for the £9,600 and not another amount, is evidence.'

'There is also the matter of the reconciliation.'

'What reconciliation?'

'You reconciled for a period during 1995.'

'No, we didn't, we made eight or nine attempts but I never could stay longer than a few days with her before she acted up.'

'That's enough. One night spent together as man and wife can nullify a separation agreement.'

'What? One night? You've got to be joking!'

But she could see me weakening, unsure of my ground and she didn't let the opportunity slip.

'Look Owen, have you any idea how many cases I've done? I know what I'm doing. This must be settled - but Colman Kelly doesn't know that of course. I told him that we're fighting this one to the last - that way we'll get a better deal. But I can't work with a client who won't take advice. If you think you know better than me, you'll have to do the case on your own.'

'I wrote out a document laying out the terms of the '94 agreement including the small variations and you have it in your files,' I replied. But she had me well on the defensive by now.

Ignoring me she pressed home.

'I see a settlement involving joint custody of Matthew and you paying Brenda a sum of money. Now, what would you pay her to become a custodial parent of your son?'

'I don't know.'

'Come on, you must have some idea, you know that being a non-custodial parent you have no rights, at all. Even your visiting rights will not be enforced as you've told me often enough. Is it important to Matthew that you have a share in his life or not?'

'Of course it is.'

'Well, how important is it?'

'Very important, he wants his daddy.'

'Well then, how much will you pay to get joint custody of your son?'

Silence.

'Will you pay anything? Is that how it is?'

'I'm reluctant to reward her for bringing these proceedings. We made an agreement in Gordon Road. We shook hands on it. She drew it up into a legal document and I kept faithfully to the bargain. You have the details in the document I gave you in April.'

'But what about your son? What would you give for his sake? Would you give anything?'

'I suppose... if it would settle things and for joint custody I'd give her twenty thousand instead of the ten.'

She smiled. 'It would be good value for money and Matthew would thank you when he gets older. I've seen him with you, he is very fond of you.'

Coming out of the office I felt weary and confused. On the way home, it occurred to me that she still hadn't told me about the barrister.

Now with only three weeks to go, it was an effort to phone her office for another appointment. Why? Every visit seemed to make me feel weak and demoralised. The next (she eventually phoned me) was no exception. Once more the pressure was subtly applied to intimidate me into an agreement I did not want. She told me how in these matters judges often gave costs to the plaintiff, so there might be an extra £20,000 to pay if we didn't come to a settlement.

In her files, she found the document detailing how I had kept to the terms of the '94 agreement and handed it to me saying 'It's best if you keep this.'

'I don't understand.'

She told me the document would expose me to cross-examination and moved on to other matters. She was in complete control of the meeting; the only exception was when I brought up the subject of the barrister.

She looked uneasy and eventually told me that Fergus Cronin couldn't take the brief and she was approaching another 'top quality' barrister and all would be well.

'Who is it?' I asked.

'I can't tell you. You'll have to trust me on this one.'

I didn't seem to have a lot of choice.

The worry was causing me to wake in the middle of the night and it was difficult to concentrate on anything for very long. Peter Tierney had not been in contact for some time, so in desperation I telephoned him one night at his home.

His advice was chilling. 'I don't do family law, Owen,' he said. 'But if you have a High Court hearing in a week and you still haven't seen a barrister then you'd better be prepared to settle.' My sleeping didn't improve.

The case was to be heard on the Wednesday. At 3.00pm on Monday, Carol Duggan brought me up to the courthouse for an hour's consultation with Sheila Rawson BL. She appeared about five minutes late in her wig and gown, looking bothered.

Our first problem was we couldn't find a consulting room. Eventually we came across a small room at the back of the building. My watch said 3.23pm.

Ms. Rawson looked at her notes. She rapped out a date and asked me to tell her about what happened. While trying to place this date among all the events that happened during the marriage, she interrupted me impatiently.

'Oh, this won't do at all,' she said. 'You must be very clear about what happened if we're to fight this case and you're being cross-examined. What do you remember regarding violence in the marriage?'

'Brenda occasionally slapped me on the cheek when she got really angry. I'm sorry to say I did the same to her. It happened very seldom and none of us ever struck the other in a way that could hurt. We got frustrated living together, that's all.'

'That's not what she says in the affidavit, are you saying that these slaps came both ways?'

'Yes I am! - And I have no problem being cross-examined on that.'

'I see,' she said doubtfully, shaking her head slightly. 'Well, *one thing* in your favour, you're making a great effort to see your son.'

'It's a seven hundred mile trip! It must stop! We'll have to share the travelling. It was only meant to last a few months. By the way, have you seen the separation agreement?'

'Yes I have but there was reconciliation after that.'

'No there wasn't, only a lot of attempts.'

'How long were the attempts?'

'A few days usually.'

'Did you sleep in the same bed?'

'Sometimes yes, mostly no.'

'Oh well, that's enough! One night together is enough to set aside a separation agreement. (There it was again!) 'And you were staying in her house until November?'

'On the couch. She used to let me stay for purposes of access to Matthew.'

'That's enough about that. I won't go in defending that agreement.'

She turned towards Carol Duggan and began speaking to her alone. Again I felt weak and uneasy. It was a relief when the clock stuck four. We had spent thirty-five minutes discussing my case.

How did I keep calm during those awful days? Three things helped me. The stables kept me occupied during the day, making and hanging the doors, fixing the gutters, laying on the water. Also, it helped a lot to discuss the case with my friends in Parental Equality. They were interested in and very supportive.

Finally, Christine was a tower of strength. We saw each other every day. She would come home from work, spend a few hours at her own place before travelling out to the mobile home with me in the truck. Then she would stay with me until I dropped her to work in the morning. I was hard company, not irritable or demanding, but distracted and unable to sleep. Although bearing it superbly, towards the end she too was feeling the strain. We decided to take a holiday in the west of Ireland when the proceedings were over.

CHAPTER 23

The halls of justice

Christine had booked us into a hostel near O'Connell Street, within walking distance of the Four Courts.

The day before, at her suggestion, I went to the doctor, and he prescribed a course of sleeping pills. That night I took half a tablet. During the day Carol Duggan had told me on the phone that the judge 'would have to make law' in order to overturn the existing separation agreement. It may have been this news or the tablet, but I had a good night's sleep.

After breakfast, we walked along the quay towards the Four Courts building where Carol Duggan was to meet me at a quarter past ten. We weren't sure if Christine would be allowed into the building because of the in-camera rule, so she decided to remain outside. The Four Courts is large and intimidating, but crossing the main foyer to meet Carol Duggan, my stride was still quick and confident.

She advanced to meet me looking very angry.

'Where have you been?' she demanded.

'In the hostel' I replied. 'What's wrong?'

'What's wrong? You're three quarters of an hour late! That's what's wrong!'

'A quarter past ten you said - it's only ten past by my watch.'

'You were supposed to be here at half past nine.'

'Half past nine? Hang on! I'll have a look in my diary.' She sounded so certain. Had I made a mistake?

'Look! "A quarter past ten!" There's no mistaking that for half past nine.'

'Well I must have said a quarter *to* ten then and you didn't hear me.'

'As far as I can remember...'

'Never mind that! There's something we must talk about.' She sounded like a hanging judge about to pass sentence and my confidence was leaving me rapidly.

'You never told me about this.' She was pulling out a piece of paper.

'What's that?'

'Your special savings account, that's what!' She put the paper on the top of her file and thrust it under my nose.

'But this account is three years old. I closed it to pay Brenda in '94.'

'That doesn't matter; you swore a false affidavit. The judge would be furious if he knew.' She sounded almost triumphant.

'You can't be serious?' I said doubtfully. 'We'll just have to tell him I made a mistake and forgot about this. Anyway it can't make a lot of difference. It's quite clear that there was nothing to gain.'

'That's not the point! Can't you see? You swore a false affidavit of means. We can't go in now; we'll have to go for a settlement.'

We were walking upstairs as we spoke. On the first floor we went through double doors to a long corridor and then stopped beside a window. The place had the atmosphere of a church. It seemed to demand reverence and hushed tones.

'No! It wasn't a false affidavit. If anything was left out it was because I forgot. In any case it's all the more evidence of the agreement.'

'Look! Are you going to let me run this case or not?' She seemed to grow bigger and more angry. 'It's not too late for me to pull out you know - and then you can deal with the judge anyway you like. But if I'm doing this case I do it *my way!* Is that clear?'

She seemed so sure of herself. It was my first time in the building and now I became conscious of the surroundings.

The silence, the high dome, the black 'bats' that fluttered by, they were all very intimidating.

'Of course you have to run the case,' I stammered, 'but...'

'Well you must be honest with me - not hiding large sums of money making my job impossible. Now we'll have to get out of this. Do they know about the special savings account I wonder?'

'Of course Brenda knows about it. There was £10,000 left in it when I closed it to pay her. Don't you think we should just come clean about this? It must be plain enough that I had no reason to deceive anyone about it.'

'No I don't! Now leave this to me! They may have forgotten about it. I'll ask Sheila Rawson.'

She disappeared, leaving me alone in the corridor and feeling more and more tense, my confident mood well and truly gone. After about ten minutes, she appeared round the corner and walked towards me shaking her head. 'The barristers have had a talk,' she confided. 'Jill Keegan jumped on it straight away.'

'Maybe it's just as well. Now we'll just have to tell the judge and be done with it.'

'No! She said hastily. 'He'll come down on us like a ton of bricks. Anyway there may be no need to tell him. Think of the joint custody. Brenda has had effective sole custody for nearly three years. If we want joint custody we'll have to negotiate. What about the offer we agreed on a few days ago? If we put it to them then at least we'll know what they have to say. Will we have a go?'

'We - ell, I suppose there's nothing to lose. We should be in court in a minute anyway.'

Sheila Rawson was approaching in her wig and gown. She looked happy. 'Hello!' she said, then added, 'I think we should approach the other side.'

'We've just been talking about it,' Carol Duggan answered. 'We've decided to go ahead and offer them £20,000.'

'Right!' And she walked back again towards the bend towards another black gown - or was it two? - with several other figures behind it. They were too far away to hear any words.

She was gone for twenty minutes or more and Carol Duggan had gone downstairs, leaving me on my own again. Was this the end of all my struggling? Perhaps I could get on with my life now - no more summonses or allegations; give Brenda the £20,000 in return for joint custody of Matthew, then rebuild my finances? The prospect held me. It seemed a happy alternative to court hearings and Matthew screaming for his father.

My reverie was interrupted as Carol Duggan appeared from behind the double doors. Sheila Rawson returned a moment later; she was smiling.

'Do we have a deal?' I asked convinced that we had.

'No, not yet,' was her reply. 'But we've had a long talk and it's looking good. There's still a lot of goodwill there and Brenda realises how important it is to preserve it, for the sake of your son. You know, in spite of all your differences she is still fond of you. It would be a pity to destroy all that goodwill in a bitter dispute in court.'

'Then why are we here? She brought the proceedings. And I'll bet she's not prepared to drop them now either. Is she?'

'Well... her legal team feels it would be better to settle matters today, once and for all.'

'So what is she not happy with? Is it the money or the joint...'

'They feel the offer is a bit low,' she interrupted hastily. 'Brenda has a huge mortgage and your properties are now quite valuable.'

'I don't think we can offer her any more. She was due just under ten thousand and now she's getting twenty. I'll have to pay my costs on top of that and whatever about my properties, my income at the moment is tiny.'

'Could you not increase it a little - for the sake of peace. You know judges in these matters often award the costs to the plaintiff. Then you'll have to pay the extra money anyway - to the lawyers.'

'Would she get costs when there's a separation agreement already? - And Brenda is a lawyer too.' Sheila Rawson winced; at the time I didn't understand why. 'She's getting thirty thousand, including what I've already paid her.'

'They're not happy with that and her team is pretty formidable. They are very confident about going into court. Alice Campbell, her senior counsel has an awesome reputation. Jill Keegan is no pushover either. Then there's Sally Donnelly, Colman Kelly, her father and of course herself.'

'Bloody Hell! She has an army, and here's me with two women trying to talk me down.' It was said jokingly, but I was worried. It felt like being on a moving stairs with no way to get off.

There was an uneasy silence. Eventually Sheila Rawson broke the ice. 'Can we go another £5,000, just to make the deal?' she coaxed.

'I don't know. That's £35,000 altogether. It wouldn't be easy to find that kind of money. Anyway they haven't said they'll accept that either. Have they?'

'I'll find out,' she said and before I could stop her she was walking away again.

Carol Duggan took my attention at the critical moment. She seemed very anxious to talk to me. 'Sheila is very good,' she said 'way ahead of their junior.'

'But not ahead of their senior? Is that what you're telling me?' It seemed right to interrupt.

'Well, Alice Campbell has made a name for herself of course. But don't worry! We're doing very well so far. All I'm afraid of is that all their war horses will want to go into battle, shouting 'false affidavit' and trying to discredit us in front of the judge.'

'Tell me where is the judge anyway? It's nearly twelve! Shouldn't we have been in court long ago?'

'Oh! There's a problem with a courtroom, so we'll have to wait until after lunch.'

'Strange! It's important enough to be heard in the High Court and the proceedings were taken out a year and a half ago.'

She gave a little laugh. 'They can be very inefficient up here. We could show them a thing or two down our way.'

Sheila Rawson was shuffling among the other wigs at the end of the corridor. They were moving out now from behind the corner, their confidence growing. Until then I had forgotten the lawyers' grapevine where they had me painted as the brutal abusive husband they all loved to hate. Now I remembered.

Eventually she came back, sat on the windowsill and assumed a cosy motherly air. 'We have no choice,' she said. We just have to up our offer to £40,000.'

I shook my head. 'No! That's it! There's no point in trying to buy joint custody with money that I can't afford to borrow. Carol says the courtroom will be free after lunch - so let's go in and be done with it!'

The mention of joint custody brought her to her feet. 'Well! It's nearly lunchtime anyway,' she said quickly. 'Perhaps we can all have a little think about it and we'll be back here at a quarter past two.'

Christine was waiting for me on the front porch. She had spotted a restaurant close by and we made our way there now as I explained that they were trying to get me to pay £40,000 to Brenda.

'Who is? The judge?' she asked. When she heard what had been happening all morning, she looked at me straight in the eye and said firmly, 'You must tell them "no way! No more deals!" Go straight into court!'

Suddenly feeling better, I began to enjoy my lunch.

'Right! I've decided what to do,' We were all back in the corridor. 'I can't afford to settle on those terms. We must go in and fight the case.'

They looked at each other in alarm.

'No! You can't do that! You can't!' They were both speaking together. The note of panic in their voices unsettled me. I hesitated to say any more and they didn't give me a second chance.

What followed was the most intense browbeating I have ever experienced in my life. It lasted a little over two hours but all I can remember are the beginning and one or two highlights further on. There seemed to be no question of the case being called or of having to talk to the other side. They had all the time they wanted to work on me.

They began by warning me of the dire consequences of going into court. It was what the other side wanted, they told me, adding that Brenda's lawyers were personally involved and spoiling for a fight. They were talking about going to the Supreme Court if they failed to get their way.

This was followed by a description of the judge who would hear the case. He was notoriously hostile to men; he would believe any story from a woman. He would take all my property and order it to be sold, including the land I got from my father. He would throw the book at me because of the special savings account.

Many other things were mentioned too but I don't remember them. I do remember their grim faces and the constant hammer of their voices. The process by which a lawyer pushes an unwilling client into an agreement is very like the technique the police use to squeeze a confession out of an unwilling suspect. Frightening him is only a small part of it. The main part is keeping him isolated and then wearing him down. The awful thing is that it works whether the suspect has committed the crime or not. The police frequently get completely innocent people to sign 'confessions' without laying a hand on them. They just relentlessly wear them down until they are prepared to sign anything.

When lawyers use these methods on their own clients they have an important advantage: trust. Trust cuts down the time it takes to persuade someone and it greatly extends the limits of what he can be persuaded to do. It was young men who trusted their superiors who went willingly 'over the top' in Flanders, only to be destroyed by the machine guns and barbed wire.

It's hard to understand people who abuse trust in this way. What kind of people deliberately use all the techniques of intense communication with another human being: pleading, eye contact, emotion, only to betray that human being for their own ends? Many bosses and so-called leaders do it. Salesmen, politicians and lawyers do it all the time; tearing the bonds of humanity that link them to other people; in the process becoming themselves living lies, sub-human.

Maybe I should have known better but I didn't. I was in a strange dangerous place, with only these two people to rely on. They were strong and confident; they knew their surroundings. I was a confused and frightened father who had been treated like a criminal in all the proceedings up to now. So I trusted these people and took the consequences.

Sometime while they were working on me during the afternoon I became bewildered and from then on they persuaded me very easily. I agreed to the £40,000 and shortly after to £45,000; finally to £50,000. I agreed to Brenda having sole custody of Matthew; I agreed to an access arrangement so awkward and expensive that it could never work and finally I agreed to pay Brenda sixty pounds a week 'for Matthew.' Even when my lawyers gave the hated Pauline Maxwell's report to the judge (apparently, he had been in his chambers all along) my protest was only a murmur. It was a bad dream and all I wanted was to escape from it.

I signed away everything I had been fighting for over the previous three years and didn't even complain. Soon after, we went into the courtroom where the judge appeared and made the arrangement into an order of the court. On our way out Carol Duggan said she would like to buy me a drink 'to celebrate our victory.' I followed her into the pub obediently.

Confidence people!

*

Poor Christine!

She thought it was going to be all over. Now, as she was questioning me about the terms of the 'settlement' it was difficult even to remember what they were. We both began to realise something was seriously wrong. Back at the hostel I fell asleep on the bed exhausted. After an hour I awoke with a moan. What happened during the afternoon would not go away. Now I was face to face with it in earnest.

Slowly, almost unwillingly I began to recall the terms of what I had signed, it felt like a huge weight being hung round my neck. £40,000 would have to be borrowed to pay Brenda and another £25,000 to pay off my debts. Then there was another £60 'for Matthew' every week and another £70 to see him and support him while he was with me.

Having found a pen Christine worked out how much I had to earn. The 'access plan' required me to move to Ireland and to earn a great deal of money. That would leave me in a double bind because of high income tax in Ireland. It worked out £500 a week just to pay my debts and see my son - and I still needed to eat after that. And it was hard to know how soon I would be able to work because of my leg. I shuddered.

'What sort of people had you advising you at all?' Christine asked incredulously.

What sort indeed? I couldn't sleep until four o' clock when Christine thought of the sleeping pills and gave me one. They were to come in very handy.

*

Next day, we were passing a phonebox on our way out of Dublin when I finally plucked up the courage to phone Carol Duggan. 'Where am I going to get the £40,000?' I came straight to the point.

'What £40,000 is that, Owen?' A split second of hope, then reality set in again.

'The rest of the money I owe Brenda of course, £39,600 to be exact.'

Chapter 23

'Oh you mean the £50,000 settlement, you were confusing me there with all those other figures. You remember yesterday when you were worried about that, I offered to go to the bank manager with you and help to negotiate a £50,000 loan.'

'All I need is £40,000. Remember I've already paid her £10,400.'

'Now we've already been through that, Owen.' She sounded like an exasperated mother talking to a child. 'Sheila Rawson told you that anything you have given her already doesn't count. You have to give her the full £50,000.'

'You mean she gets £60,000 altogether?'

'She gets £50,000 now; what you gave her earlier is another matter. Sheila told you that yesterday; I heard her.'

'She did? When did she tell me?' The pause was tiny, just a fraction of a second, but it was enough.

'...About twelve o' clock.'

'You mean before lunch'

' That's right.'

'No way Carol! I remember everything that happened up to lunch perfectly and there was no mention of it whatsoever.'

'Look Owen! I think you should read the court order. I'll post you a copy. There's no way to get out of it. You'll just have to pay up and that's that. You got off lightly in my opinion. There's a client with me now. It was only because it was yourself that I agreed to take the call. Bye now!'

Click! The receiver went down. For a second or two I felt under the spell again, but Christine's voice from the truck rescued me and I realised we were no longer lost in 'the halls of justice.' Now there was time to reflect and analyse what was going on.

In the truck I was silent for well over an hour. Until the phone call I had not been sure. Even though I knew that solicitors often bamboozle their clients in small ways, it was still hard to believe that my own lawyers, the people taking my money, would go to such lengths to betray their own client. Why would they want to do that? But now the answers were all too clear.

First of all, there was no way that they mentioned the money that had been paid to Brenda. Telling me that it didn't count, effectively telling me to accept that Brenda had tricked me out of it, would have made me angry; angry enough to break off all negotiations on the spot - and that was the last thing they wanted.

Above all, they were determined that the case be settled without a full hearing. The tiny amount of preparation, the one short interview with the barrister, the fact that my case was not called, the softeners - 'one night is enough to...' telling me I was late and that my affidavit was false. These all added up to one thing. My lawyers did not want the case to be heard in court; they were going to do all in their power to force a settlement. And from the way that Carol Duggan had bullied me about Pauline Maxwell's report it was going to be a settlement with nothing in it for me. They had decided long ago that Brenda must get more money and that I was not to get joint custody of my son.

Only for the telephone conversation I would still have found it hard to believe. After all, what was their motive? Why would they want to do something like that? But Carol's cheerful tone and her phrase 'you *got off* lightly' showed her true feelings about me. The lawyers' grapevine again! I was the criminal, the brutal husband, the villain. *She had believed these stories all along.* The number of lawyers practising family law in Ireland is quite small. Women, including Brenda, make up about two thirds of them. In such a group, a piece of gossip like that can be powerful. Even if Carol Duggan had not believed the stories, it could be awkward for her if Brenda's application had been dismissed in court. She could have found herself unpopular among her colleagues, a difficult position for negotiating future cases.

Instead, both herself and Sheila Rawson took part in a consensus with the lawyers (all women!) on the other side. Brenda had to be looked after. All decency demanded it! How could they let down a poor abused mother - and one of their own? Besides, there was no need for joint custody. They could guarantee that *as long as Mr. Sheridan behaved himself,* he would have no problem seeing his son. No need either, to put the poor thing in the witness box in front of her colleagues, *'hasn't she suffered enough?'* So it was all arranged.

Family law is so covered in secrecy that family lawyers are almost unaccountable. The in-camera rule in Ireland is so draconian that nobody is allowed to say anything whatsoever about any family case. Lawyers drafted it, of course.

We were nearly at the Monastery of Clonmacnoise when I spoke. 'What do we do now? Any ideas?'

Christine's response was ready; she had been thinking too. 'You must get out of that settlement! You didn't really agree to it in the first place.'

'Right! I'll get a letter off to Carol Duggan today. They seem terrified of going in front of a judge; so that's the very place we'll bring them!'

Pandora's box had opened for the second time and our visit to the ruined monastery was surprisingly pleasant. We took some photographs.

CHAPTER 24

Appeal

The letter was not written that day. My mind needed time to clear, to take it all in; so for the moment, it was best to stop thinking about it entirely.

Clonmacnoise, in its day, was a kind of Oxford University; the biggest learning centre of the Coptic-Atlantic Christianity known to us as 'The Celtic Church.' We both found it fascinating.

That evening in a guesthouse near Aughrim (another historic town), we had a good discussion on Irish history with a retired headmaster before going to bed. It helped.

The following morning, driving through the Connamara countryside, I was ready to think about it again. Could family lawyers really be such a law unto themselves? The idea was contrary to everything we were taught. But going over what happened again, piece by piece, there was no doubt about it. I had been tricked into signing away the '94 agreement - *and custody of my son.*

The stories we were hearing from other dads were similar. A small number had left their homes out of a sense of guilt or duty. (Men can be made to feel so guilty!) Those ordered out by a judge were even fewer. The majority had been pressurised into leaving by the solicitors acting for them and taking their money. Putting up a fight on the dad's side makes cases complicated and *unprofitable*. It makes things *awkward* for the judge and discourages women from bringing proceedings. That's not in the lawyers' interest – especially as the solicitor acting for the man today is acting for the woman tomorrow.

We were driving through a landscape that is considered to be one of the most spectacular in Europe, but it was wasted on me. Around two o' clock we arrived in Cong, the setting for John Wayne's film 'The Quiet Man.' It was in 'The Quiet Man Tea Rooms' that the note was finally written. It read:

Dear Carol,
I can't believe that you got me to sign what I signed two days ago. Please arrange for another hearing as soon as possible.
    Owen Sheridan

'Pity we can't see her face when she gets it.' Christine said

It made me feel better but my worries remained. That night the sleeping pill was forgotten. Sometime after three in the morning, having got in and out of bed half a dozen times, Christine gave me an ultimatum: either take a sleeping pill within the next sixty seconds and read quietly until drowsy, or find alternative accommodation!

And so it was for the rest of the holiday. During the day, there were things to keep me occupied, but at night the awful consequences of what I had signed came back to haunt me. The £50,000 had to be paid within a few weeks. What if the money couldn't be borrowed before then? Or if the repayments could not be met? My father's property was all that was left in the family. If it was lost now *through me*, how would my father feel? The sleeping pills were very necessary.

Worst of all, there was no hope of sustaining my relationship with Matthew under those terms. With the repayments on a huge loan to be made, there was no question of taking two days off every fortnight and spending over £200 on a trip to Dublin. It was going to be six days a week every week, until my debts got under control. A flight from London a few times a year perhaps, and all by kind permission of his mother.

Shame added to my worry. How could I have been so gullible, so weak? Why did I not understand what was happening until it was too late? My friends in Parental

Equality were expecting me to telephone them and let them know what happened, but I was too depressed and ashamed to make the call. It took me nearly a week to pick up the phone. Tony, at the other end was very understanding and supportive. It made me feel sorry immediately for not phoning sooner. But that was the least of my mistakes.

Christine helped me through the depressions and was philosophical when she noticed me becoming distracted and remote. 'So you're off on a tangent again,' she would say good-humouredly. Thanks to her, by the end of the week I was looking forward to the time with Matthew in Limerick.

We picked him up on the Friday and the three of us had a happy time travelling southwards in the truck. We all stayed together in the mobile home.

But something was wrong. The following evening, when Matthew had gone to sleep, I spoke to Christine about it. 'Matthew is moving away from me,' I said. 'He doesn't seem to be enjoying this trip as much as usual. The bond between us is weakening; the same feeling doesn't seem to be there.'

'No! No! A bond doesn't go away like that. It's just how you're feeling now. Of course he loves you as much as ever.'

But she failed to convince me. This was the one night that the sleeping pills didn't work and I woke suddenly at three o' clock. Was it the fact that I had just been asleep and was still close to my subconscious mind? Probably - because all of a sudden I understood. *It wasn't Matthew holding back - it was myself.* Knowing how impossible the access 'agreement' was, I was afraid to get too close to him, protecting myself from the pain of 'the dark days' now that it looked like I would lose him again.

The poor child! He had sensed my aloofness and reacted accordingly. Without a word I crept out of bed to where he was sleeping. Sensing my nearness he woke up and reached out both arms. He knew! He knew everything! I gave him a long hug.

'I love you Daddy!'

'And I'll always love you Matthew! Always!'

Chapter 24

Carol Duggan phoned early on Monday morning. She spoke in a hearty casual tone. She had my letter and would I come into her office? She would explain things to me and we would sort it out.

'Is the hearing arranged?' From my tone of voice, she knew that the game was up; I trusted her no longer.

'No!' she said after a short pause.

'Have you done anything about it?'

'No!' this time she faltered.

'Then I won't be going near your office.'

'I see.'

There was silence, then a click as she put the phone down.

'The story of my life,' I said smiling.

'What's the story of your life, Daddy?' Matthew was eating his cereal. My smile became a big grin.

Later in the week I wrote another letter to Carol Duggan.

> Dear Carol,
> On the ninth of this month you and Ms Rawson intimidated and tricked me into signing a document at the Four Courts in Dublin. The terms set out in the document are the opposite of everything I have been trying to achieve for the past three years.
> I forbid you from acting for me as of now and since I am unable to comply with this 'agreement' I hold you responsible for any consequences that may arise as a result.
>   Regretfully,
>   Owen Sheridan.

I delivered the letter by hand.

Christine and I had a long talk. One thing was quite clear. No solicitor could be trusted to act against a colleague. They were too accountable to one another; they had too much to hide. Anyway I was broke, and lawyers don't work for nothing. If this so-called agreement was going to be overturned, I would have to represent myself.

Matthew had to be back in Dublin by six o' clock on Saturday, so we decided to drive him up in the truck. Brenda met us in Jurys Hotel, all smiles as if the court proceedings had never happened. She had been trained well.

My reply was cold; I was having none of it. It was Matthew who broke the ice. 'Mummy! Do you like my daddy?' he asked suspiciously.

'No, Matthew! She hates my guts.' It came out automatically.

'Did you *have* to say that in front of him?' she demanded.

'He asked me, and he wouldn't have, unless he sensed what was going on in the first place. I'm not going to lie to him. One of us is enough to do that. By the way, you won't be getting the £40,000 or the £50,000 or whatever it is. I retracted that so-called agreement the following day.'

'Oh, you did? Did you?' There was no friendliness now.

The bitterness was too much for me as my child was being taken away yet again. I didn't want to part with him and he didn't want to go, but our wishes counted for nothing in the great system of family law that operates 'in the interest of the child.' We gave each other a hug and then I turned away, afraid to look back. Christine told me Matthew didn't look back either.

On Monday, we made straight for the Four Courts. The sight of the big building made me feel nervous again and almost glad to see the front doors closed. 'The summer recess,' I muttered, relief mixed with my disappointment. But Christine was made of sterner stuff and she gripped my arm firmly. Round the back, there seemed to be a lot of building work going on but men and women in suits were coming out a doorway at the far end of the building. One of them told me obligingly that even though it was the recess, emergency hearings were still taking place.

We went through the door, down a corridor that led to a huge reception area and joined a long queue. Eventually our turn came and I spoke to a pleasant looking girl behind the counter explaining that I wanted the court order stopped.

'Oh, you mean you want it set aside' she said. That will require a special sitting of the High Court since we are now in summer recess.' She handed me some forms.

'Oh...right! So how do I go about that?'

'Well... the first thing you have to do is talk to the registrar. Then you have to go in front of a judge to get leave to bring the application. Then, you have to bring the application (with its accompanying affidavit) in here to be stamped, initialled by the registrar and lodged with the court.' She was positively cheerful, the benign face of bureaucracy showing off its power. 'And by the way, since this is the summer recess, we close at one o' clock,' she finished with a smile

'And the registrar is...?'

'Upstairs, straight ahead, right when you come to a T in the corridor, last door on the left.' She beamed.

We found the registrar exactly where she told us. A youngish forty, he had the look of power common to all court clerks.

'You have to go in front of a judge and you'll have to hurry, he said. We're closing at one o' clock. Have you a jacket? No? Well I suppose you'll have to do as you are.'

We followed him down some more corridors and stairs that brought us to a small courtroom on the ground floor. It was empty apart from the three of us.

'All rise!' the registrar said, about ten minutes later as the judge came in. He didn't waste any time. Having asked me why I was bringing the application and heard my reasons, he explained that I would have to serve the summons in person, as the £50,000 was due to be paid in a week and the hearing had to take place before then. After that he gave me leave to bring the application, the registrar called 'all rise!' once again. The judge left the courtroom and we went out the way we came in, feeling rather bemused.

The afternoon was one of the busiest of our lives. There was no time for lunch and barely enough to buy the blue paper on which all the documents had to be written. Our next stop was the R.T.E. television studios, where a programme called 'Signpost' about changing patterns of family life was about to be recorded. Parental Equality had three people on the panel including myself. I explained how the courts effectively encourage a married woman to break up a child's home by giving her the house, the children and most of her husband's wages.....

'Regardless of who is to blame,' a woman beside me added. There was a clap. A man added that soon there would be a system of joint custody where the children would not be taken away from either parent and nobody would be rewarded for breaking up the home. It was very encouraging.

Back at the hostel, it was hard to knuckle down to writing the application and the long affidavit. It seemed such an anticlimax after the television show and there were all kinds of reasons to get up from the table. But Christine kept my nose to the grindstone until twelve o' clock. It was just over halfway done.

By 6.45am we were both awake - and starving. But Christine kept me at it until 9.00am when we both ate a huge breakfast, not having eaten for a whole day. At 10.00am when the cleaners finally ushered us out of the room, there were only a few lines to go. I finished them in The Gresham Hotel while Christine ordered coffee. The result was coherent and (for me) surprisingly legible, but it was now 11.35.

We were lucky to find a brass sign for commissioner of oaths a few doors down from The Gresham. Within ten minutes my affidavit was stamped and sworn: 11.54.

A running walk up the Quay, and by 12.05pm we were at the side door of the Four Courts building. Minutes later, we reached the head of the queue. Here we ran into our first problem. The application was incorrectly worded, the girl told me. It would have to be written out again on a new sheet of paper and sworn in front of a commissioner of oaths again. Seeing the dismay written all over my face she noticed a space on top of the page. 'Here!' she said pointing, 'If you write it in carefully, we can let it go ahead. Now, as you know, it must be stamped and initialled by the registrar before it can be lodged at the court.'

'Where do you go to stamp it?' My voice was weary.

'You must leave the building. The stamping office is just a short walk up the quay.' I groaned.

It was now 12.25; leaving Christine, I started to run. The queue in the stamping office was even longer; so at 12.45 there was no option but to gulp back my shyness and ask to be allowed up to the front as my case was urgent. The solicitors obliged, smiling. The clerk stamped my affidavit and the application, then took the money with a look of disapproval: 12.51.

A run back to the Four Courts and up to the registrar's office at the end of the corridor; he quickly initialled the two documents at the margin. Sweat was running down my face as I strode back down the stairs to join the queue once more. It was less than a minute to one o' clock.

Seconds later a bell rang and the double doors were closed ceremoniously. The others in the queue were chatting calmly. So we had made it! Those of us inside the room were going to be served. This time the girl accepted the documents without a word and we made our way out the door in triumph. It was 1.08pm. At a pub nearby we had soup and a sandwich. After that it was time to set about serving the summons. We weren't done yet!

A pang of guilt came unexpectedly. Brenda had once asked me to serve a summons on a man in London. At his home, it suddenly became clear to me what I was doing. This man had done me no wrong. But my piece of paper would deliver him into the hands of the lawyers and their courts. I couldn't go through with it and drove away.

Now, looking at my summons for Brenda, the same guilty feeling returned. It didn't last long. The thought of Matthew screaming 'I want my daddy!' was more than enough to change my mind. But the memory of July 1994 when Brenda had been so nice to me on the phone while preparing the papers to be thrust at me in the airport made me lose the last of my remorse. Here was a solicitor, an officer of the court,

Appeal

getting a taste of her own medicine. No harm! No harm at all!

At her office Brenda couldn't talk to me as 'she was in a hurry' No! She couldn't see me later, or in the evening. Things were busy just now. Click! (Again!) She knew something was up.

We decided to go to her office before she left. The quickest way through the Dublin traffic is often to walk, and we were outside the office in twenty minutes having stopped to photocopy the documents on the way. Brenda was out, or so the receptionist told us, until tomorrow.

Next we tried the house. This meant two long walks and a trip by train but we did not hurry; she was not likely to be there. To my surprise, her car (my old Volvo!) was parked outside. I knocked firmly on the door.

It was Margaret who answered. 'Hello Owen' she said coldly. 'If you've come for Matthew, you can't have him. I have no permission to hand him over.'

'I want to go out to my daddy.' Matthew's voice was firm and angry, but the door was on a chain.

The last thing I wanted was to have my son screaming again. Quickly I said 'Matthew! They won't let me see you today. But I'll be back soon OK?'

'OK Daddy.' His voice was small and very disappointed. - 'Damn!'

'Damn! Damn! Damn! Why did my little son always have to pay for his parents' mistakes?'

'Because his mother used the legal system to deprive him of his father,' my mind answered at once. Now as we made our way to the train station, my feelings were anything but guilt.

Looking at my watch, I took a deep breath: 4.30pm. Brenda was out; her mother was at home; so was Matthew and so was her car. She would be coming home herself soon, and almost certainly by train. We waited by the station in silence.

Early or late, it didn't matter now; she was going to get that summons if we had to stay there until next morning.

She was on the second train. There was no mistaking the quick bold stride or the tall formidable figure walking straight towards me.

'Brenda Newman!' my voice was loud; 'I'm serving these documents on you!'

She gave a gasp, followed by a look of pure horror and remained fixed to the ground.

I was pitiless. 'What goes around, comes around,' I thought grimly.

The tables had been turned.

CHAPTER 25

Standing alone

'All professions are a conspiracy against the laity' G.B.S

We expect judges to be wise and kind.
    Those of us who grew up with television have been in courtrooms many times. It is a frequent setting for a dramatic script with 'good guys' and 'bad guys', the latter usually trying every kind of trickery and deceit. Of course the deceit gets them nowhere; the wise, kind judge sees through it all, and justice prevails in the end.

That is an average layman's impression of a courtroom scene. It's an impression formed at an early age. Although we may know intellectually that the reality is probably different, deep inside we still expect to see justice win the day under a benevolent judge. To know something intellectually is not really to know it at all; otherwise teenagers would be the wisest people on the planet. To the more analytical teenager, with all kinds of answers, understanding often comes slowly.

At the age of forty I was still learning. In spite of all that had happened, in spite of having lived with a solicitor for four years I still trusted the system and expected a happy outcome to my case. But then, I had never really met the system face to face before now.

The week was spent preparing. I put together cross-examinations of Brenda and of Carol Duggan, then made out an affidavit of means and wrote down my reasons for overturning the court order in a document that showed that it was an arrangement to which I would never knowingly agree. It all added up to a powerful case.

Ignoring my doctor's advice, I did two days work with a builder in order to pay for the trip to Dublin. There was very little choice; my credit was exhausted and I was broke. The two days passed cheerfully in spite of the pain in my leg because all that week my mood was happy and confident.

That was before coming face to face with Judge Warren.

He was a small man with steel grey hair, middle aged, not old, and with an air that reeked of self-importance. His accent had an affected nasal quality.

The case began with Jill Keegan objecting to Christine's being in the courtroom during the hearing. I stood up to make the point that there was a precedent for having an assistant in court in matters of family law when a layman appears for himself. But Judge Warren snapped that since it was set in an English court, it didn't apply here. What worried me, was that he was looking at Ms. Keegan as he spoke, almost deliberately away from me.

In fact the precedent was McKenzie Vs McKenzie in England in 1971 and it established the right of a lay litigant to have the support of a 'McKenzie Friend' during a hearing, though the friend is not allowed to speak to the court.

'Who is this person?' demanded Judge Warren.

'Some new girlfriend my lord,' answered Ms Keegan.

At this stage Christine stood up to her full 4'10". 'I'm not *some new girlfriend*, I'm his partner,' she said firmly.

'And you didn't even ask my permission!' Judge Warren replied.

'I was about to my lord, but didn't get the chance.'

'She must leave the court before we can proceed,' was the curt reply. So Christine indicated to me where the files were and went outside the door.

The clerk then handed my affidavit of means to the judge. He looked at it with distaste. 'What's this? Some handwritten document?' he said in a sneering tone, and put it down beside him on the desk.

The next part of the hearing was more successful. Ms Keegan stood up again. 'My lord,' she began. 'We have a very serious matter to bring up here. Mr. Sheridan is speaking about his case in the media. He has appeared twice on RTE television including last Monday on the "Signpost" programme.'

On my feet again. 'My lord, my wife has also mentioned this in her affidavit. May I cross-examine her? I have evidence here that will disprove the allegation.'

'No' snapped the judge. 'Just give your evidence!'

'My lord, here are transcripts of both my appearances on RTE backed up by full video recordings of the programmes, and they will show that while speaking about the situation of fathers in family law, I took pains to avoid any mention of my own case.'

'That will do!' interrupted the judge, at least it was not a snap. Judges hate falling foul of the media. Had he applied any penalty for my speaking on television, it is quite possible that journalists, as a body, would have rallied to my side. He was very glad of my answer.

There followed a brief interrogation by the judge on the circumstances of my signing the document that became the consent order. He enquired if I had had a solicitor and if so, who?

'Murphy Duggan and Bell,' I answered.

He asked me if I had read the document and understood what I was signing. No! I told him and the document was signed in the courtroom when Sheila Rawson handed it to me over her left shoulder shortly before the judge appeared. Then he asked me my reasons for wanting the court order changed.

'Because I didn't agree to it, and because it effectively prohibits my having a relationship with my son,' was my reply.

'Haven't you an access order?'

'It's not practical, my lord.'

The judge then scrutinised both my main affidavit and my affidavit of means and eventually pronounced. 'I won't set aside the order on grounds of financial hardship, and as regards the other ground that you were pressurised into signing, I will have to hear the evidence of your solicitor. Can we say Wednesday?'

Jill Keegan promptly offered to contact Carol Duggan on her mobile phone. She left the courtroom. Presently she came back in. Yes, Ms Duggan was in; yes, she was free on Wednesday and no, of course she knew nothing about these proceedings. All very convenient!

Judge Warren then set the date for Wednesday at ten o'clock. 'The idea!' he added. 'Reputable solicitors bamboozling clients!' and then he went on to have a one to one chat with Jill Keegan in low tones.

My heart sank; they were the only two barristers in the courtroom. I knew then what a judge is, another lawyer behind the bench, one of the club, answerable to the others and anxious to preserve the club's privileges and power.

Lawyers hate people conducting their own cases, it throws the market wide open. They regard it as 'other people playing with *their* ball'. Judges particularly hate it. Lay people are not taught the respect for the bench that is drilled into a lawyer and they tend to have a sense of justice that judges find particularly constraining.

When Judge Warren finished his tête-à-tête with Ms Keegan the clerk called 'all rise!' and the proceedings were over for the day.

I came out of the courtroom shaking my head. Christine was waiting for me; we headed straight for the train.

*

That day and the next were spent in a kind of tense foreboding. It was a kind of creepy feeling, an animal instinct of danger. The same feeling came over me once while driving through South London; soon afterwards a police car flagged me down. It turned out that they had been following me for a quarter of an hour.

In fact I was being discussed in two overlapping legal circles at the time. Brenda and her legal advisers (including her family) were talking to Sheila Rawson and Carol Duggan. They were determined to quash my appeal at all costs. Carol Duggan was livid. *A mere layman* questioning her work and showing her up in front of all her colleagues! Clients ought to be grateful to their lawyers and if they lose they must learn to take their beating! *How dare they be angry!*

On Tuesday, Christine helped me prepare my case even more thoroughly, and on Wednesday morning we both boarded the early train to Dublin. We were the first to arrive outside the courtroom. One by one the lawyers walked past me. They looked confident but avoided my eyes.

The door closed and we were back in court again. This time there were many other cases and the courtroom was full of people. We rose, and Judge Warren entered again looking smaller, more bad tempered and even more self-important.

When the list of cases was read, he ordered the court to be cleared 'so they could deal with the matter of family law first'. Again Christine stayed in court and again Jill Keegan stood up to object. I also stood up again to suggest the precedent, but the judge didn't give me the chance to open my mouth 'I've ruled on this already,' he snarled. 'She must leave my court!'

Christine got up and left quietly. There was no point in antagonising the judge.

I was a Black American at a meeting of the Ku Klux Klan. All the lawyers were furious with me for challenging their system - especially the lawyer behind the bench. If ever I needed Christine beside me for moral support it was then, and her organising skills would have been invaluable. But it was not to be. Judge Warren was not the type of human being to look objectively on someone who disagreed with him.

He continued as soon as the door closed, 'Ms. Rawson, Mr. Sheridan made certain allegations against you and his solicitor in his affidavit. Of course I would not allow the case to proceed without your having a hearing; but first of all, she must come off record. You have no objection Mr. Sheridan?'

'None, my Lord! I requested it when she was dismissed.'

The registrar raised the question of no stenographer being present and Jill Keegan offered to take notes.

'That will be satisfactory,' said the judge with a smirk. He was now virtually unaccountable.

The proceedings then took on the appearance of a well-rehearsed play. Carol Duggan was called to the witness box. Giving the judge a nice smile, she sat down on her seat crossing her legs. The short skirt she was wearing did them full justice. Judge Warren's expression softened. He returned the smile, as she began to answer questions from Sheila Rawson.

'How long have you been practising family law, Ms Duggan?'

'Ten years, my lord.' The judge gave a nod of approval.

'Can you describe what happened outside the courtroom in July?'

'Yes I can. We were all in a corridor outside the upstairs court. There was nothing intimidating about the place. A very serious matter arose on the morning of the hearing, so Mr Sheridan indicated that he wanted to settle the case and the barristers met to negotiate a settlement. Counsel on the other side offered to settle for what was an unacceptable amount. Before lunchtime a more acceptable figure was suggested. Of course I explained to Mr. Sheridan that any monies he had already paid to his wife would not be taken into account.'

'There was a report from Dr. Maxwell. Weren't the access terms in the settlement even more liberal than in the report?'

'- And these terms were read over to him and he understood them?' - from the judge.

'Yes he did. I read the document out *twice* to him in the corridor before he signed it.'

The judge's voice was low and confiding; he leant towards Carol Duggan as he spoke. She played it for all it was worth.

When Sheila Rawson had finished her questions, the judge turned forward again and looked at me. His face changed completely; there was no attempt to conceal his anger. 'Have you questions Mr. Sheridan?' he snapped.

'A few, my lord.'

'Very well then,' he said curtly; so I began.

'Do you recognise this document?' I asked handing her a copy of the '94 agreement which the clerk in turn handed to the judge.

He glanced at it and cut in, 'Mr Sheridan! You must confine your questions to the settlement and any reasons why the court might not accept it.'

'My lord, I'm trying to make the case that Ms Duggan for her own reasons did not want to fight my case and so she decided to put pressure on her own client to settle it instead.'

'No!' the judge said firmly. 'I won't allow that.'

Half my case gone already! There was no option now, but to change course. 'Ms Duggan if I wanted the case settled, why wait until the day of the hearing? Why not settle it during the previous ten months?'

'Mr. Sheridan!' barked the judge. 'I cannot allow questions like that. This is a very busy court. We must get on with this case. I'll only admit questions that concern whether Ms. Duggan intimidated you *on the day*.'

It was at that point that I knew there was no chance. Ever since Matthew had been taken away, hope had kept me going. Now, the hope was draining away, to be replaced by helpless despair. My confidence evaporated. All I wanted was to get away from that room and all the people in it.

I fumbled with my files.

'Well? Are you going to carry on?' from the judge. Somehow I pulled my self together.

'Did I not state plainly on my coming back from lunch that I could not afford the kind of a settlement being proposed and that we would have to go in and fight the case?'

'Are you saying she's lying?' Judge Warren was almost screaming.

I should have told him the truth: Yes, of course she was lying! But I was so nervous and intimidated that I had almost given up. The judge's anger was obvious; it seemed that he would have liked to send me to prison, so I replied, 'Perhaps she's mistaken, my lord,' in lame tones.

I'm not sure how, but I managed to pull myself together for one last go.

'When did you take on my case?'

'January '97'

'When did I see a barrister?'

'You saw Fergus Cronin in early '96'

'When did I see a barrister who had anything to do with the hearing?'

'The seventh of July'

'Two days before the hearing! Do you think that was adequate?'

'She was briefed about the case before then'

'Did I tell you, before our meeting with Ms. Rawson that I had spoken to a barrister myself?'

'You did.'

'Who was the barrister?'

'Peter Tierney'

'Mr Sheridan!' The judge felt it was time to interrupt again. 'You can't blame her if you couldn't get the barrister you wanted.'

'That wasn't the nature of my question, my lord.' This time it was I who spoke sharply and it silenced the judge.

'Did I not say to you,' I went on, 'that he told me that if there was a High Court hearing in six days and I still hadn't seen a barrister then I had better be prepared to settle, because something was seriously wrong?'

There was no reply to this, and I let the silence continue while searching through my files to find the letter written in Cong requesting another hearing. Carol Duggan looked embarrassed, but the judge came to her rescue once again.

'Is that all, Mr Sheridan?' he demanded.

'One more question, my lord' I handed her the letter. 'Do you recognise this?'

'Yes, but I didn't get it until four days after the date.' I passed it to the judge. He put on his glasses, read it then pushed it to one side.

'Mr. Sheridan,' this times in the tone of a long-suffering adult whose patience is being tried by a tiresome child, 'You gave evidence in this case that you were intimidated will you please keep to that?'

'Then I have no more questions, my lord.'

'Have you finished?' he demanded, slightly surprised.

'I have.'

Judge Warren lost no time in summing up. He said that there were no grounds for setting aside the order and I was wasting the time of the court. 'Motion denied!' he pronounced. Then Jill Keegan asked for costs and the Judge asked me if I had anything to say about them. This time his tone was sarcastic; he was baiting me.

'There will be serious difficulty meeting them, my lord,' I replied.

'I have no problem awarding costs in this matter,' he added in his most pompous voice and that was that.

At last it was finished! I came out of the courtroom feeling weak and walked over to Christine. She didn't need to ask me anything. It was written all over my face.

Calming down, it suddenly occurred to me that I had not been given any chance to give my own evidence. Being the applicant, I should have been asked to take the stand before Carol Duggan. Judge Warren not only denied me that opportunity; he didn't see fit to hear me at any time.

For a split second I almost burst into the courtroom again, but Jill Keegan interrupted me with the announcement that Brenda was changing the access plan. We had arranged that Matthew come with me to Limerick that day. As Brenda was spending the weekend with her parents, she would pick him up on the Friday. Now she was changing it to the following weekend 'as it would upset his schooling.' Brenda knew my financial situation from my affidavit; there was no money to pay for another trip up and down from Dublin. Once again she was offering me access I could not use.

'You know very well that I can't afford the trip,' I said. 'What about letting me see him today for a few hours instead?'

At first the answer was 'No' but then I said that that left me no choice but to apply to the court for a different access order.

'We might as well apply now that we are here,' Christine chimed in. That set the alarm bells ringing and there was a whispered exchange between Jill Keegan and Brenda. Eventually she came back and said that we could collect him from Blackrock Station at half-past two - provided he was back there again by half-past-four. Two hours! But I agreed.

'Come on! Let's get out of here! We need some fresh air,' said Christine

After a light lunch my mind was still trying to get around all that happened. The disappointment was beginning to make itself felt. It has a bitter taste not like any other. Deep down I had still been expecting a wise kind judge, and then to be confronted with this pompous, pathetic little wretch; it was quite a shock.

Christine, Matthew and I spent the two hours playing and chasing one another in the park. We forgot our troubles for awhile until it was time to hand him back once more.

For weeks afterwards I kept analysing and mulling over my failure. My biggest mistake was not realising the implications of the in-camera rule. It meant that the whole thing was going to be heard in secret and the lawyers could do what they liked.

If my appeal had succeeded it would raise serious questions about how lawyers treat their clients. More important, it would cast doubt on the validity of a great many 'consent orders' where dads had 'agreed' to sign away their homes and custody of their children, leading to a flood of applications and undermining the whole process of family law. Judge Warren knew what he had to do. Perhaps I could have been spared a lot of expense and humiliation by realising that it was not going to be the same kind of hearing as in open court.

It took me some time to become glad about taking the appeal, but finally it became clear to me that it was the only way to be happy with myself. At least I had fought for my son; otherwise I would have blamed myself for not trying.

I had taken my own case in the High Court and done my best when the whole system was out to frighten and crush me. I had come face to face with the people who operate the system and had watched them close ranks against an outsider, heard the hypocrisy in their voices and seen the fear and hatred in their eyes. They would not frighten me again!

A few months later we discovered that Carol Duggan had an uncle, a circuit court judge, who was well known to Judge Warren.

I hadn't a hope.

CHAPTER 26

Where is my son?

('And a sword shall pierce thy heart,
Thine also')
                                T.S. Elliot

*I*t was over.
I had lost the fight for my son. There were no expectations now; no daydreams about the camping trips or the little workshop I was going to build for him; only the awful clarity that comes with the dying of hope.

First to go were any ideas about returning to live in Ireland. It just wasn't an option. London is my home and I had no urge to build a new one now that my son would not be there. Ireland had nothing to offer me but very unhappy memories, so I made arrangements to go back to Gordon Road.

Christine decided to go with me and stay until Christmas, in spite of my protests about her having to give up her job.

'I hate my job!' she replied. 'I've been trying to give it up for years. Anyway you need looking after right now.'

I suppose I did, so she gave two weeks' notice and quit. We went out to dinner to celebrate. It was to be our last meal out for some time.

During the weeks that remained, there were two access visits, which I couldn't afford. Tony took pity on me and offered to travel up to Dublin in order to bring Matthew down. He is entitled to free travel with his disability pass. However Brenda refused point blank to hand him over.

'You must collect him yourself at the station,' she said. 'I'm not going to have him handed to a stranger.'

'But whoever is *bringing* him to the station will be a stranger to me,' I said.

'But not to me, and I won't give him to someone I don't know!'

It was the confident note in her voice that made me see the writing on the wall. She was part of the system and the system would look after her. Any dispute between us would be decided by *her* people at a secret hearing in Dublin. She had broken every access order up to now, and she could break the High Court order too - with impunity.

I was powerless. Brenda on the other hand, could pull out a form and summon me in front of a solicitor-judge anytime she wanted, on any pretext whatsoever. A word with the court clerk could make sure it was a judge of her choosing, and the secrecy would cover things up when he sided with his own, just as it did under Judge Warren. It was time to get out.

Christine and I loaded our belongings in the truck. We took the ferry to Fishguard and drove down to London. It was a bleak cold day in late autumn, with the odd shower, as we drove eastwards on the M4. But Gordon Road was warm and welcoming as ever. Bob Wilson organised a welcome home drink in Gustav's. Stephen Clarke came and Jimmy Nagle; we had a good evening.

The building trade was now much better in London, and a single phone call got me a job. By working a lot of overtime and keeping lodgers in the house, my mountain of debt gradually got under control, and four months later my credit cards could be used again. It felt strange, taking them out of the drawer and putting them back in my wallet.

'For emergency use only!' Christine warned, as if I needed telling. Now the bills could be faced every month without worrying. Believe me, it's not something to take for granted!

I started building. I demolished the cheap pillars holding up the front gate and built new ones using the yellow-stock bricks, stored since Stephen Clarke knocked down the hall partition with me (a lifetime ago!). They matched the house beautifully. By pulling down a stud wall, there was enough room for a toilet under the stairs. With wood salvaged from skips, I built cupboards and a desk in my bedroom. It did me good. Building bits of my house helped to build me up too.

The following summer, a neighbour telephoned me. His son-in-law kept a few horses and wanted to make me an offer for (sadly!) my stables. We agreed a price; the £50,000 was cleared and my father's land was safe. With no huge interest bill to pay every month, my short-term debt (almost £30,000) could be tackled. It should be paid off sometime next year.

Christine is still here. She found a very good job in a laboratory in Battersea and forgot to go home. The lab is close enough to walk to work in the mornings. She misses Ireland but has no plans to go back. I'm glad.

Carol Duggan sued me for fees. I refused to pay her the last batch of almost £5,000. There was no hope of finding the money and I wouldn't have paid it anyway. She took out the proceedings, confident that they would be no more than a formality, that her own people would look after her in court. There were various delays before the case was finally heard, after more than a year. - Another trip to Ireland!

She, or her firm, had a word with the court clerk, so no other cases were heard that day. It was the nearest thing to an 'in camera' hearing they could arrange. We had a judge and a court all to ourselves, courtesy of the Irish taxpayer and of all those people whose cases had to wait. But now she was dealing with someone who knew the rules of the game. (It was expensive knowledge!) I brought a well-known Irish journalist to the hearing as well as some supporters from Parental Equality. The judge, recognising the journalist, realised that he had to be seen to be fair, so I was allowed to bring the entire case that had been suppressed by Judge Warren.

Carol Duggan marched into the witness box, her head high in the air. She was to remain there for three hours. After a few short questions from one of her partners she was cross-examined by me once again. Her testimony broke down completely, and it was quite clear that nobody believed her. Nevertheless she got just over half of what she was demanding, and of course she was spared the humiliation of being shown up in front of her colleagues. But she shook visibly as she stepped from the box and her head was down. I had clearly won the day. A small victory, but a very sweet one - the only one I've had.

Matthew and I have not lost contact. We see each other three or four times a year. He is now eight and can fly from Dublin on his own. Lately, I can occasionally afford to fly over to see him. The bond between us is still strong, but Matthew now holds himself back a little He is not quite so affectionate, more self contained. He understands that his time with me is short. Should he try to stay, the power of the state will be called in to prevent him.

Access is not a parental relationship and we both know it. You can't be a parent to your child if you can only be with him in McDonalds on a Saturday afternoon. Seeing him just a few times a year your chances are even smaller. Matthew's closest parent has been turned into a visiting uncle by the law. No wonder he tries to protect himself from getting hurt! All the same, he usually manages to prolong his visits by several days. As far as negotiating access is concerned, he is the best solicitor I ever had.

The inquisition continues. 'Family law' is a clever name for a system of secret courts whose main business is removing fathers from their homes and taking their children away. It all happens 'in the interest of the child' we are told. The cruelty is covered up by the in-camera rule and by 'visiting rights'. These are pieces of paper saying we are allowed to see our children at certain times. They are treated with contempt by mothers who know that they are neither enforced nor intended to be.

They take away our children and they don't even give us the right to visit them; it's as simple as that.

Sole custody is judicial kidnapping. And turning the family home and the children into a prize to be fought over means that most separating couples are at war. For lawyers it is a highly profitable business. All they need is a steady supply of legal proceedings to keep it going. Women are bringing the proceedings, so they must be rewarded. They know it - and it's hard to blame them. If two children are fighting, then an adult puts a knife into one child's hand and the other gets hurt, neither child is to blame - the adult is.

It doesn't have to be like that. If residency was shared between parents after break-up and if they were encouraged to live near one another, then a great deal of pain would not happen. But lawyers would lose a lot of money...

Advocacy is poison in disputes. In family matters it creates so much suffering and bitterness that mothers and fathers can never again co-operate to parent their children.

Advocacy and judiciary are incompatible; there should be no lawyer-judges. Where a body of professional advocates comes to control the judicial process, the law is out of balance. Courts tend to resemble lawyers' clubs and to make decisions which encourage people to sue, enabling lawyers to make money out of almost anything – even taking children away from parents. What happened to Matthew and to so many other children like him, happened because the law is in the hands of a small private group. It's the kind of injustice that's unlikely to change without serious legal reform.

As for my own emotions, I have come to terms with them over the years, but the scars remain.

One of them is a fear of the mail; a counsellor told me it's common among dispossessed dads. Because of all the summonses, threats and court orders, the sound makes me shudder every time letters drop through the door.

And my voice did not come back; I don't sing now.

A parent should support his child, but handing money over to the woman who took his child away is not the same thing at all. Recently I gave more than two thousand pounds to Matthew's mother. (The courts have no problem enforcing the law here!) She spent it on a foreign holiday for herself and her new boyfriend. Child support or child ransom? – The price of being allowed to see my son.

Worst of all is seeing Matthew so seldom - and by permission of the woman who took him away. Even speaking on the telephone is difficult with a 'gatekeeper' supervising the calls. The truly awful thing about being a dispossessed dad is that it is not one, but several dispossessions. Every time Matthew comes to see me, he must be handed back in a few days. A glimpse, and then he is gone, leaving his toys and the pattern of his presence behind.

Losing my son has brought me in touch with reserves of strength and talents, such as being able to speak on television and to offer hope and comfort to parents in despair. Many of my friends advise me strongly against spending my time in this way and urge me to get on with *my own life*.

Viewing one's own life as something isolated from other human beings only makes sense to those people indoctrinated in the selfish religion of consumer-capitalism. There is no point in trying to retreat into my own little world, pretending not to feel the pain of other dads.

Looking back, my last twenty years are not short of interesting memories. Working as a carpenter, as a farmer and for short periods as a milkman, a labourer and a truck driver; in Ireland, England, Canada, The United States and Australia; advising, counselling, running meetings, speaking on radio and television - and now I have written a book. Four times I looked at policemen in the eye as they came to arrest me; I conducted my own case in the High Court in Dublin, was disabled once and injured many times; I know the feel and the smell of my own flesh burning around me.

Of all these experiences, none was so profound as being a parent; seeing my tiny child brought into the world, bonding with him, loving him and having my love returned.

For me the experience was short - barely two years before he was wrenched away. But the bond between us has not gone, and in the future we can make up for some of the time that has been taken from us.

Where is my son now? Who is with him? Is he safe? Is he happy? Is he feeling sick or well? What is he thinking about? What is he doing? Has he something to ask me? To tell me? Is anything worrying him? Does he miss me? Does he need me?

These are things I must learn how not to know - for my son's sake as well as my own.